Official Know-It-All Guide™

RELATIONSHIP $ELLING

Orv Owens, Ph.D.

Frederick Fell Publishers, Inc.
2131 Hollywood Blvd., Suite 305, Hollywood, FL 33020
Phone: (954) 925-5242   Fax: (954) 925-5244
Web Site: www.Fellpub.com

Fell's Official Know-It-All Guide

Frederick Fell Publishers, Inc.

2131 Hollywood Boulevard, Suite 305

Hollywood, Florida 33020

954-925-5242

e-mail: fellpub@aol.com

Visit our Web site at www.fellpub.com

This publication is designed to provide accurate and authoritative information in regard to the subject matter covered. It is sold with the understanding that the publisher is not engaged in rendering legal, accounting, or other professional service. If legal advice or other assistance is required, the services of a competent professional person should be sought. From *A Declaration of Principles jointly adopted by a Committee of the American Bar Association and a Committee of Publishers*.

Library of Congress Cataloging in Publication Data

Owens, Orv.

    The psychology of relationship selling : developing repeat and referral business / by Orv Owens.

     p.   cm.

   ISBN 0-88391-069-1 (alk. paper)
   1. Selling--Psychological aspects. 2. Customer relations. I. Title
HF5438.8.P75094   1996, New 2002 Edition
658.85--dc20   96-5051
                        CIP

Cover Design by Elena Solis
Editorial by Olég Alexander

· Endorsements ·
and Testimonials

"In this day of high-tech, and often times, impersonal communications, people are increasingly feeling out of touch with the people they do business with. That's why it is so important now to develop effective personal relationships with your customers and employees. Orv Owens's Relationship Selling captures that process as well as anything I've seen. He has the insight to help an executive develop that important communications edge that will build lasting relationships which in turn build lasting sales potential."

—Don A. Harris
Executive Vice President
National Independent Automobile Dealers Association

"In Relationship Selling Orv Owens reveals timeless principles of Master Salesmanship. If repeat business and more sales are important to you…you'll want to read this book."

—Ralph Palmen
Professional Speaker, Author of Principles and Success Strategies for Everyday Living,
Founder-The Palmen Institute

"Over the years in my teaching sales organizations I have asked the question, 'On a scale of 1 to 10, where does our society place sales people?' Most sales people respond with, 'Somewhere between 2 and 3.' Then I ask, 'On a scale of 1 to 10, where is the level of trust on a referral?' Most of the answers are from 8 to 10. If the sales people of the world will read this book, it will raise their reputation several degrees on the list of the most respected professions."

—Dave Grant
Author or Ultimate Power, A Portrait of a Loving Heart
Teacher on 'Learning to Love' Radio Program, Seminar Speaker

"I now have a better understanding of the psychology and relationship of people. I was able to build a better environment for my team to work in, which enabled me to increase my team's productivity."

—Bill Klaus
General Motors
North American Operations

"Dr. Owens has been helping us as a consultant for more than ten years, and this book simply and clearly unfolds his powerful concepts and unique insights that have been central to giving us the leading edge in our market and with clients. Anyone who values equipping their sales people and/or technicians with these vital, tangible 'tools of the people trade,' would do well to absorb this book and use it as their primary training manual."

—Bruce A. Davis, Sr.
President Day & Nite Plumbing & Heating, Inc.

"I use the principles taught in this book on a daily basis. I feel it gives me an edge on other real estate agents. And I often use this book as a gift to people who have a great desire to be successful."

—D.C.F.
Remax Realty

"Seminars, books, and conferences related to increasing employee productivity come and go, but there is something different about the material in this book…[It has] proven to be invaluable in helping create an environment of love and trust in the work place. Our business today is a great success, in large part due to the tools, keys, and philosophies presented in these pages."

—Gary Williams
President Coakley & Williams Hotel Management Co.
Operators of Hiltons, Hilton Garden Inns, Holiday Inns, Sheratons, Days Inns, Wingate Inns, Comfort Inns, Sleep Inns, Quality Suites, and Independent Resort hotels. Currently managing 23 hotels in ten states.

"I cannot imagine selling real estate without understanding and using the principles on 'selling value' and 'motivations of life' taught so clearly in these pages. I am confident that much of my success has been a direct result of this material."

—C. Reeves
Six Million Dollar Sales Club
Real Estate

"Orv Owens's principles helped me to sell merchandise to clients, ideas to co-workers, and build stronger relationships in all walks of life."

—Karen Twilla
Finance Department
City of Marco Island

"There are few writers that can get the message across from two points of view, this book does it. You can read it from the relationship side and from the selling side, and you get two great lessons. I have recommended it to hundreds of people. It's a fantastic read."

—Dan Gaub
CEO Kay Productions (Children's Media Co.)
National Trainer and Speaker

"The concepts and principles that Dr. Owens teaches have been highly valuable in allowing me to achieve success in my personal and business environments."

—Ed Naujoks
Massachusetts Mutual Insurance
Hartford, CN

"Reading the book gave me the skills to understand people and the ability to build more effective personal relationships. These skills gave me the ability to increase my customer and organization base, which, in turn, increased my sales."

—Pat Klaus
Millionaire Member
Independent Distributor of Herbalife International

"By understanding the psychological basis of people's behavior, encouraging employees to achieve their highest level of performance has become much easier. Dr. Owens is 'right on' with his understanding of people's motivations."

—George H. Myers
C.F.O. G&A Label, Inc.
El Paso, TX

"Your book has been extremely helpful in my real estate career. It is so insightful in terms of human behavior relating to selling. Relationship selling has made me one of the top realtors in my company and the upper 3% of the agents in the Prudential Real Estate Network in the country!"

—Anna Pusz
Prudential Florida WCI Realty
President Macro Island Association of Realtors

• Dedication •

To my wife Lee who has put up with me over the years, and our six children, Corey, Kirby, Kris, Codey, Candace, and Kenny, who have had to go through the good and bad times and often found themselves a proving ground for most of the principles contained in the book.

To Carol and Don Fenimore, Fred and Karen Twilla and Jimmy Huddleston who stuck with me through some very difficult times, often putting this teaching ahead of their own welfare.

· Table of Contents ·

INTRODUCTION: What Is Relationship Selling?

Achieving the ability to establish long-lasting relationships with prospects, resulting in repeat and referral business.

The successful salesperson understands that the sales field is a people business and success is based upon understanding the prospect's emotions. There are four relationships that determine these emotions.

Two basic emotions, "love" and "fear," control all emotions: Love — giving without expecting anything in return; and Fear — an emotional response to a belief of loss.

The first six years of life create a pattern that dictates a lifestyle for a lifetime. An under standing of how this pattern is formed gives answers on correcting deficiencies that restrict personal development and sales abilities.

A successful salesperson will continually examine his or her values to be sure they are based on a love-motivation. He or she will also learn the prospect's values and create a sales presentation based upon the prospect's value system.

The subconscious mind has been labeled "the greatest computer known to mankind." Yet, a very small percentage of this potential is used. As this power is developed, the sales person can double or triple effectiveness in dealing with prospects.

Fear is the greatest destroyer of sales success. There is a formula for conquering fear:

Repetition x Acceptance = Renewed Mind. When this formula is used, fear is no longer a roadblock to a successful sales relationship.

True salesmanship is shown in the ability to determine the outcome of a sales situation. The clerk puts the responsibility of decision-making on the prospect. The successful salesperson sells the decision to the prospect.

Studies have shown that decisions are made in five minutes or less. All other thought on a subject is to justify the decision. If the decision is acceptance of the salesperson and the presentation, the pressure is off both the salesperson and the prospect. The signing of a contract is a natural response to the presentation.

Prospects are looking for a salesperson they can believe. The salesperson must develop an attitude of professionalism that projects confidence and competence.

Time and money are never a problem when a high value is placed on your product or service. When a salesperson creates value higher than cost, cost no longer remains an objection of whether or not to buy.

Salespeople are not in a sales situation until they have established their sales authority. Most salespeople work from a prospecting position rather than a sales position. It is impossible to sell until a position of authority is established.

The mechanism used to control the emotional environment is a series of daily check points and evaluation of responses to events. This awareness gives the feedback neces sary to maintain an attitude that projects enthusiasm and excitement and yet can handle the negatives that arise.

A salesperson has only one opportunity to make a first impression. A checklist of the ten most important areas of concern will help the salesperson be aware of the first impression they will make and what to do to make corrections where needed.

CHAPTER 14: Sales Interview159

Sales are lost when the salesperson "shoots from the hip," hoping something good will come from the presentation. Understanding what makes a presentation go smoothly (making the prospect comfortable and creating a sales atmosphere) is vital to success in sales.

CHAPTER 15: Personal Air Space171

We communicate with others by our body movements (actions and reactions) and our responses to touching or closeness. The ability to read the prospect's body language and react positively, can turn negative situations into sales situations.

CHAPTER 16: Telephone Success177

The telephone is one of the most valuable instruments created by man for the salesperson. A salesperson's ability to use the telephone effectively will determine his or her appointment setting skills.

CHAPTER 17: Motivations of Life185

Four basic "fear-motivations" control most of our behavior. The ability to recognize the prospect's fear-motivation and lift him or her above the fear will determine the ability to establish a sales relationship.

CHAPTER 18: The Prospect's Needs205

A salesperson must go beyond listening to what a prospect is saying, to a higher communication level of hearing why they are saying what they say. This ensures a presentation tailored to the needs of each prospect or client.

CHAPTER 19: Behavioral Deficiencies223

The difference between a strong salesperson and an unsuccessful salesperson is the ability to be the "doctor of sales." Closing ratios increase when the salesperson corrects his or her own areas of weakness and becomes a true "salesperson" rather than a "clerk."

EPILOGUE239

· Foreword ·

Relationship Selling is a stirring account of nearly 30 years of Dr. Orv Owens' ability to capture the very essence of selling—the ability to establish a meaningful and productive relationship.

Dr. Owens has made an exhaustive research into selling and relationships, as well as interviewing many outstanding successful salespersons who have used his most unique strategies. As a result of this successful operation, Dr. Owens has outlined his book, **RELATIONSHIP SELLING** and he has brilliantly pointed out the fact that there are four relationships that determine how successful a salesperson can become: Inward Relationship, Upward Relationship, Downward Relationship, and Outward Relationship. Dr. Owens has stated, "These principles are a must in establishing long-lasting relationships."

Dr. Owens also explains the difference between a salesperson and a clerk. Simply stated, a salesperson has the ability to establish a relationship in which the prospect recognizes the salesperson as a professional in his or her sales field. This is a "how to" book. It teaches relationship techniques rather than sales techniques. It proves that anyone can be successful in the sales field if he or she utilizes these relationship techniques.

I truly believe that this book is a book whose time has come to guide its readers to the understanding that success can be for everyone, and everyone can succeed with the right attitude and the right relationships.

We must hereby understand that a right attitude is everything; however, a right attitude can only be obtained through instant forgiveness and unconditional love, and that we as a people do not have the right to do as we please, except when we "please" to do right.

I believe as we have opportunities and successes through relationship selling, that we will always do good unto all mankind, and finally we will do good for our country, the greatest country in all the world, The United States of America.

To those readers who are already great salespersons, I say to you that reading Dr. Owens' book will only make you a better salesperson. And for those readers who will take pride in the achievement of great things in their lives, I commend their reading, **FELL'S OFFICIAL KNOW-IT-ALL GUIDE: RELATIONSHIP SELLING.**

—Dr. James "Johnny" Johnson
Former Under Secretary of the Navy,
Former Director U.S. Civil Service

· Editor's Statement ·

Before you contemplate closing your next deal read this book!

The world of sales is more than just product and price. It is about salesperson and customer and the relationship they have with one another. And when we talk of sales, it is not just about cars, homes or stocks. Sales can also mean services, such as financial, medical or educational.

FELL'S RELATIONSHIP SELLING will allow you to master the art of developing a relationship in a sales situation in five minutes or less! This book is for anyone who needs to build a professional relationship or market a service. This is for the individual seeking to develop repeat and referral business, for the true sales pros who understand that 80% of their business comes from just 20% of their clients.

You are in great hands with the sage advice of Orv Owens. When Orv first proposed doing this book he told me "Don't let the reader know I have a Ph.D." I asked him why he would want to keep such a proud accomplishment a secret. "Because they'll think I'm just spewing a bunch of theoretical and hypothetical garbage at them."

Let me assure you, in addition to his educational credentials, his most qualifying attribute is that he comes from thirty years of experience in helping hundreds of companies and thousands of individuals increase their productivity. As a result, sales forces multiply their closing ratios, and individuals become more effective in their family and personal life. His teachings are far from hypothetical. This man is proven and tested.

Orv proves time and again that you can make a sale, not by product, price or promise alone, but by building up a friendly but obligatory "can't-turn-you-down" relationship with the client or customer.

As a lecturer and consultant, Orv's popular seminars and 30-hour video cassette training package cost up to $10,000 but now, released for the first time in book form, here are the sales and motivational secrets of personal and professional success.

"This book teaches relationship techniques rather than sales techniques," says Orv. "This is about how to relate to the wants, needs and desires of a customer and present a service or product based upon that person's frame of reference. People do not buy a product or service until they have established a relationship with a salesperson."

Orv also serves as a trainer and convention speaker on the art of developing more productive relationships. His experience in research, sales and management include working with Fortune 500 corporations such as General Foods, IT&T, DuPont, Hughes, Xerox, as well as various federal government agencies, plus a wide variety of small businesses and associations.

Owens has appeared on most major broadcast news media as a sales expert.

Whatever your service or product, Orv offers you strategies that create a higher closing ratio, increase repeat and referral business and help you relate to each client, customer or patient. You overcome the greatest killer of sales relationships: FEAR, enabling you to analyze a sales situation, determine the person's inner motivations and make a presentation which is specially designed for the client's psychological make-up.

Offered here is the practical application of concepts and principles that have made people successful in business and in their professions.

Frederick Fell Publishers wishes you good luck in improving your sales efforts.

—Donald L. Lessne
Publisher

· Acknowledgments ·

Because I am far more comfortable as a speaker rather than an author, I wish to give recognition to the many people who have been a part of creating this book. To Erin Morris who helped me turn spoken word into written word. To Carol Fenimore who worked long hours polishing the manuscript and making me look like a writer. To Ron Winter, Bennie Harris, Virginia Schneider, Dick and Margie Hammer, Jerry Hammer, Lurline Halmo, Tom Rockwood, Carolyn Rockwood, Mildred Yeager, and Sherilynn Mason who came to my assistance when I needed them the most. To Bob Shaw and Anna Pusz for their encouragement. It was much appreciated. To the Gold Card Family that have been friends and supporters and a sounding board for the development of new material over many years. To the thousands of people who have sat under my teaching and have encouraged me to write a book. Also special thanks to Frederick Fell Publishers and all of their helpers: Brian Feinblum, Vicki Heil, Donald Lessne and Chris Pearl. Most of all, to the Grace of God who has led me to this point in my life where I can offer something of value to any person that reads these pages. I will forever appreciate each of you.

· Introduction ·

What Is Relationship Selling

I will never forget hearing my first sales manager say, "Remember guys, you're not selling grass shavers, you're selling yourself." I was confused, because we, at age twelve and ten (my brother Dave was my partner) thought we were selling grass shavers.

Now, in case you have never heard of a grass shaver, it was a handy little invention which used six discarded Gillette double-edged razor blades on an aluminum sickle-type gadget and was great for trimming the lawn or the tall grass which grew along the sidewalk. Our training was to memorize a complete sales presentation in how to sell this new invention, door-to-door. Most of the sales staff were in their late teens or early twenties, but Dave and I proved we could sell, even though we were young.

"You see," said the sales manager, "if the prospects buy you, they will buy what you say, and if they buy what you say in your presentation, they will buy a grass shaver."

Well, I wasn't sure what he meant; however, when Dave and I would walk up to a door, I did the best I could to sell myself. "Good afternoon ma'am, may we have a few minutes of your time to show you a new product which will save you time and hard work. We represent the "Grass Shaver Company" and we are offering this new time-saving product to you at a special introductory price." In most cases at about this spot in my presentation, the lady of the house would say, "Just a minute son. Harold, come here quick! Now, tell us again so that my husband can hear about it." She wanted to have her husband hear these little kids talking like big businessmen. I would start all over and normally before I could get through the presentation we would be handed green money, sometimes with a tip for doing such a good job, and we would walk down the sidewalk saying to each other, this is the easiest money we have ever made. One lady said, "I will take two," and gave us a five dollar tip, which was a lot of money in those days.

Both Dave and I have been in sales of some type most of our adult lives, and I think both of us have never forgotten, "You don't sell grass shavers, you sell yourself."

Selling a Relationship

In my research and studies for material in the development of sales seminars I have changed that a bit to say, you don't sell a product or a service, you sell a relationship. In this relationship, prospects buy you as an authority in your field—a person who can be trusted to do the best possible job for them. I often ask the question, "What kind of automobile insurance do you have? What are the limits and the coverage?" Most people do not know, but they do know the name of their insurance agent. In fact, in most cases they have the agent's business card handy in their wallet. You see, they didn't buy insurance, they bought an agent who takes care of all of their insurance needs.

Turning a Prospect Into a Client

When the salesperson establishes a sales relationship with the prospect, the prospect becomes a client. The client will buy, give referrals and repeat business and will remain a client as long as the relationship is in place.

In this book you will learn how to establish so strong a relationship that the prospect believes in you. You become the answer to their problem, the supplier of their needs, and the person who can be counted on to do the best job possible for that person you now call your client.

When this belief exists there is no longer any competition. You have established a legalized monopoly and your client would never think of talking to another salesperson about your product or service. You have become what I call the "Doctor of Sales."

If you have a family physician you do not shop around each time you have medical needs. If you have a family dentist, attorney, or chiropractor, you do not leaf through the Yellow Pages to discover what the competition is offering. When it comes time to use one of those services, you go to your professional.

If you are the doctor of sales, your clients will inform the competition that they are not interested in a presentation because they already have a salesperson who takes care of that business for them.

Relationship selling is not based upon how long you have been in sales, how knowledgeable you are in your field, or how many answers to questions you have memorized. I am not saying knowledge and experience is not valuable, but I am saying very few of your clients know how knowledgeable you are, and probably very few, if any, new prospects ask the question, "How long have you been in sales?"

Relationship selling does not require you to develop a long list of closes which you can plug into just about any sales situation. The most important aspect of success in sales is how to establish a sales relationship and maintain it throughout your career.

A young salesman, Michael J. Griffith, attended a seminar I gave to his firm in Anaheim, California some years back, and the next day he made a sale — his first.

After settlement, the buyer wrote the owner, congratulating him on hiring such outstanding talent as Michael Griffith. He went on to say that he had done a great deal of house-hunting in Southern California and that Mike was the most knowledgeable and professional salesperson he had ever met. He also said his firm was moving many new employees into the area and he would certainly encourage them to call on his company and Mike Griffith for all of their real estate needs.

Was Mike the most knowledgeable real estate salesperson in Southern California at that time? He would tell you, "No." But he did know how to establish a relationship with a prospect so that the prospect became a client. The referral business which came to Mike over the next few years was proof of Mike's success with this client.

I would say Mike was successful with this person because he established a relationship, causing the prospect to believe in him. The client bought Mike, making Mike his doctor of sales. With his position established in their relationship, Mike was able to meet the prospect's wants and needs. Mike was able to sell based upon the prospect's frame of reference and conquer all the fears which had caused the prospect not to buy from other well-meaning salespeople.

Each chapter in this book will give you psychological concepts and principles which will, when applied, cause you to be effective in relationship selling. They will help you develop such a strong relationship with your prospects that they will believe in you, believe what you say, and buy what you sell.

Being a Sales Professional

When you develop your abilities in relationship selling, over 50% of your sales will be from repeat and referral business. You will be a part of the elite 20% of the sales force which makes 80% of the sales. You can expect your customers to think of you as the professional in your business, and you will enjoy the financial rewards which come with success in the sales field.

Turning Ability Into Capability

You were born with the ability to walk but you had to develop the capability. You were born with the ability to talk, but you had to develop the capability. I believe everyone is born with the ability to sell, but it is up to us to develop and maximize that capability. Our study of successful salespeople—what they are doing that unsuccessful salespeople fail to do—will give you the concepts and principles of relationship selling that you will need to reach your personal goals in the sales field.

CHAPTER 1

FOUNDATION RELATIONSHIPS

☞ *Success Defined*
☞ *Four Key Relationships*
☞ *Selling Yourself*
☞ *How to Sell*

As a consultant to marketing and sales organizations for over 20 years, I have seen salespeople double, triple and quadruple their closing ratio by applying basic psychological principles in the area of relationship selling.

In the most simple form, "relationship selling" is changing a prospect into a client in five minutes or less, by establishing a relationship in which the prospect trusts the salesperson. When I become your customer, you become my source. Then I can believe you will do for me what I cannot do for myself. This belief eliminates the need for me to look around, shop, talk to others, or see what other firms have on the market. I have bought you and with that decision came the trust that you will look out for my good, that your knowledge will become dependable advice, and that I will get a *fair shake* in all of my dealings with you.

I had an appointment at the home of the vice president of a corporation for which I was doing management consulting. As I approached his home I noticed a *"For Sale"* sign in the yard. The sign caught my interest because it had been placed there by a firm that had been using our sales training for several years. I asked the owner how he had chosen that particular real estate firm to list his home. "That's an interesting story," he said. "We bought this home seven years ago and the salesman did a great job for us. When it was time to sell, my wife thought we should list it with the same salesperson. Upon calling his office we discovered he no longer worked for that firm. We asked for information concerning his new place of employment, but they indicated they were not at liberty to give us that information. Finally, we found him in the white pages of the telephone directory. When we called his home, his wife gave us his place of employment. That's how we chose this company to list our home."

I couldn't point to our outstanding training program and take credit for this listing. I could, however, point to a *real* salesperson who had developed a sales relationship that was so successful it brought repeat business -- the hard way. I might also add here that the firm which couldn't help this couple find their salesperson will never have another opportunity to do business with these people. In later chapters we will deal with fear motivations, and you will see how this firm created a *wall* rather than a *relationship,* and how those walls destroy potential business.

When a salesperson creates a strong relationship with a client, success in sales is guaranteed. Whether or not the market is good, business will be strong for any salesperson who uses relationship selling principles.

Most salespeople in the corporate world today are not really salespeople at all; they simply are *clerks*. They present their product or service and hope the prospects will select what they want to buy, and take it away with them. However, *real* salespeople have the ability to get out of their own shoes and into the shoes of their prospects in order to establish relationships which translates prospects into clients. With a relationship established the customer can relate to the salesperson's principles of selling. The program, product or service is presented based upon the prospect's frame of reference rather than that of the salesperson.

Frame of Reference

All of Life's Experiences Focused on a Now Decision

In relationship selling you must be able to see and feel what the client is seeing and feeling, and know the reason. Your ability to relate to each client, individually, is dependent upon your understanding of his or her *frame of reference.*

Most salespeople sell the way they would like to be sold, but a true salesperson will sell the way the client *needs* to be sold. All of us are different. There are no two of us just alike; therefore, getting into the shoes of your prospects determines how successful you will be in making a presentation that will relate to their values. Until you can relate to the prospect's values and relate them to your product or service, they cannot buy.

Bennie Harris, one of the most successful insurance agents I know, had a prospect who believed he would outlive his wife and children; so, why should he need life insurance? Bennie had to create a scenario where he *also* outlived his finances. He showed his prospect an insured savings program that would guarantee him a lifetime income which would never stop, even if he lived to be 110! The man bought the program. The reason to buy must be in harmony with the client's frame of reference. You will only discover this truism when you have first established a relationship.

I want to help you be more effective in establishing relationships with customers so that you can relate your presentation to their area of need.

I know a copy machine salesperson who finds little corners in offices which are not being used and sells small desk top copiers to fit the empty spot. I also know a real estate agent who, when showing a home, has her male clients get into the shower (with their clothes on, of course), bend over, and pretend to pick up the soap without bumping anything. There are hundreds of illustrations I could use, but in every case, the salesperson is relating to the client's "needs," and not their own interests.

Just to establish some common ground, and to make sure we are all going in the same direction, I would like to give you my definition of *success.* If you cannot relate to it at this time, you will be able to do so after you have read this book.

Success

Your ability to establish long-lasting relationships

Every measure of success you have experienced in your life is a result of the fact that you first established a relationship. If you developed a good relationship with a school teacher you learned a great deal from that person. You established a relationship with an employer to get a job and kept that relationship strong in order to be productive in the job. If you have ever quit or been fired from a position, it was because of the breakdown in a relationship.

You must have a good self-concept, a high self-esteem, and high self-acceptance to achieve growth and reach goals in life. That means having a strong relationship with yourself. It is vitally important that you understand how to establish relationships with people, and this is especially true in a sales situation.

Selling Yourself

If you establish a relationship with me, you have *sold* yourself to me. People have told me, "I'm just not a salesperson," or "I can't sell." That is *not* true! Everybody sells. You sold yourself to your friends. Those friendships were established based upon you selling yourself. A woman said to me, "I can't sell. I've never been able to sell anything." I asked her if she was married, and she replied, "Yes." I told her she was one of the greatest salespeople in the world. She sold some guy on the idea of living with her the rest of her life. That's a pretty good sales job!

If you are a parent, you are in the sales field because you have to sell principles to your children 24 hours a day, 7 days a week. You *are* in sales. If you are in management today you are *really* in sales. Whenever you present a new idea to your employees you are selling that idea to them. So, don't say you are not in sales. I want you to relate to the material in this book, regardless of your position in life. Your ability to be successful in sales is based upon your ability to establish long-lasting relationships.

Four Relationships

1. Inward Relationship:

There are four basic relationships in your world. The first is an *inward relationship* -- how you relate to yourself, or who you think you are. It is the most important relationship you will ever establish. Your ability to establish relationships in the other areas of your life is based upon your ability to first establish a relationship with yourself.

Self-Confidence

Self-confidence creates confidence in a prospect's mind. Self-doubt, likewise, is projected to a prospect and creates doubt or fear in the prospect, which is reflected back as sales resistance, objection, and a lost sale. *You* must believe in *you* before I can believe in *you*. If I am going to buy from you, you must help me conquer my fear rather than create fear within me. Your inward relationship is measured in self-acceptance, a strong self-image and high self-esteem.

Self-Acceptance

Self-acceptance is when you know who you are (both strengths and weaknesses) and focus on using your strengths and conquering your weaknesses. Weakness is created by a failure to develop natural abilities into capabilities. In reality, you don't have weaknesses, you have undeveloped areas in your life.

A young woman in California talked to me at a break in one of my seminars. She had always wanted to be in management but did not believe people would take her seriously. She did not have experience in leadership and had never really pushed herself to become a manager. I told her that leadership abilities are developed by assuming responsibility, and that this could start in small areas of her life and then continue to grow as she gained confidence. If you fail to assume responsibility you will never develop your natural leadership abilities. I had opportunity to see this woman three times over a period of five years, and each time she had been promoted to a higher level of management. When she could accept herself as a *leader,* she was recognized *as* a leader. I believe the only limits you and I have are the limits we place upon ourselves in our *inward relationship*. In later chapters we will focus on creating a continual development of self-acceptance.

Self-Image

Self-Image is a mental picture of your ability to perform -- what you can or cannot do. "I have always been clumsy," or "Math has never been my subject," are expressions of a negative self-image. Hypnosis has proven our limitations are caused by belief rather than physical ability or intelligence.

Building a strong self-image in sales is vital to your success. You must believe in your ability to relate your presentation to your prospect, your ability to answer any question your prospect might ask, and your ability to close sales. You *can* develop your self-image, and it will, in turn, become a motivating force within you. This is the importance of the inward relationship. It will be a motivating force if it is positive or a debilitating fear if it is negative.

Self-Esteem

Another dimension of the inward relationship is *self-esteem,* or how much value you place upon who you are. This is not conceit or bragging about how great you are; it is a realization of your own uniqueness and unlimited potential. You take care of the things in your life that have high value. Family heirlooms, jewelry, fine automobiles or purebred animals are well provided for and protected. When you place a high value on yourself, you become more aware of the productive use of your time, your creativity, and your abilities. You are careful to avoid things which can destroy you, such as drugs, alcohol, smoking, being overweight, etc. The best way to control these areas of your life is to increase your self-esteem to the point that you would not do anything to destroy yourself. This also will become a source of self-discipline which will cause you to develop your abilities in sales which will make you successful. The fact that you are reading this book is an indication that your inward relationship is strong. In the next few chapters I will give you some methods to increase your inward relationship.

2. *Upward Relationship:*

The second is the upward relationship - how you relate to those in authority over you and those for whom you work.

Our basketball coach was fired at the end of a losing season. Some felt it was a bad decision. We liked him, and if he had not lost several *stars* to injuries, or even had a little more talent on the team it might have been different. This year a new coach was hired and he's making the athletic director look like a genius. The team hasn't lost a game, and has dominated most of its opponents. How can a coach with pretty much the same players turn a team around so quickly? The reason is, the coach is the source of motivation, direction, correction and team building. The team which relates well to the coach has the best chance of winning.

Power comes from the top down, and a good working relationship with the boss will move you toward success. If you don't like your sales manager you will have difficulty wanting to go to work. If you don't relate well with your sales manager, you will not learn and develop. If you are not subordinate to your sales manager you will not be effective in your relationship with fellow salespeople, and, most assuredly, you will have difficulty with your clients. I would say, if you cannot establish a good working relationship with your sales manager, do yourself, your manager, your fellow salespeople and your customers a favor. *Find a new job!*

Your source of authority and power and your source of opportunity is a strong upward relationship. You must work to enhance it every day because your sales success is dependent upon this relationship. I am not speaking of friendships or being a buddy. I'm not even referring to liking the boss. The important ingredient is a strong working relationship which carries mutual respect, good communication, and common values and goals. If this is all in place, you can grow and be productive. Perhaps you would change a lot of things if you were the sales manager. However, until you are, work on establishing good relationships.

3. *Downward Relationship:*

The third is the *downward relationship,* which is the reverse of the upwards—how you relate to those you have responsibility for or authority over. As a salesperson, you were given sales authority to market your product or service. This may have required a license, training, or technical knowledge. However, in all cases, you were commissioned by your employer to be a salesperson. This authority gives you a position to assume responsibility and be of service to your prospects. A sales relationship is based upon your ability to fulfill the wants, needs, and desires of your prospect. Your ability to sell is dependent upon establishing a downward relationship. Most of this book is directed toward this relationship.

4. *Outward Relationship:*

And the fourth relationship is how you relate outwardly, or how you relate to people on a peer level or socially. In the field of sales the outward relationship will be a great source of knowledge and personal growth. Your fellow salespeople, as well as salespeople you meet at conventions, conferences, association meetings and seminars can give you great insight into what does and does not work. You can draw from their experiences to develop your sales ability and knowledge. Learning one idea which you can use repetitively can move you toward a higher level of success in the sales field. Work at developing strong outward relationships

Tom had been working on a large commercial real estate deal but had bumped into what seemed to be a stone wall. The deal looked good except for the amounts of cash the buyer was able to put together for the down payment. While attending a Board of Realtors luncheon, a salesperson, representing another firm, described a similar deal he had made and how he had solved the problem. Within two days, Tom had his sale. Tom believes if he had not attended that luncheon, had not developed a relationship with a salesperson from another firm, or had just kept the problem to himself, he would have lost the sale. The *outward relationships* in your field of sales need to be developed and nurtured.

If you are successful in these four areas of your life, you will be successful in sales. If you are *lacking* in any one of these areas then we would say you are not really successful. It detracts from your sales ability and you are not really happy either. You need to achieve a balance in these four areas.

We have found in our research of successful salespeople that one of the common threads woven into the fabric of success is the ability to establish relationships in these four areas. In the following chapters, you will learn how to develop your capabilities in each area. This will be manifested in your sales volume, as well as repeat and referral business.

CHAPTER 2

EMOTIONS OF SUCCESS

☞ *Pressure Selling*
☞ *Love Motivation*
☞ *Fear Motivation*
☞ *Winning Prospects*

We are emotional beings. Therefore, controlling our emotions and recognizing the emotions of our prospects will give us the control in a sales presentation which we must have to be productive and effective.

There are two basic emotions which are the basis of your motivations in life and all emotions are based upon these two—*Love Motivation* and *Fear Motivation*. I will share with you my definition of these emotions and how I believe they effect and influence your ability to sell.

Love Motivation

Total Giving Without Expecting Anything in Return

Many people talk about *love*. There have been thousands of songs written about love. I want to look at *"love motivation,"* which is the emotion behind all positive actions and reactions. It is not *the norm* in the sales field or in our

9

world. In our society, we operate on what we call the *law of fair exchange*. "I'll do something for you if you will do something for me." Or, you have probably heard this one, "I'll scratch your back if you'll scratch mine." Or perhaps, "I'll be nice to you if you'll be nice to me." And then, "I'll say nice things about you if you'll say nice things about me."

Then the reverse possibly would be, "If you are going to talk about me that way, I'll talk about you that way, too." I will make it a bit worse than what was said about me.

The *law of fair exchange* always says, "What's in it for me?" There are bumper stickers that talk about the law of fair exchange. Things like, "If it feels good do it," or "Do unto others before they do unto you." The majority of people in our world today don't know what *real love* is.

Love is an important emotion because your ability to love—especially yourself first and then others—is your ability to sell. Your ability to give of yourself based upon who people are rather than what they have done or how they look or how intelligent they are will determine how successful you will be in establishing relationships within your sales field.

I choose to love my wife, my children, and my friends, simply because of who they are. That alone qualifies them for my love. I would tell you something else. You have to love yourself on that same basis. If you try accepting yourself for all the great things you do (and you know all the mistakes you make) you will find you have trouble loving yourself. Until you accept yourself, you cannot accept anyone else. Until you accept yourself you cannot accept me. Until you accept yourself you cannot accept your sales manager, your prospect, your client, your spouse, your children, or your God. It's important that you choose to love yourself.

I choose to accept you today simply because you are who you are. You don't have to qualify. You don't have to meet any standard. Just because you are breathing air and are alive, I choose to love you. I might not like everything you do, but I accept you for who you are. I can do that with a prospect I have never met. I can do that on the telephone when setting an appointment. I can even accept someone who hangs up on me when I am trying to set an appointment, or someone who says, "no" in a sales presentation. If I can't accept them in that situation I'm going to have trouble accepting them when they say, "Yes." If I can only accept them when they say "Yes," then I am not accepting them at all. It is merely a love for the money they are going to put in my pocket by buying from me —not a love for them as people.

Have you ever had a salesman come up to you and you could see dollar signs in his eyes? "How are you doing today?" he asks. "Can I help you with something?" There is no doubt in your mind that this person's only interest in you is making a sale. And, if he sees you on the street tomorrow, he won't even recognize or remember you.

You like to buy from people who believe in you, who accept you and who relate to you. And people like to buy from you when you can relate to them. You have to be able to give of yourself, not because you are going to get money, but because you believe you offer your client what is best for them. Your function in life as a sales person is to love people, whether or not they buy from you. When you accept people who don't buy from you there is a better chance that someday they *will* buy from you, because they did not feel pressure from you. When you accept people, more people will buy from you because it is a *pure* love motivation, as opposed to a calculated or coercive grabbing which the prospect can feel.

The main concern of the real estate firm which had the policy to never give the new employment of a past salesperson was the possibility of losing a prospect. Guess what happened? They lost a prospect!!

You have never really been fooled when someone really loved you and accepted you. Your customers can also feel it when there is a wall between you and them or when they feel pushed into something.

Pressure Selling

Have you ever heard the words *pressure selling?* That is simply a situation where salespeople do not accept their prospects. They love the sale rather than the customer. If you believe your product or service represents an opportunity for your prospect, then you are doing them a favor by making your sales presentation to them. You are expressing love by selling. Incidentally, if you do not love your product, service, or company that much, (sales managers, hang on to your chair while I say this), then you should *quit!* You're not going to do a good job for yourself, your company, or your products, anyway!

You must believe in your product or the service you sell in order to sell that product or service. If you don't, the principles in this book will not work for you. You cannot use what I teach to *coerce* people into buying.

The opposite of love motivation is *fear motivation.* In looking for a definition of the word *"fear"* I consulted the dictionary. The dictionary's definition is *being fearful.* I didn't find that definition very helpful, so I have a *definition* that I believe will be more meaningful to you as a salesperson.

Fear Motivation
An Emotional Response to a Belief of Loss

If I believe you are going to take advantage of me, if I believe I am not going to get what is rightfully mine, or if I think I'm going to lose face, fear takes over and I start building fear emotions. This causes me to set up defense mechanisms which ultimately push you away.

Fear destroys relationships as much as love builds relationships. We have known for years that dogs will bite people who are afraid of dogs. Bees will sting people who fear them, and horses will throw you if you are afraid. Studies have shown that fear in a salesperson will create fear in the prospect. Sales people who fear they will blow the sale or say the wrong thing at the wrong time will create resistance in their prospects. They can sense tension, which in turn, creates defense mechanisms. Sales are lost because the salesperson is projecting fear. On the other hand, most people go into a sales situation fearful of making a *wrong* decision.

There is a relatively new business in the United States and many people are doing very well with it. It is that of a professional car buying service. When you are ready to buy a car, you hire this person to purchase the car for you. You tell your buyer what you want and the entire deal is handled for a percentage of the savings. The reason for the success in this new venture is that most people are afraid to buy a car because they do not understand how to play the game. The *"pro"* saves them money because he knows how car salespeople work. He plays by their rules and wins. These stories are causing greater fear in prospects and *you* must deal with it. Your job as a salesperson is to help prospects conquer the apprehension and fear they bring into a buying situation. If you make a presentation to me today and I say, "I'll have to think about it," I am telling you I still have fears; therefore, I have to think about it. If I say, "I'd like to shop around a little bit," I am really saying that I am afraid I am going to buy the wrong product from the wrong person. Therefore, I better shop around a little more. And if I say, "No, I'm not interested," and you know I really should be interested because your product is so good and your service is so great, then what I am really telling you is that I have fears stronger than the reasons you have given me to buy.

The salesperson's job, therefore, is to help people conquer fears because once fear is eliminated there is no longer a reason not to buy. Do you want to increase your closing ratio? It's very simple. Conquer your prospects' fears and in conquering their fears you will help them solve a problem in their lives, and that is an expression of love.

A stockbroker once told me about one of his clients who lost a great amount of money on Black Tuesday. He was thinking about getting out of all his stock investments and switching to real estate. He felt, "At least, the property is still there, no matter what!" The broker asked him if he thought all of the companies in which he had invested were going to fold? The answer, of course, was "No." The broker then encouraged the investor with the fact that his investments were going to come back stronger than ever, and that this was the time to buy, not to sell. That is what his client did, and, incidentally, he did well with his investments. When fear is conquered, the total attitude changes, and there is more reason to buy than not to buy.

Love Dispels Fear

Scientists have discovered that love motivated thoughts programmed into the subconscious mind dispels the effect of fear which exists there. Where *love is,* fear cannot exist. Where *fear is,* there is no love. It is like darkness and light. Where there is light, darkness is dispelled. It is interesting that light is real and darkness is not real. Darkness is simply the absence of light. If there were reality to darkness we could create darkness. You could go to a switch on the wall and turn on darkness. We can't do that. All we can do is close out light.

There is no *reality* to fear. Fear is an emotional response to a belief of loss. It is not after the fact, it is before the fact. It is a projection. The word *belief* here means it has not happened yet. It is well-defined in the old saying, "Don't cross bridges before you get to them," or "Don't count your chickens before they hatch."

You cannot be afraid of a car accident you had yesterday. You might be afraid you will have another tomorrow, but that is merely a projection—once burned, twice shy. Do you know why you are shy? You are afraid it is going to happen again, and that is fear. You are not afraid of the burn. That has already happened. There is nothing to be afraid of there. It is that it might happen again; therefore, fear is never a reality!

On the other hand, love is a *now* emotion. It is something you can experience right now and as you experience love, you conquer fear. The more love you have the less you will have to fear. The greater your fears, the less love you will have. Therefore, we can *measure* your *love motivation* by your level of fear. If you are a fearful person, you will literally create fears in other people with whom you come in contact. If you are a love-motivated person, you will create a relaxed, love-motivated feeling in others. You will cause people to relax and be comfortable around you. Have you met people and upon meeting them it was as though you had known them all your life and you were very relaxed in their presence? You probably felt they were "just as common as an old shoe." That was because they projected love and when you received that love it caused you to feel comfortable with them.

Your ability to become successful in sales is based upon your ability to become a love-motivated person - to project love into a sales situation and cause people to relax. I want you to understand these definitions and if you did not catch it in this chapter, go back over it again and again, because until you conquer fear, and until you know what love motivation *is,* you will never be successful in sales. You will never be happy, and you will never be successful in any relationships in your life.*Success is based upon relationships.* Relationships are based upon a love motivation and fear causes a destruction of relationships.

In your lifetime you have experienced fears from way back in your childhood, and you continue to respond to those fears today. Many of these fears are unknown to you because they are unconscious fears. In fact, if you were afraid of the dark when you were a child, there's a good chance you're afraid of commissioned sales as an adult. Can you see it as a relative fear. Fear of the dark is an unknown, and what is commissioned selling? It is *really* an unknown! However, if you know who you are and if you love the person you are, you will love commissioned selling because you know you will be a success. If you conquer your fears, commissioned sales is far more positive than a salaried position and much less confining.

You see, the most successful people in the world don't worry about how much money they are going to make because they know they are going to make *plenty.* They are going to give so much service that money will automatically follow.

When my wife and I were first married we were very poor. In fact, we were so poor, that poor folks called us poor. That is poor! We did not eat well. I remember one dinner my wife fixed was lima beans. That was not the main dish—it was the *dinner.* One morning we found five boxes of groceries on our porch. Someone, in the middle of the night, had brought groceries to these poor kids who were "starving to death." We did not know who it was, because there was not a note with the groceries. We could not even call someone and say, "Oh, thank you, you shouldn't have." But we did enjoy the groceries!

After studying these principles over the years, I have thought often of those people. I can envision them shopping for these kids...going down a grocery aisle, picking up five of these and 10 of those, and saying, "Oh, I know they will love these." They bought things they probably would never buy for themselves. They most likely did not even look at the prices as they shopped. When they paid for the groceries they probably smiled at the clerk! People *never* do that, unless, of course, they are expressing *love*. Then at 2:00 a.m. they come coasting up to our front door. They do not want the engine noise to awaken us, because their surprise would be ruined. So, they tip-toe up to our doorstep, leave the boxes, and drive off into the night, feeling good. Why? Because when you are giving without expecting anything in return, you automatically receive *joy*. Many years have passed since this event occurred in our life, but, wherever those people are today, they can think back to the time when they bought groceries for the hungry kids, and they will feel as good today as on the day they bought the groceries. The joy of giving never dilutes. It never disappears. It never weakens. It is a *forever* thing.

It is also true with you in sales. You will be successful in sales when you know who you are, love yourself, love the person for whom you work, love your prospects, express love in offering your service, and conquer your prospects' fears so they can experience your service. When you have done that you will live on repeat and referral business. You will have relationships which will continue through the years. You will have clients rather than just prospects, and you will *truly be* a salesperson. We would choose to call you a "Doctor of Sales."

Rather than selling a product or service you sell yourself. You sell a relationship and you sell or give love. When you give love, I have to buy from you because I believe in you. That is real salesmanship. When you love, you sell. When you are fear-motivated you fail. Do not *choose* to be a failure. *Choose to love yourself* and those you meet and you will be a *super*-successful salesperson, no matter what you do.

CHAPTER 3

CHILDHOOD SHADOWS

☞ *Pure Learning*
☞ *Inferiority Complex*
☞ *Identifying Mistakes*
☞ *Identifying With Mistakes*

At a very young age, we take into our subconscious mind ideas and thoughts about ourselves. These thoughts come as a result of our successes and failures and from this information our self-image is created. This mental picture of yourself affects your sales ability and how your prospects and clients will respond to your sales presentation. In this chapter we will take a look at how fear is created—its causes— and discuss the basic problems salespeople must deal with as a result of these fears.

We will learn how to conquer those fears later. Let's begin by discussing how *fears* are *created*.

Pure Learning

The first two years of life are considered *pure learning* years. These are the highest impact years in a child's development. It is so strong in the first two years of life because in those years children believe everything they are told. If you tell them the moon is made of blue cheese, Santa Claus comes down the chimney, or the Easter Bunny brings eggs, they will believe you.

My youngest son, Kenny, illustrated this clearly to me a few years ago at the age of two. Often my wife will buy me a box of chocolate covered cherries (my favorite). On one occasion Kenny asked if he could have a piece of candy and I gave him a cherry. About ten minutes later, he came back with chocolate all over his face, running off his chin, and on his hands and asked, "Can I have another chocolate?" I said, "No. If you eat too many chocolates you will get pimples." The next day, he came back to me and said, "Daddy, can I have another pimple?"

You believe most of what you hear between birth and age two, and that information becomes a vital part of your life. We believe that in the first two years over 50% of our self-image is developed. Now you might say, "Wait a minute. I can do a lot of things today that I couldn't do at age two." I'm not talking about what you are capable of doing. I'm talking about who you think you are—the person you believe you are.

Most of the person you identify as being *you* was developed by age two and the interesting thing is that you now act as though all that you learned in the first two years is true.

If, as a small child, your parents took you along to functions which included people in a variety of social settings, you probably have felt comfortable meeting new people, which is a great asset in the sales field. If on the other hand, you were left with baby sitters and was not exposed to strangers, you might have difficulty meeting new people, which creates problems for you in prospecting, making cold calls and first appointments.

The impact your first two years of life had upon your sales ability is hard to measure. We do know, however, that your personality, whether or not you are outgoing or reserved, have a sense of humor or are quiet and stoic, had its beginning in those years. That is why we often hear people say, "He or she is a born salesperson." The fact is, there is *no* born salesperson; but, personality traits developed in the first two years of life can enhance a person's ability to sell.

If you developed people skills as a child, that is great. If you did not, the chapters ahead will help you do the necessary steps to develop those skills.

Strong Learning

The years from age two to six are *strong learning* years. Strong learning is when you believe *most* of what you hear. How often have you heard parents say that when their children were small they believed everything they were told but now that they are older they just argue all the time. Well, they just *grew out* of those strong learning years.

We also believe that by age six, over 80% of our psychological makeup is developed. That means for the rest of your life approximately 20% of your self-image changes. Needless to say, we are generalizing, but we do know that most of what you believe about who you are was established at an early age. Try thinking about the changes in your self-image that you have made since the age of six. There are still fears in areas where you had fear at age six, and in areas where you were confident you still experience *confidence*. These fears can have a *debilitating* effect on you as a salesperson today. Fear of *rejection,* fear of the *unknown,* and fear of *failure* are three which can cause you not to set appointments, fail to ask for the order, be weak on the phone, and *most popular,* waste time talking to other salespeople rather than pursuing new customers.

These childhood fears can destroy your sales potential and have caused many people to give up the sales field. How many fears do *you have* holding you back from the success you should be experiencing? Any changes have come as a result of effort on your part to change and develop.

The problem is, as parents we *abuse* rather than *use* those first six years, the *pure learning* and *strong learning* years. Rather than creating the type of self-image we want in our children, we tend to create problems *for* the children which will stay with them their entire lives.

Here is a good illustration about little Johnny, who is two years old. He is sitting in his high chair having breakfast and decides he wants to drink his milk all by himself, and he has never *flown solo!* This is his first try and no one is watching. The glass slips out of his hand because it is too heavy and, of course, the glass hits the table and breaks into a hundred pieces. The milk runs off the end of the table and down his leg and it is *cold.* Now, remember, Johnny was not *trying* to fail. He was *trying* to succeed. He was merely trying to drink like a "big person." And then, while he is feeling like a failure, his mother says to him, "You stupid idiot, you spilled your milk. How can you be so dumb?" And so, now little Johnny, who believes *everything,* thinks he is a stupid idiot who spills milk! You must admit that is a pretty poor start in life.

I know you would never say anything like that to your children but many people *do.* If you think about it, it is a pretty dumb statement because Johnny knows he spilled his milk, he can feel it running down his legs. Secondly, he was not trying to spill the milk. He was trying to be a *big boy,* but he felt like a *failure,* because he spilled the milk. Now, it is even worse because he believes everything he hears.

A little bit later he is outside playing and runs into the house and across the new carpets with mud on his shoes. And his dad says, "Look what you're doing. Were you born in a barn? What a pig! Get out of here." So, now Johnny knows he is a stupid idiot who spills milk, who was born in a barn and is a pig. He has accepted as fact that he is a loser. Because of that belief, Johnny will *identify with mistakes* he makes in life rather than *identify his mistakes*. And that is a problem!

Inferiority Complex

By the time Johnny reaches age ten, he will have an inferiority complex. We believe 99.9% of our population (I would say 100% but that would be an absolute, so we back off and say 99.9%) have an *inferiority complex* by age *ten*. If I were to ask you if at any time in your life you had an inferiority complex, I already know you would have to answer, "Yes." If you did not answer, "Yes," I would know you have *two problems*. You are a liar *and* you have an inferiority complex!

The sad part of this scenario is that only 5% of our population ever conquer these feelings of inadequacy, learn who they really are, and become what we call love-motivated. That means 95% of our population goes through an entire lifetime limited by some degree of fear of inadequacy which we call an *inferiority complex*. And, we would say, they are *fear-motivated*.

They say things, buy things, wear things, and react to things, based upon a fear-motivation which literally destroys their ability to be successful and happy. This is the reason only 20% of most sales forces make 80% of the sales. The interesting thing about that statistic, however, is that salespeople, on an average, have less fears than people in most other professions. It is impossible to be successful in sales if fear *controls your thinking*. So salespeople either conquer their fear *before* they enter the sales field, or are working to conquer fear as they grow in experience.

Identifying Mistakes

A love-motivated person, the 5%, *identifies mistakes*. When we identify mistakes we simply say, "Whoops, I spilled the milk" and we clean it up and try again. Or, "Whoops, I tracked the carpets" and we clean it up and try again. "I lost that sale, but I learned a lesson that will help me be more effective as a salesperson next time." You will lose some sales because of mistakes you will make. It is important to *identify the mistake* and learn from it, but not to allow the mistake to shake your confidence by creating a fear that you might repeat the mistake. Home run hitters also strike out a lot. Successful salespeople have learned a lot of lessons the hard way, but have not identified *with* the mistakes. When we *identify mistakes* we can then make a correction. "It's not who I am, it's just what I did." And so, we correct the mistake and move on to a higher level of success and actually learn from the mistake.

The *principle* is simply this. If you are setting appointments, making presentations, and making cold calls, you will make a few mistakes. A person who is not doing anything will not make mistakes except the mistake of not doing anything. *The more productive you are in sales, the* more mistakes you will make.

Identifying with Mistakes

The fear motivated person *identifies WITH mistakes,* and when you do so, you identify with failure. "That's me. What can you expect from a stupid idiot who spills milk, was born in a barn and is a pig?" Here are a few quotes from a salesperson who identifies with mistakes. "I am weak in the close," "I'm not very good at setting appointments," or "That person is not my kind of prospect." There are many I could add to the list and you could probably list some of your *own*. In all cases, it is accepting the mistake or lost sale as a measurement of sales ability, and that can stop your growth and personal development as a salesperson. If you *identify with mistakes*, then every time you make a mistake, you will believe, in your mind, that you are stupid or dumb.

I tell my children that I make more mistakes than anyone else in the world. I do not know if that is accurate but I do not know anyone who makes more mistakes than me. I want my children to understand there is nothing wrong with making mistakes. That does not make me a failure. It makes me a self-educated man—it is learning the hard way. There are two ways to learn: from my own mistakes or from someone else's mistakes. I like to listen to other people as much as I can because it saves me from making the same mistake.

I find in talking to teenagers that the biggest problem they have is that they have identified with their mistakes. "I'm just stupid," "I'm just a 'D' student,"

"I'm second string. Nobody wants me on their team," or "I'm not very popular." These statements are identifying with failure or mistakes. And, as a result, they *are* a failure. You want to conquer these feelings of inadequacy. As you do, your ability to develop successful relationships with prospects and clients will increase. You will discover a higher level of consistency in your attitude, less negative impact when you lose a sale, greater confidence in your sales ability, and negative situations will challenge you rather than defeat you. The end result will be a greater consistency in sales productivity. How do you change all of this negative information you have believed most of your life? We will focus later on an in-depth method of conquering fear, but there is something you can do today -- begin working with your *self-talk*.

Self-Talk

Approximately 75% of our day we talk to ourselves. The problem is, we *believe* most of what we say. And, most of what we say is negative. For instance, "I'm just stupid," "I'm so dumb," or "I'm clumsy." And you can imagine what we all do—we prove it! We will *be* what we say we are.

"That's just the way I am." You cannot change something if that is just the way you are, can you? "I give up trying to change." The fact is, you should be *changing* every day. How about this one, "I can't remember names." As a salesperson, if you cannot remember names, you are in trouble. The most important word in the English language is your *customer's name*. You *must* remember names. "I'm weak in the close." That is enough to make your deodorant kick out in the middle of a presentation, and cause a little trickle to go down your side, because now you know you are coming to *the close.* You are moving along in your presentation... "Well, this is a very good product"....and you know you are coming to the end of your presentation. Your voice changes, and all kinds of things begin to happen when you get fearful or nervous about the close.

To compensate for this problem, there are sales trainers who teach people how "to close." This is merely a bandaid method of correcting this problem.

"I'm weak on the telephone." If you say you *are,* then you *are!* It becomes truth to you. "Cold calls scare me." They *will!*

Whatever you say *will happen.* "The new presentation won't work," and it *won't.* I've seen some fantastic sales presentation ideas go down the tube simply because salespeople could not buy the idea that it would work. If they make a presentation with the new idea and they miss the first one, that is it! They *identify with the failure.* So then, they believe it is a bad presentation. Or, how about this excuse: "This is a bad time of the year. Nobody wants to buy *now*!"

If you believe that, you will prove you are right. Bennie Harris, my life insurance friend, loves selling in the month of December because everyone is in a *buying* mood. There are so many of these. Here is another one: "Money is tight." You've never heard that one, I'm sure. Or, "This is a weak prospect." If you believe your prospects are weak, they *will* be weak. "It will never sell at this price." You probably have a few others to add to this list. I want you to *eliminate* those phrases from your vocabulary. Remember, you believe most of what you say. In fact, neurologists have told us that as we speak (our speech center controls the nervous system in our body) our body puts into action the very thing we say is happening in our life. You literally *speak* your thoughts into existence. Make sure your thoughts are positive.

As you talk to yourself, say the things you wish to be true. "I am a successful person. I relate well to my customers." "I am strong in the close because I have the ability to create desire for my product or service, in the mind of my customer." "I am developing my sales ability every day, and I am learning new lessons from each presentation I make."

When you make a mistake, lose a sale, or experience a fear that shakes your confidence, attack those situations with *positive self-talk.* Negatives are so easy to think, but it takes determination and hard work to turn them into positives. It is worth it, however, because you will see the results almost immediately. Your confidence will grow, your closing ratio will increase, and your commissions will be the evidence of your own personal growth. Speak into existence that which you want to be true.

CHAPTER 4
VALUES, PRINCIPLES AND BEHAVIOR

☞ *Values*
☞ *Customer's Needs*
☞ *Behavior*
☞ *Principles*

L et me introduce you to a formula that will help you understand why you are who you are today, and what you can do to change or develop yourself so you can become the person you want to be. **The Formula is** V = P = B.

Values

Your values are those things you hold most dear. Every deed, thought and reaction is based upon your values. You place a *high* or *low* value on your personage as well as the people and things in your world. Listening closely to what you say and understanding why you are saying it will determine where your values lie.

25

If your conversation revolves around your home, car, or airplane, this indicates that you are a materialistic person and you place a high value on *things*. If you generally speak of your family or business associates, then you are more people-oriented and your values are based upon what people will think of you, how they will respond to you, or how you appear to them. If you talk about personal growth, giving of yourself, accomplishing goals, or changing peoples' lives for the better, then you will tend to be productivity-oriented and relationship-oriented, showing concern about success and productivity of others.

If your values are based on physical *things* you are probably in sales because it offers the greatest financial opportunity to obtain the things you want, need, or desire. If your values are people-oriented, I would say you are in sales because you enjoy meeting and working with people, as well as developing new friendships. However, if your values are based on productivity, you are in sales because it offers you the opportunity to fulfill your customers' wants, needs, and desires which, in turn, creates a *"win-win"* situation for you, your prospect or client, and your company.

Everything you do, including every response you make, and every thought you think, is determined by your values. You have complete control of choice in setting values. However, once you have chosen your values, they will control *you*. Therefore, it becomes imperative that you think about your values, change those that will deter you from your desired success and focus on the ones that will cause you to be a professional salesperson.

I met a young real estate salesperson recently who said she was having difficulty closing sales. She was successful in getting a buyer excited about a specific property, but could not close the sale. I asked her why I should purchase a home from her rather than from a *"For Sale By Owner"* or another salesperson. She stumbled with her answer and never gave me a reason to buy from her. It was evident that she did not understand the value she brought to the sales relationship.

I suggested she list all the positive things she brings to her customers as a real estate professional without comparing herself to any other salesperson. When you compare yourself to someone else you will sell yourself short because you will focus on that person's strengths and your own perceived weaknesses. This, then, locks you into a false sense of inadequacy because you do not *know* that person's weaknesses. So, it is important that you focus on your strong points, which is precisely what your prospects and clients need to see in you.

Once she was able to do this, she articulated the value she offers her buyers and approached the sales situation with an entirely different attitude. The change was immediate; both her sales closing ratio and her referral business increased. This is an indication of the high professional value her customers perceived.

Self-value is all you really have to offer your prospects, so make sure what you project is what you want them to believe about you.

The other side of this scenario is to understand the *values* of your prospect or client. Your entire presentation, from beginning to end, must be in harmony with the values of the prospect or you will not relate to that person's interest and concerns. A sales presentation based upon *your* values will not, in most cases, be the values of your prospect, and rather than creating a sales situation you might create objections, which are indications of psychological blocks and fears.

Recently, while visiting a Lincoln automobile dealership, I watched a salesperson working with a prospect. The salesperson was trying to create interest in a new Lincoln Town Car. He said to the customer: "The thing you will love most about this car is that it has a beautiful interior, with soft, velour upholstery." The prospect's reply was, "I like leather!" Then the salesperson said, "Isn't this a beautiful shade of blue?" The prospect replied, "I have never liked blue!" He continued trying with, "You will love the smooth ride of this luxurious automobile." As the prospect departed the showroom he said, "I want economy!" The salesperson stood there for a moment and then muttered to himself, "I couldn't find one thing he liked." The problem was that he was expressing his own values rather than determining the values of the prospect and then relating to *his* wants, needs and desires.

In later chapters you will learn how to determine the prospect's values before you start your presentation so that everything you say and do will move the prospect toward the knowledge that you are a salesperson who can be trusted to do a good job. Remember, the most important aspect of your presentation is how it relates to the prospect's values.

Principles

Your values create principles which are the rules by which you choose to live. Everything you do is based upon a principle that you have embraced because of your values. It is either a fear-motivated principle such as "grab and get while the getting is good" or a love-motivated principle that causes you to give of yourself. If your values are on a productivity level then your sales principles will be on that  level as well. You will be productivity and service-oriented and edify people. You will help them feel comfortable about their purchase by satisfying their wants, needs and desires. This will be your goal.

If your values focus on people, your sales principles will be people- oriented and more on the emotional level. There is great concern for what people will think and what they will like. You will not be pushy and will attempt to make every customer a friend. In this case your sales presentation will be governed by whether or not the prospect likes what you are offering, which is a reflection, in your mind, of how much they *like* you. This sounds pretty good, until you fail to ask for the order because you feel you might offend the prospect. Or, you breeze over the presentation because you don't want to bore them. It is even weaker if you suggest they think about it for a few days. You do this because you do not want to seem too pushy. Be careful not to allow your high value of people create within you a principle of *clerking* rather than *selling*.

If your values are on the *physical* level, then your sales principles will be focused on the physical aspects and you will tend to be product-oriented. You will sell price or savings rather than value. Your prospects will not become clients, even if you make the sale, because you have caused them to become *good deal*-seekers rather than customers who purchase based upon high value. This means you have destroyed the repeat and referral business that you must have for real success in the sales field.

This was illustrated recently by a saleswoman who told me of a telephone call from one of her customers. The customer was quite excited that she had found a new home at a terrific price and knew her real estate friend would be happy to hear the news. The salesperson had talked *price* so much that the customer had gone *"price hunting"* alone and had found a better deal than the salesperson had shown her. Incidentally, the home she purchased, from another agent, is one this salesperson could have sold as well. Be very careful in the *physical* side of the sales field. You must deal with it, but you do not want price to become the reason to buy, or not to buy.

This kind of principle creates the attitude of, "making a sale no matter what it takes," which has created a bad name for salespeople in general. Some years back I worked with a sales organization that sold vacuum cleaners, door to door. This was an organization that took pride in the fact that they could *"sell anything to anyone."* They had the old hard sell, foot in the door, type of sales approach. They would send a salesperson down one side of the street and another down the opposite. When they got to the corner they would compare success stories of how many sales they had made. I heard some of the stories, and they illustrate this "make a sale no matter what it takes" principle. One salesperson said there was a sign indicating, "No Solicitors Allowed." So, he removed the sign and knocked on the door. When a woman answered he held up the sign and asked, "Do you really mean this?" She said, "Well, No!" He sold her a vacuum that day. This principle has no concern about client satisfaction, repeat or referral business. In fact, there is no repeat business, so the sales person must plow new ground everyday. In place of referral business, the customer will instead, call the neighbors and warn them not to open the door.

When you hear the phrase, *door to door* sales, this is the image you get, and it is not positive. The newspaper cartoon character, "Dagwood Bumstead," has had to deal with this type of salesperson for years. As a result, it has created a bad name in the *real* sales field. You certainly want to close sales. That is what the sales field is all about; however, you don't want to pressure the customer for the *close.*

Leonard Llewellyn, a highly successful Realtor in Marco Island, Florida says, "You must help people make a wise buying decision." When you have done this they will be clients for life and will send all their friends to buy from you." I call that a *love-motivated* principle because it is *giving* rather than *taking.* It is fulfilling dreams rather than just making a sale. You must ask yourself these questions: "What is the best buy for this customer," "What best fits their wants, needs, and desires," and "How can I best tell the story so they can see the value? When you make this your approach to sales, you will never have to worry about closes, answers to objections, or even how much money you are going to make this month. You will be highly successful and enjoy repeat and referral business.

So, principles are a reflection of a person's values. Therefore, if you can understand a prospect's principles, you will have insight into their values. Or, if you can know their values, you can predict their principles. By recognizing a prospect's principles, you will be able to relate your presentation, conversation and responses to that person's values, which is their reason to buy. Everything they say, every action, and reaction tells you what you need to know to establish a sales relationship, because *behavior* is a result of a person's principles.

Behavior

Behavior is how a person acts and reacts to certain situations. Choice of words, dress, likes and dislikes are all behavioral. Because principles determine behavior, our job is to be aware constantly of what our customers are telling us about their principles and values by way of their actions and reactions.

"Effective Interviewing," one of our 12-hour seminars, teaches interviewers how to predict habitual behavior in an interviewee. We teach the questions to ask to assist the company in determining how well a person will fit a specific job description. In a sales relationship you can understand the clients wants, needs and desires and their values and principles by asking

questions and listening to what they say; but more importantly by *hearing why* they are saying it.

In later chapters you will learn the *inner motivations* that create *values, principles, behavior,* and *wants, needs* and *desires*. In this chapter, I want you to understand how your values determine your principles and behavior and how much your behavior tells your prospect whether or not to trust you. You have heard the old saying, "Your actions speak so loud I can't hear a word you are saying." I would say, your behavior tells me the principles by which you live, and your principles tell me how much you value me as a customer. Understand I'm not suggesting that your clients or prospects must study you before they can buy from you, but I would say that all of us can sense whether or not we can trust a person because of a *projection of attitudes*. Defense mechanisms arise when we sense you have your own agenda rather than our best interest at heart.

Customers Want, Need and Desire a Sales Relationship

An executive of a company told me of an incident involving his purchase of a new automobile through a local dealership. He relayed how throughout the entire transaction he was shuffled from person to person throughout the company and at each stop he had to relate to a new person or manager, each having a different reason for being a part of the sale. He said, "I never felt anyone got to know me or even cared about my wife and I. To them we were merely customers buying a car." He said he went back to the dealership the following day to pick up the license plate and his salesperson walked past him without recognition. Of course he will never again buy a car from that dealership or refer anyone he knows to that company.

Successful salespeople project such positive presence that we trust them, and buy the product they offer. Your mind projects *attitudes* which develop a positive *presence* and that projection causes the prospect to accept you as the professional in your field.

Since the *cause* is a person's values, and everything else that follows is the effect, it is important that we develop correctly the values of giving to our clients the best of service, and product: who we are. Then we will be able to relate our presentation to their values, and we will enjoy real success.

When time permits, list your values. In doing this, consider all aspects of your life, starting with your *inward relationship*—the value you place upon who you are, what you have accomplished in personal growth, and what you offer your world. Consider your *upward relationships*—wherein we find the value you place on your employer, your value to your religious heritage, and the value you bring to any other organization. Also determine your values in your *downward relationships*—those with your children, your customers and any other person for whom you may be responsible. And lastly, you need to think about your *outward relationships*—those with your peers and friends.

All four of these relationships and the numbers of people included are the basis of your world. If you can determine the value you bring in each of these areas of your life, you will begin to see that you are someone special. If you will accept that fact, it will affect everything you do, including how you approach relationship selling.

CHAPTER 5
USING YOUR HEAD

☞ *Judging Performance*
☞ *Subconscious Success*
☞ *Believing in Yourself*
☞ *Creating a Strong Presence*

In this chapter we will approach the fears we harbor subconsciously, and how to conquer them. If we can understand how they were created, we can attempt to do what is necessary to rid their effects in our approach to *relationship selling.* We will look at the inner attitudes and beliefs that make up the person you are today. When others look at you, what they actually see is an outward expression of your inner self. Let us go back to Psychology 101 and determine the relationship of these concepts and principles to your ability to be successful in a sales relationship.

One-tenth (1/10) of our brain is believed to be the conscious mind and nine-tenths (9/10) is the unconscious or subconscious mind. In studying this, we learn that the conscious mind has the decision-making function of the brain. When we think a thought consciously, we are actually making a decision; that is, we are recognizing and evaluating the value of the thought that is being processed through the five senses. Our conscious brain is determining its value to us and how much we should allow into our conscious state. This is the controlling factor of the thought process...how important the information is, how it fits in with individual values, and what can be done with the information. God gave us free will. Yet most of us forget that with this *free will* we determine who we will become. If we allow ourselves to dwell on fear-motivated thoughts, we ultimately destroy our potential and relationships at their best. When studying successful people in any field, the one common thread is their ability to find positives in almost all situations. I have found through studying success patterns in sales people that they learn from their mistakes and grow as a result of them. They look for good in everyone they meet, and usually find it. They choose to work harder when things go wrong, and keep the faith when it seems hopeless. You cannot make me think something I choose not to think and, likewise, I cannot make you think something you choose not to think. So, I ask the question, *"Who do you think you are?"* And your answer to that question determines the person you are becoming. I once taught a seminar to the Gold Card Family, a group of families that meet each summer to study some of these concepts and determine how they apply to every area of their lives. One such theme, *"Becoming* Becoming"...how to continually work at becoming a "more becoming" person, was taught in classes for each age group.

The answer to *becoming* more "becoming" is to think positively. Then, the fruit of our thinking will be more creative and productive, and our inner self will be outwardly expressed, thus making us agreeable to others. It is imperative that we guard our *thinking* for it is the doorway to our soul.

The subconscious mind is the memory portion of our brain, much like that of a computer. In fact, if we were to compare our brain to a computer, the *conscious* would be the keyboard and the *subconscious* would be the memory. Everything that has ever entered your conscious mind has been programmed into the subconscious mind and will be there forever. You were created with a photographic mind; therefore, you have forgotten nothing. You may think that is impossible, but it's entirely true. Everything you have ever been exposed to has been recorded subconsciously. When the year *"1986"* is mentioned in your presence, an event or possibly several events which occurred in that year will jump from your subconscious to your conscious mind. This might be a thought you have not recalled for some time, but the mention of that year brings it back to your thinking. Every piece of data was stored in your memory and can be recalled at will. I can mention a person's name, and an image of someone with that name, and thoughts of your relationship with that person, will be recalled to your conscious mind. I will not go into a long  dissertation on the power of the subconscious mind, but it is important for your sales success to realize how powerful it is to you, *and* the effect it can have on your sales relationship capabilities. The person you are today is the sum total of all that has been programmed into your subconscious.

Because the subconscious mind is the storehouse of all memory, it is also the source of your habitual behavior. Do you remember when you learned to drive an automobile, and especially if you learned on a stick-shift? You had to coordinate the clutch and the gas, and it was probably a leapfrog-type experience for a while. But through practice, you learned to let out the clutch, while putting just the right pressure on the throttle, so that it was a smooth shift. What actually happened was that you programmed the subconscious mind to coordinate the left and right foot so you could drive, shift gears and be thinking about something entirely different. It was a completely unconscious effort. You were not thinking consciously about it as you went through the motions of shifting those gears, but you did it mechanically. Do you ever drive along the highway and forget that you are driving? You are in a completely different world thinking about some other situation or problem, and suddenly realize you have driven several miles and don't remember the trip. Then you wonder what would have happened if an emergency had arisen. Well, I've got good news for you. The eye can pick up 72,000 characters per minute and programs that information into the subconscious mind, sending a warning to your conscious mind, alerting you. Recently, I experienced this phenomenon as I was driving quite late one evening. I rounded the corner on a dark highway, with my mind on the day's business, and suddenly, I came upon a large deer standing in the middle of my lane. Immediately, I was in my conscious mind which told me to

35

move into the other lane to avoid an accident, and to warn the oncoming traffic of the impending danger by honking my horn. That caused the deer to run toward the forest, and I continued my drive. This all happened in seconds. There were only tenths of seconds between the time I recognized the problem and responded to it. The subconscious mind is a tremendous instrument.

The conscious brain places a value on every thought and then programs that information into the subconscious mind. It then becomes a subconscious attitudinal belief. Once that imprint is made subconsciously, it is there forever, never to be erased. So, of all the problems you may face in your world, memory is not one of them. You may not have developed your recall ability so that you have easy random access to your memory, but that is an altogether different problem!

Someone said to me recently, "I can't remember names." I asked her to tell me her name. She responded with her name and I laughingly replied, "There you go! Now you can't say *that* again!" The fact is, you *can* and *do* remember names. It is simply a matter of importance. You don't forget the name of someone you love, or someone you greatly dislike. You will never forget the name of that person who owes you money or spoke badly about you to your friends. Remembering names is only a matter of how much value, positively or negatively, you relate to that name.

You must understand that in a sales situation the prospect's name is the most important word in the English language. As a salesperson you must be able to remember names (because the customers will remember *your* name) and when you do, they believe you have placed a high value on your relationship with them. If you fail to remember a customer's name, that is an indication that he or she is not important to you. Do you expect your insurance agent, your physician, or dentist to remember you when you walk into their offices? Of course you do, and your customers expect the same. When a name becomes valuable to you, you certainly don't forget it. If I were to tell you that I had a prospect for you who wanted to purchase your product, you would not have a difficult time remembering that name. In fact, you would make *sure* you remember that name. You would write it down, and possibly read it over several times prior to meeting that customer. Normally, you shake hands when you first meet someone, and also exchange names. However in most cases, the name is forgotten within minutes. Try this technique the next time you meet someone new. Shake hands and mumble your name so that it is unintelligible. In most cases, people will act as if they heard what you said, when you really didn't say anything. The fear of embarrassment will cause most people not to ask for clarification of a name. We are so concerned about what people will think of us that we fail to clarify the most important information of the conversation, the customer's name. What we *should* say if we miss a name is, "Could you repeat that? I didn't catch it." I'm sure they won't mind repeating it. It is actually a little flattering, if you ask me. It lets the customer know you are interested in getting acquainted. And, if you still don't catch the name, ask for the correct spelling of the name. This can only reinforce your interest.

Remember, everything you have experienced is recorded in your subconscious mind. This is your *frame of reference*, and the outflow of that material is the person we see when we meet you. Your prospect's first impression is based upon this outward expression of your inner attitudinal beliefs, and this is who you believe you are, in your own mind.

When I meet you, I look at three dimensions of who you are. These dimensions total up to what we call your *personage*. The first of these dimensions is *personality*.

Personality

Your personality is an outward expression of what you think of yourself subconsciously. It is a projection of your attitudes and values. So to develop a better personality, we must start by working on our subconscious attitudes, including our *self-esteem*, our *self-image*, and our *self-acceptance*. These are the three dimensions of the inward relationship we discussed in an earlier chapter. The problem with most salespeople is that they have many fears which were created at a young age. Then, even though they are maturing, their fears are not. They continue to attack the way they feel about themselves, ultimately affecting their personality. Those fears must be conquered before there will be any positive change. You cannot change your personality by working on your personality; personality is only an outward expression of an inner attitude. It is like a flashlight shining a beam of light onto the wall. You cannot erase the beam of light. You must turn off the flashlight. Since we are dealing with inner causes, personality can only be developed by creating subconscious change (this change will be discussed in the next chapter).

Performance

The corporate world judges people by *performance*. Commissions are also based upon performance. In fact, some organizations give *performance bonuses,* meaning the higher the performance, the higher the bonus paid. The problem comes when we start judging ourselves based upon our performance. Notice that I used the word *judging* instead of *accepting.* If you know who you are, then you are not discouraged when you make a mistake. If your self-image is weak, you  will identify *with* mistakes and consider yourself a failure. When you identify with mistakes or failures, you are actually identifying with poor performance. When you *identify* mistakes and make corrections, you will succeed. There are many illustrations of people who believed they could succeed and proved it. There are many others who were afraid they would fail and gave up, proving they were right.

Have you ever been surprised by something you accomplished? In most cases, when you have done something well, it is because you thought you could do it before you started. The top salesperson on your staff is never surprised at being at the top. Incidentally, the person at the bottom, with the lowest sales volume, is never really surprised either. It is interesting to me as I reteach seminars for corporations, that the persons on the bottom of the charts do not change a great deal; and the persons at the top of the production charts remain top producers. We would like to think that the people on top are there because they are dedicated, but what really keeps them on top is their positive attitude. The people at the bottom think poorly of themselves and give up.

A wise man once said in Proverbs 23:7, *"As a man thinks in his heart, so is he."* In layman's language, he is saying, *"If salespeople believe subconsciously they can succeed, they will."*

Your capability to close sales is directly related to your self-image, or to what you believe you can do. I read about a study of salespeople and how their thinking controlled their ability to close sales. In this study the people who played the role of prospects were *all* instructed to purchase the product, no matter what the salesperson said or offered them. By noon these sales people had reached their quota for the week, and by early afternoon they were talking people out of buying. Why? They had a mental picture of what they were capable of selling, and on this day they had far exceeded their expectations. As the day passed, the salespeople began saying things like: *"Think about this. You don't need to make a decision today,"* or *"You might be more comfortable if you looked around and compared prices."* They were actually voicing the objections they had been trained to overcome. Why would any salesperson do such a thing? The answer is simple. They were uncomfortable producing more than they believed they could produce. Of course, this was not a conscious reaction. In fact, when asked why they talked their customers out of buying that day they could not believe they had actually done that. If I believe I am a mediocre salesperson and suddenly I am a superstar, my self-image short-circuits and without knowing what I am doing, I begin reverting to my comfort level, the way it has always been. It is human nature to want to remain in your comfort-zone, but in order to grow, you must break out of the realm of comfort. Fear is a destructive force for it destroys the ability to grow and develop unless it is recognized and controlled. A good comparison is learning to walk on the ground and then suddenly finding yourself on a highwire. These salespeople could not accept the fact that they were selling so *well* on that day; therefore, they literally talked prospects out of buying!

What you believe you can do determines what you *will* do. Hypnosis, which changes only what a person believes, has proven that theory over the years. A man under hypnosis was told that he was as stiff as a board. He was told to put his feet on one chair, his head on another chair, and allow his torso to span the distance between the two chairs. Another man weighing 250 pounds was asked to stand on the hypnotized man's stomach. Was the man under hypnosis strong enough to hold a 250-pound man on his stomach while suspended in air? The answer is *yes* if he believed he could. Without the belief level he would not have been able to hold the weight.

When you think positive thoughts, you have more strength, you are more creative, and you accomplish more than when you are thinking negatively. For years, no one could run the mile in less than four minutes. Then, in 1959 Roger Bannister broke the four-minute record. From that point onward, a male mile-runner is not considered to be a world-class mile runner unless he can run a sub-four-minute mile. Today it is not uncommon to have the top four or five mile-runners break the four-minute mark. You see, they now believe it can be done. We are breaking new ground daily and are actually developing technology so quickly that most new developments are nearly obsolete before they come off the production line. There is more being created today than in any other day in the history of the world. If we did so much yesterday, we can do much more today, and the more we believe we can do, the more we *will* do. Therefore, I'm telling you today that what you believe about your sales abilities and capabilities needs to be expanded. Your self-image will determine how well you will sell because your performance is based upon what *you* think about *you*. If you like who you are and believe in yourself, you will perform up to that expectation. Henry Ford once said, *"If you think you can, or if you think you can't, you're right."* And he was right!

Presence

The third dimension of personage is *presence.* This is more difficult to understand than *personality* or *performance.* Presence is an outward projection of attitude into the atmosphere which causes people to sense when we are upset, angry, or happy. This is how it works. As you think a thought subconsciously, you immediately experience a corresponding body chemistry. This chemistry is controlled by your thinking. If you think negative thoughts you have a negative body chemistry. A saliva

test with litmus paper or nitrogen paper, a blood or urine test, or any other body secretions, will register this if you are having a bad day, and conversely will register that everything is in check if you are having a good day. Nitrogen paper, on a tape dispenser, with pH level labeling, can be purchased at any drugstore. You can test your saliva and determine the pH factor which influences your behavior, actions, and reactions all day. If you have a positive body chemistry, you are less likely to catch colds, the flu, and other diseases. That means if you are positive of thought, you will have a greater resistance to those and other sicknesses. If you are negative and fear-motivated, then you will be more susceptible to sickness.   According to the American Medical Association, the major cause of heart disease, cancer, allergies, ulcers and strokes is stress, caused by fear on a subconscious level.

When body chemistry is negative it is destructive to the body in several ways. It affects the physical condition, creativity, productivity, energy level and relationships with other people.

Physical Reactions

When body chemistry is negative, resistance is low and thus it is destructive to the body, causing an aging effect. We generally think people who are sickly have a right to be negative. This comes from the belief that negativity causes illness. Studies indicate that a negative attitude can make people ill, or at least make them more susceptible to sickness.

Creativity

If body chemistry is negative, it causes lack of creativity. Attempt to write a letter to a friend on a bad day and most probably you will not mail the letter. Creativity is a prerequisite for success in sales. You must be able to create a relationship, create value, create good communication, and create a visualization of your product or service; satisfying the wants, needs, and desires of the prospect. You *must* be creative to be successful in sales and *creativity* is also your primary source of happiness.

Productivity

When body chemistry is negative due to fear, *productivity* is destroyed. Nothing seems to get done. You will have trouble closing sales, people will not show up for appointments, and nothing will seem to fit together. In the sales field you are paid for productivity; and the more productive you are as a salesperson, the more you earn. You cannot afford to have a *bad day.* Change your attitude and monitor the results of your sales volume. They are directly related.

Energy Supply

When body chemistry is negative, it destroys energy supply so that by about two or three o'clock in the afternoon, exhaustion sets in. It is as if the *gas runs out* both emotionally and physically. Fear is a tremendous energy drain because it causes worry, which is a negative feeling. However, a positive attitude will produce tremendous energy throughout the day. If you find yourself running out of energy, take a short break and review your thoughts over the past few hours. Were you thinking about negative circumstances that you cannot control? Then stop! If you cannot change it, forget it! Have you been thinking about circumstances you *can* change? Then make a plan and set it into motion. Make the corrections or changes. Did the plan increase your energy? Of course it did! There is always a reason for lost energy. Check it out!

Relationships

And finally a negative body chemistry destroys the ability to relate to other people. No one likes to be around a negative person. If you have lunch with someone who is negative, it takes about two or three hours to *get over them* and you think twice before you accept their invitation again.

Negative salespeople can pull you down and cause you to refuse to purchase from that person, even if you want the product being sold. More sales are lost because of fear in the mind of the salesperson than fear in the mind of the prospect. It is not difficult to understand why so many salespeople are not successful. They literally chase people away with their negative attitude. If you are having a bad day, do yourself and your prospect a favor—cancel the appointment! Correct your attitude before you destroy your sales relationships.

In the next chapter on conquering fear, we will cover some things that can be done to extinguish the fears that would destroy potential sales relationships. An interesting suggestion might be to carry along some nitrogen paper on your next sales appointment and occasionally check your customer's saliva. If the paper is gold, they are ready to buy, if it is blue, don't try closing the sale, because they will not buy!! Of course, you have to be a pretty good salesperson to get them to stick out their tongue!!!

Seriously, let me carry this one step further and tell you that your body chemistry projects an atmosphere that will be in accord with your thinking, whether negative or positive. This atmosphere either draws people to you and creates a relaxed, comfortable environment, or it repels people with a feeling that "something is not quite right." If you are having a bad day your body language will tell the world.

You may have read some studies by American scientists who have studied plant life and how it responds to people. Positive people make plants grow well and negative people cause them to wilt. A friend of mine has a plastic plant in his office and it is wilted!! I would say he has a *real* problem!

One of these studies was in a greenhouse, in which a man was directed to destroy a plant. Other plants in the greenhouse were wired to electronic equipment that would measure any chemistry change in the plants. Fifty people walked through the greenhouse, one at a time, and as the man who destroyed the plant walked into the room, the plants measured a drastic change—a wilting sensation. These studies tend to be spooky and not easy to believe, but perhaps you can relate to this fact: dogs will bite some people and not bite others. If you are afraid of dogs, they may bite you. You can say, "nice doggie," and even smile at the dog, but if you are afraid of dogs, they sense that fear. This causes a negative vibe and the dog senses it, causing it to be afraid of *you.* Dogs only bite people they fear, and that fear is created by the person. It is merely a defense mechanism. Bees sting some people while others can take honey from a hive without ever being stung. My brother, Dave, has worked around animals all of his adult life. He is able to walk through a dairy barn, work around the cows, and very little attention is paid to him by the animals. If he has a guest with him who is not familiar with large animals, the cows become nervous. Animals can sense the fear or uneasiness of the person.

Likewise, a salesperson can walk into a room and some prospects will be drawn to that salesperson while another salesperson walks into the same room and the prospect will feel uncomfortable. They are sensing a negative presence that causes them to be fear-motivated, and they set up a barrier or a psychological block toward the salesperson. This is not based on nationality, race, physical appearance, gender, religion, or education. Charisma comes in all sizes, colors, and both sexes. To be successful in sales, you must project a positive presence, and in order to have a positive presence it is required that you conquer fear on a subconscious level. You need to be so positive and love-motivated that fear does not influence your life, your sales ability, or any part of your vocabulary!

As you think a thought subconsciously you have an outward projection that is manifested by your *personality, performance, and presence.* I will not buy your product or service until I have first bought you, and these three factors of *personage,* determine whether I can trust you, believe in you, and let you be my *"doctor of sales."* Therefore, I can safely say that if you are successful in sales, it is because you have been successful in establishing a good relationship with yourself; conquering your subconscious fears so that you are projecting a positive attitude. It is then that we will call you the *"doctor of sales"* and send you repeat and referral business. At that time you will enjoy servicing clients instead of searching for prospects.

CHAPTER 6
CONQUERING FEAR

☞ *Repetition*
☞ *Acceptance*
☞ *Beliefs*
☞ *Renewal*

We must conquer the fears that have been programmed into our mind since birth that keep us from being successful in sales. The best way to conquer fear subconsciously is to use the same method that caused the fear initially, *except* we will replace fear motivations with love motivations. The Holy Scriptures read, "Perfect love casts out fear." Psychologists would tell us that love dispels the effects of fear. Some of the fears that plague us are inferiority, rejection, inadequacies, loss of power, and failure. To dispel the fears that keep us from being everything we want to be, we must reprogram our self-talk, replacing the negatives with positives. The importance of this is that until we believe in ourselves, others cannot believe in us. In order to *make a sale,* our customers must be able to believe in us. Then they will believe in our product.

R x A = RM

You have used this formula repeatedly in your lifetime. Let us define how this tool can be used *on purpose,* rather than by accident. We all have been brain-washed with this formula, and it works both negatively and positively. Every fear that exists in our subconscious mind is there as a result of the power of this equation.

R = Repetition

For the purpose of understanding this formula, *repetition* is the number of times we are exposed to the same element through the five senses. There are two variables to consider:

(1) How often we are exposed to something or someone.

Each time we are made aware of something or someone, our mind records that information. The conscious mind makes a decision for us about the value of the information, and then records that information subconsciously. Whenever that same information enters the brain, it is a *repetition* and has either a positive or negative impact on us.

(2) How many of the senses are affected.

We see something once and it makes an imprint in our mind. When we see that same picture again, we have a repetition. And every time thereafter that we see, hear, touch, smell or feel that same exposure, there are multiple repetitions. *Each* time I have a repetition, it is programmed into my subconscious mind, it becomes a subconscious attitudinal belief, and is forever imprinted. Because the subconscious is the memory area of the brain, it will never be erased. As an attitudinal belief, it controls what we think about others and how they act—their level of personality and performance. We abuse this formula by allowing negative or fear-motivated thoughts into our subconscious on a repetitive basis. So, to reverse the negatives, we need to dilute them with repetitive positive reinforcements. Later we will cover a method to accomplish this.

After using this repetitive method every day for one week, you will *feel* different. Within two weeks people will begin *sensing* something different about you, and within three weeks it will affect your sales closing ratio. You will definitely see a positive impact if you resolve to discipline yourself to concentrate *on* yourself over a three-week period. If you will not commit to this exercise, you are wasting your time reading this book, and you probably should get into some other field of work. Furthermore, if you are not willing to work on *yourself* as a salesperson, then forget about sales, because it is among the most demanding career fields. It demands continual self-discipline and tremendous dedication to creating a better self-concept.

We must work on ourselves twenty-four hours a day, seven days a week, if we desire to be a successful salesperson. Three out of five of the most financially successful people in the world are salespeople, or are in their current position as a result of their sales success. The sales field is tremendous because it gives us the flexibility to earn whatever we need to meet our own goals. If we need to earn more, we work a little harder. If we face inflation, our commissions increase and our spendable income keeps up with the economy. Many network marketing companies, have given people on fixed incomes an opportunity to operate a business, and develop it to their desired level of personal income, based upon their level of effort. I personally find the sales field extremely rewarding and will always be involved to some degree, for my own personal gratification.

It is important to *your* success that you constantly remind yourself that you *are* in a great career field. This reminder will keep your enthusiasm high. Put positive rather than negative repetitions into your subconscious!

A = Acceptance

Acceptance is how much you believe of what you receive through the five senses. If I tell you that you are "good looking" and you cannot accept my compliment, then it will have very little impact in changing your self-concept. However, if I compliment you every day, that continual repetition will begin to make *slight* changes. If I continue to compliment you, repeatedly, throughout the day, you will start *recognizing* changes. On the other hand, if you can immediately *accept* the compliment, it will make a change the first time it is said. This is why we have a "multiple" in the formula: *the number of repetitions multiplied by the acceptance level.* If you believe one hundred percent of what you hear, then the first exposure will have great impact. However, if your belief level is only at five percent, then you will have to hear it many times to compensate for the low belief level. Have you ever complimented someone and they could not accept the compliment? They were telling you that they have a poor self-concept and a low self-esteem.

Every time we sell ourselves short because of fear, it is simply an indication we have chosen to *accept* fabrications regarding our personage rather than truth.

There are four *beliefs* to consider in assuring acceptance of a thought:

(1) "Belief" in the Teacher

Our ability to learn, grow and accept training is determined by how much we believe in the teacher. This teacher may be our sales manager, a sales associate, or our own self-talk. I remember in High School my peers warned me not to take English from Mrs. Benson, because her class was really tough! Somehow I ended up in Mrs. Benson's class and sure enough, my friends were right. We *didn't like* this instructor because she was too strict. It had absolutely nothing to do with her skills as an English teacher. However, upon successfully completing the course, everyone thought she was terrific. We do not have to like our teachers in order to learn from them. We need only to respect their knowledge and position. As salespeople, *we* are teachers because one of our functions is to teach others the value of our product or service. This thought will be covered more thoroughly in a later chapter. Having a belief in the teacher increases our learning experience. For instance, two-year-old children believe everything they hear. Therefore they have a high level of *acceptance.*

(2) "Belief" That the Information is True

To have real acceptance we must believe that the information being taught is the truth. Do you ever have difficulty remembering jokes? Sometimes if we don't write them down and read them over several times we will not remember them. That is because they are not *truth.* To have success in accepting positive programming into our subconscious mind, we must *believe* that the new information is true.

(3) "Belief" That We Need the Information

We must believe we need what we are hearing in order to have a high acceptance level. If we believe we need what we are hearing, our acceptance will increase. Probably the most difficult learning process you have experienced was when you were required to take a class that you did not feel you needed. I trust this book will create so great a need for growth within you that you will become a consistent student of personal growth.

(4) Belief in "Use" of the Information

Finally, we must believe we can use what we are learning. If I tell you that you have tremendous abilities, and that you can make a great living in sales, you must be able to believe that what I am saying is *true,* believe in me as your *teacher,* believe you *need* to make more money, and believe you can *use* that information to do what I suggest.

When all of these beliefs are present then you will have 100% acceptance. However, if you take away any of those factors, it will lessen your ability to change what you believe about yourself subconsciously. To make this formula work for you, you must have a high acceptance of the love-motivated information being programmed into your mind.

RM = Renewed Mind

As we study the power of the subconscious mind, that great storehouse of all memory, and the controller of our habitual behavior, we must realize the controlling factor is the decisions we make consciously. As information flows through the five senses, the conscious mind makes a decision to accept or reject that input. Then an imprint is made subconsciously that can never be erased. And so we might say, "If that is true, why try to change?" For years people have said, "That's just the way I am." With that statement they are accepting an existence far below their capabilities. We *can* make changes, development *is* possible, and fears *can be overcome* by using this formula. We can create a *renewed mind.* We are unable to erase the beliefs that are already there, but we can imprint new beliefs that will dilute the effects of those fears.

To illustrate this, put an inch of water in a gallon jug. Then dispense two drops of blue ink into the jug. The water will turn blue. Would you drink that water? Probably not! It is full of blue ink. Pouring a glass of clear water into the jug would dilute the ink to some degree. It will still be blue, but not as blue. The more water added, the clearer the water, and eventually there would be a gallon of clear water. It might be slightly blue, but two drops of ink in a gallon of water would be significantly diluted. If you were thirsty you might even drink the water. Now, take that gallon of water and pour it into a swimming pool containing thousands of gallons of water and take another sample of the water. How much ink will there be in that sample? It is doubtful that a trace could be found. There remains the same amount of ink, but it is so diluted, it cannot be detected.

We all have fears in our subconscious mind that have been with us from birth, and they will be there forever. The good news is, we can pour in so many love-motivated thoughts that we will dilute the effects of the fears on a subconscious level, and they will no longer affect us.

Create a New, Love-Motivated You!

We cannot restart but we *can* recreate. For you of the Christian faith, I am not speaking here of a spiritual recreation but rather using our God-given ability to think, make decisions and choose thoughts that will build, rather than destroy, our personage. You renew your mind by not allowing yourself to think fear-motivated or negative thoughts, but instead, love-motivated positives. Using this formula causes a beautiful thing to happen. Then there is no open door to negatives, which would tend to establish within us an inferiority complex.The love-motivated thoughts will build up and bring out the best in us. We were created by God as a totally unique individual. There is no one in the world just like us. We  have known for many years that everyone has different fingerprints, and recently we have found that everyone has a unique voice. When voice tapes are graphed, there are no two voice prints that are exactly the same. We are very unique beings. From the top of our head to the bottom of our feet, we are different. Yet most people go through life comparing themselves to others.

If I ask you the question, "Are you good looking? and your response is, "I'm not bad," you really are saying you are not bad compared to everyone else in the world. Your response should be, "I am the best looking, most creative, intelligent *me* in the world." That is not bragging, it is a fact. So do not put yourself in the trap of comparing yourself to others. Just be the best *you* that you can be, and you will find that with that positive reinforcement and repetition, you will begin to recreate your personage.

Most of our day we talk to ourselves. The problem is, we believe most of what we say—and most of what we say is *negative*! Listen to your self-talk and determine whether what you are hearing is what you want to believe about yourself. Stop saying the negative and begin to fill your mind with positive repetition. The new, positive repetitions will dilute the original fears.The more positives you put into your mind to dilute the fears, the more positive the outflow will be. It is important to continually fill our minds with love-motivated thoughts and stay away from the negative thoughts that we have practiced since birth.

Using the Preconscious State

Between the conscious and unconscious mind there is an area we call the *preconscious state*. In this state we believe everything we hear. This is the area of the brain used by hypnotists. When hypnotized, we move from a conscious level to a preconscious state and in that state we believe everything we hear.

Have you ever experienced a daydream or a deep thought process where you were concentrating so strongly about something that you were no longer aware of your surroundings? If so, when that occurred, you moved into a preconscious state.

When we fall asleep we move from a conscious level, through the preconscious, into a deep sleep. Normally, it takes fifteen to thirty minutes to pass from the conscious to the subconscious. As we pass through that area, we believe everything we hear. This is the area where *sleep learning* is effective.

In the late 60's a couple in San Jose, California, approached me concerning their seven-year-old son who had a bed-wetting problem. I suggested they try using a sleep tape telling him how great he was. We told him in the tape that he was special, and that there was no one in the world just like him. We did not mention bed wetting in the tape. I suggested they play the tape as their son began to fall asleep. The following morning the parents found a wet bed. The second morning they found a wet bed as well. On the third night, however, the boy got up in the night and used the bathroom, and his bed was dry the next morning. He never had a bed-wetting problem after that night. For years, his parents had tried everything possible to cause him to stop wetting the bed, and in three nights it was conquered through the use of a simple sleep tape, with thoughts of how special he was, planted into his subconscious mind. The child realized by himself that *special* people don't wet the bed. His subconscious mind told him to wake up and go to the bathroom, or else he would not be performing in context with what he believed about himself.

Since that time, children all over the country have listened to similar sleep tapes, with equally fantastic results. Sales people also can make sleep tapes to help conquer fears subconsciously. There are sleep tapes to help create a higher belief level in abilities by conquering fear of the telephone, closing sales, making cold calls, and numerous other fears that would deter us from being successful. Try it! Listen to a 30-minute sales tape as you are falling asleep. Fill your mind with positive, love-motivated thoughts while you are in that preconscious state, and within a very short time you will have positive results.

A man in Portland, Maine, told me he listened to our Salesman's Sleep Tape every night for a period of years because he had a strong fear of using the telephone for cold sales calls. He said his hands would perspire whenever he dialed the telephone to call a prospect. He realized the sleep tape was working, when, one day as he ended his phone conversation, he looked at his hands and they were dry! Now he *enjoys* telephone sales calls.

If I could guarantee that everyone you call tomorrow will purchase from you, how many calls would you make? If the number in your mind is different than the number of calls you made yesterday, you have just measured your fear of the phone. We *all* have fears we must conquer, and in the field of sales, they can be debilitating.

When we use sleep tapes we are working on diluting subconscious fears while we are at a high-belief level.

Weeds and Seeds

Earlier in this chapter I promised you an exercise to assist you in conquering your subconscious fears. This is a very simple exercise, but it will take consistent *self-discipline* to see results.

With two sheets of paper and a pencil, find a private spot where no one will bother you, and make two lists. Title the first list, *"Weeds."* Write down everything that you don't like about yourself, including attitudes, fears and behavioral patterns. Don't leave anything off that list! Then title the second sheet, *"Seeds."* On this list, you will translate all of the *weeds* into *seeds.* If you wrote a weed, "I am not organized," you will translate that weed into a seed by writing, "I am an organized person." Continue through your list changing negative thoughts (weeds) about *you* and your *sales ability* into positive thoughts (seeds). After you have translated all of your weeds into seeds, destroy the weed list. Now comes the self-discipline! You must read your seed list *aloud* (to yourself) *ten times a day.* This is positive repetition, and by reading it aloud, you *see* it and *hear* it, which doubles each repetition.

This exercise may appear to be a childish game to some, but I will assure you that I have seen thousands of people, from the "boardroom" to the "mailroom," enjoy tremendous personal growth by using this method to conquer fear. As you do this each day, the seed list will become part of *who you are,* and will become reality in your world. Eventually, the weed list will fade away into forgetfulness.

Imagine a farmer sitting on a tractor, plowing his field. As the tractor moves across the field, the farmer keeps looking backward at the plow to make sure everything is going well. When he gets half-way across the field, he stops and looks back at the furrow he has dug, and it is crooked! This is definitely a problem, because on his next pass he will put the tractor wheel into that furrow and the remainder of the furrows will be as crooked as his first. It is obvious he must do something different, so he decides to look ahead. He puts his eyes on a fence post ahead of him and lines the tractor's hood ornament up with the fence post. As long as he looks at the fence post, he plows a straight line.

Relating that on a more personal level, I would say he was looking at his past problems and failures, which were causing problems for his future success.

The fence post is our *seed list* and the plow is our *weed list*. Let us forget about the plow and look at the fence post.

Each time *you* look at the *plow*, you will repeat your problems and mistakes, but as you look at the *fence post* you will begin to gain victory over your fears and failures and be more successful in every area of your life. Everyone in your world will recognize the change and you will be the *"doctor of sales."*

CHAPTER 7
CONTROLLING THE DECISION

☞ *A Closed Mind*
☞ *Frame of Reference*
☞ *Closing the Sale*
☞ *Losing the Sale*

*D*ecision-making in the sales presentation is a critical time because this is when we test our level of success. We ask ourselves, "Have we been able to show enough value in our service or product that the customer will say, "*Yes*." Most salespeople do not realize that there are a series of *decisions* throughout the presentation, beginning with the initial greeting.

Every Thought is a Decision

The smallest element of thought is a decision. Every time we think a thought we make a decision. When we awoke this morning, we made a decision about our spouse, the weather, the day of the week, what we would wear and what we would do. We make thousands of decisions each day. Therefore, any decision we or our customers will make is really a series of decisions, ultimately leading to a final decision.

"Decision-making" time leads most salespeople to think about "closing the sale." We must realize, however, that when prospects first meet us, or they first hear our voice on the telephone, they are making decisions about us. They are concerned that we can be trusted to be their doctor of sales. They subconsciously question our professionalism, tone of voice, choice of words, friendliness, and knowledge of our product. An accumulation of decisions about us will determine what our prospects will think about our presentation. And, what they think will determine whether they will be open to a sales relationship with us. So there is a lot to consider in decision-making before we ever get to the close. Each element or small decision will determine our success.

In this chapter, we will consider how decisions are made and how to recognize decisions that are based on a fear motivation. We need the ability to lift others above their fear so their mind is open to the value of our product, service, or opportunity.

Intensity of Emotion

Whenever a person is in the decision-making process, the two basic emotions of thought, love and fear, will be determining the conclusion. Every thought (decision) stems from a love-motivation or a fear-motivation.

There are things that are okay and there are things that are fantastic. Some things are not so good, and other things are terrible. The greater the intensity of emotion, the greater the impact that decision will have upon the person making the decision. In all cases, this process is based upon the individual's values, principles, wants, needs, and desires.

Let me illustrate this concept. You have reached the conclusion that the family automobile is on its last leg, and it is time to make a trade for the new model. So, you clean and polish the old clunker, drive it to the dealership, and they are pleased to assist you in driving away in your dream car! As you drive away, you say to yourself, "This is great! It's just what I wanted, and it's loaded!" You are flying higher than a kite.

"Value" is a Decision

That same day, the car dealer "details" your old trade-in, puts four new tires on the old rims, sprays a little "new car smell" on the upholstery, and puts it on the used car lot with a sign in the window reading, "Low Mileage Executive Car."In this scenario, a young newlywed couple, in desperate need of an automobile eyes your old "junker" and falls in love.

It is perfect for them -- the car they have been dreaming of. And, best of all, it is within their budget. As they drive their new car from the used car lot, they say: "This is great! It's just want we wanted, and it's loaded!" They have experienced the same intensity of emotion as you did with your "new" purchase.

The decisions we make have little to do with the product or service, but have everything to do with the intensity of emotion that we attach to the value we have placed on the product or service. The two automobiles in this illustration are not the cause of the decision, or the positive response. The value of what the new car could do for you, and what the old car offered the young couple, created positive emotions in both of you and each of you made a value decision.

We have total control of our decisions. I cannot make you think something you do not want to think, and you cannot control my decision- making. You can, however, help people make "a wise buying decision." By determining your prospects' values and relating your product or service to their value system, you can lead prospects into a clear understanding of the value of your product. When each of you as buyers were thinking about purchasing a new car, you were creating a value system regarding automobiles. Decisions were made regarding price, style, use, color, financing, gas mileage, and many other factors.

When we as salespeople can determine the value judgments (decisions) made by our prospects, and relate the sales presentation to those values, the final decision (the close) will be positive for everyone. There will be no need for coercion or sales techniques.

57

Impressions Affect Decisions

An important principle to understand is that everything you (including your staff) say, and every action and reaction, is impacting the decision the customer is making about you, your company, and your product or service.

Most people do not know why they say, "I want to think about it," because in many cases they have made an effort to become knowledgeable about the product and know what they want and need. However, they do need to think about how much they can trust the person, and the company offering the product.

One of my principles is that when I meet new people, I look for three things I like about them. By choosing to look for positives rather than negatives, I always find what I am seeking. I have never met a person who did not have at least three good qualities. This exercise is done for my benefit, not the other person's benefit. Once my decisions are made, my day is either more positive or more negative. I have found by the time I have discovered three things I like about a person, our time together may be over, and I leave the relationship feeling good about that prospect.

Look for Positives

It is important to remember this principle when you are qualifying a prospect. A few years back, while selling real estate, I had the misfortune (or perhaps fortune) to have floor duty on a Holiday. As is the custom with most firms, the persons on duty share the "ups" (customers walking through the door). On this particular day, my associate was "up" when a pickup truck pulled into the parking lot, and a man got out wearing dingy work clothes and high top boots. My associate did not think she would enjoy showing property to this particular person and asked if I would mind trading "ups." I feel anyone who is breathing air is a good prospect, so I traded. You can guess what happened! I made a sale that day to a very unsuspecting prospect.

Don't fall into the trap of judging others by looking for something wrong. Accept *everyone* as a prospect. You will waste some time with a few, but you will remain in a position to be successful, if you will look for the *positives* in every prospect you meet.

How Was Your Day?

Your decisions determine the quality of day you will have. You either will be a positive person from whom prospects want to purchase, or a negative person to be avoided at all costs. These decisions are made hour by hour, and moment by moment. If you decide, "It's a lousy day," you will be right. On the other hand of you decide, "It's a beautiful day," you will be right as well. So, if you had a lousy day yesterday, it serves you right!!

Remember, it is important that you choose a love-motivated lifestyle, if you choose a career in sales. Otherwise, it is not possible to be successful in sales.

Decision-Making by Bias

There are two types of decision-making. The first is *decision-making by bias.*Decisions made by bias occurs when we come into contact with something or someone and make a decision based upon past experiences. I often make the following statements and receive the standard response: "All redheads have ....? *(tempers)*, or "All Irish have ....? *(tempers)*.

Are these statements always true? Do all redheads and Irish have tempers? Of course not! I have not seen a study confirming this as truth; yet, most people give the same response. We have many *biases* that are quick decisions without any foundation that they are accurate. A few others are: "All Germans drink....? *(beer)*; "All Scots are ....? *(penny pinchers)*; and "All French are ...? *(lovers)*. (My wife is French and I know that one happens to be true, but all others possibly are not!!)

There are thousands of these biases and most of them have to do with race, religion, politics or gender. We have pre-drawn conclusions that affect our daily decisions. You possibly have met someone who has the same name as someone you dislike, and you have trouble liking that person. That is a decision by *bias*.

Immediately upon making contact with someone or something, our bias will cause us to make an instant decision (negative or positive) and we will accept that decision as truth. This type of decision-making represents about 80% of our decisions each day. Knowing this, you can see how problems can be created when a prospect comes to you carrying negative biases regarding salespeople.

Open-Minded Decision-Making

The other type of decision-making is the *open-minded* or *rational* approach. This is when a person looks at the good and the bad, and then makes a decision, positively or negatively, based upon the input received through a series of small decisions or thoughts. If there is more good than bad, there will be a positive decision. If there is more bad than good, based upon that person's values, there will be a negative decision.

Would it not be great if all your prospects were in this state of mind? Then they would be able to accept your presentation and relate it to their own values. The problem we face each day is that only 20% of our decisions are based upon an open-minded approach to decision-making.

Defense Mechanisms

Once a decision is made, a *defense mechanism* is created to protect that decision. This mechanism will block out any information that contradicts or opposes the decision that has been made. Once this *block* is in place, all input is censored to be in agreement with the decision or disagreement. When I disagree with something you say, it is because you are in opposition to that which I already believe to be true. In sales, we call these blocks *"objections."* Therefore, most sales courses teach "answers to objections" to overcome the block. We memorize hundreds of these answers to objections, and try to pull them out at just the right moment to convince our prospect to make the purchase.

Creating an Open Mind

I want to introduce a way that you can understand the cause of the objection —or fear— and dissolve the fear in the mind of the prospect, so the objection no longer exists. This creates an open mind in your prospects, and they can hear and accept your presentation.

We all defend our decisions. If I like something and know I am right, I will stand against any opposition to my *"positive"* decision. If you don't like something, you will do the same. Therefore, *objections* are always decisions made by the prospect, which are not in accord with what we want them to believe. We then *perceive* their response as being negative. Always remember, the prospects believe they are right. They do not think of their decision as being negative, and that is why they protect that decision with their defenses. If a prospect has a *closed mind,* it is impossible to communicate any thought not in total agreement with the decision they have already made. It does not matter that it make sense. As long as they have a closed mind, they cannot accept the presentation. Many sales have been lost, not because the prospect was unqualified, but rather because the mind was closed, blocking out the information they needed to understand in order to be an interested buyer. Being able to bring your prospects from behind a *block* or *closed mind,* thereby creating an open mind, is vital to you in presenting your product or service.

Curiosity

If a closed mind is created by a series of decisions leading to a final decision, you must also use the same principle to create *curiosity* or openness about your product.

Illustration:

George is a broker and has received a referral from a client. He was told that Bob and Sally Hefner had made a comment indicating that they had talked about making a move. George, being a professional sales broker was calling his clients for referrals. Now with the prospect's name and number he made the call. When Bob answered the phone George said, "Hello Bob, this is George

Rice. You don't know me, but we have a mutual friend, Mike Stevens." (*At this point George has picked up the good will of the relationship which Bob has with Mike.)* George continued, "I talked to Mike recently and he suggested I give you a call.I am a broker with Reliance Realty, and Mike told me you are thinking about *(making a decision)* relocating in the near future. Since I handle all of Mike's real estate business, he thought you might be interested in hearing what we can do for you *(offering a service)* when it comes time to sell. I would like to set a time *(an "appointment" could create fear)* when I can meet with you and your wife and answer any questions you might have concerning real estate, and today's market. When is the best time to catch you both at home?" *(This question asks for a positive response).* Bob's response was, "I'm not ready to sell right now. Mike must have misunderstood my comment when we were talking. I'm not prepared to sell, buy, or even discuss real estate at this point!" Bob now has a closed mind and as far as he is concerned a meeting would be a waste of his time. We would say the "block" was a fear of wasting his as well as George's time. George now has the task of opening Bob's mind. If his prospects are making positive decisions (thinking about the move) now is the time to establish a sales relationship. First, George must diffuse the negative decision, or soften the *"block."* His conversation continues: "Bob, Mike said you had merely mentioned you might be *thinking* about a move, and I asked if he would mind me giving you a call to offer my services." *(This softened the block because he was saying he was not expecting anything from him; he was only offering his services.)* "I've found that when people begin to think about relocating, that's the time they need the latest information on real estate. You might find this is not a good time to sell or buy. On the other hand, you might find the timing is perfect. Either way, your thinking would be influenced, wouldn't it?" George then can ask the closing question, "Bob, if I could show you a way that you would have all the information you need concerning selling or buying, would you be interested?" When George gets a "yes" answer to this question, all that remains is to set an appointment.

Remember, George asked the question, "If I could show you a way that you could know all there is to know about real estate so that you could make an accurate decision, would you be interested?" When Bob said *"yes"* he was really saying, "I'm coming out from behind my block and my mind is open to you." Now, George can set an appointment that will establish a relationship, which ultimately should result in a listing and sale of Bob's present home, and a sale on the purchase of his new home.

I Can't Afford It!

Price is often the cause of a *closed mind.* Many sales have been lost because of a price tag. "We just can't afford it right now," is a statement we have all heard many times. Let me give you another illustration dealing with this fear of paying too much, or over-committing. Understand, if the customers are qualified buyers, then they can afford to pay for the product or service. If not, the sales person is wasting time.

Illustration:

Connie Hartley is a real estate broker who showed Dave and Sue their dream home. When they returned to Connie's office, she gave them an estimated breakdown of the monthly costs for this home. Her conversation was, "Here are the figures we have to work with." Dave replied, "The bad news?" This was an indication of fear, and fear can close a prospect's mind very quickly. Connie replied, "No, it's not bad news, but it *is* a starting place." A starting place means you cannot close your mind *here;* we are just getting started, which is a neutralizing statement. Connie then tells them, "Excluding taxes and closing costs, and less your downpayment, the total amount to be financed would be $109,000. Now, this is subject to change, but on a thirty-year contract, your payments would be approximately $1,000.00 per month." She had left the door open for adjustment or change. At this point she must watch for a response and be prepared to deal with any negative. The first response comes from Sue, telling her husband, Dave: "I told you it was too much house for us. There's no way we can make that kind of payment." Dave agreed, "You're right. That's way over our heads." He apologized for taking Connie's time and arose to leave. When a prospect is leaning toward the door, you know you have a problem; the mind is closed and the deal is off. Connie interjected, "Tell me, how much *could* you spend monthly in order to make this your home?" Questions open the mind, and in this case, they will give her the bottom line of their budget for a home. They told Connie that they were paying $800.00 a month in rent at this time and that they could stretch to $850.00 or $900.00 if they were purchasing their *own* home. It would have been most difficult to get this information prior to this point. Now Connie asks the *mind-opening* question, "If I could show you a way that you could buy this house and save money over what you're now paying, would you be interested?" At this point Dave relaxed and replied, "Well, yes, but can you?" Dave was saying, "We will open our mind if you will show us how we can trust you to help us." Then, Connie used her negotiating skills to put the deal together and make the sale.

Fear Induced Blocks

"We always sleep on it," "I have a friend in this business," "We want to look around," or "We always talk over these decisions," are among the list of hundreds of *fear*-induced blocks we encounter in the sales field. The only way to dissolve these *blocks* and create an open mind in our prospects is by asking the question, "If I could show you a way to ... (satisfy the fear) would you be interested?" The answer will be "yes" if you have found the fear that is causing the block. If the response is "No," you need to ask more questions because you missed what they were indicating to you as being their fear. Keep in mind that *statements* can close a mind, but *questions* open it. A professional in any field will find a way to satisfy the wants, needs, and desires of a customer, but the customer's *mind* must be *open* before the answer to the fear can be *accepted*.

I mentioned earlier my friend, Bennie Harris. Bennie is a Life Insurance Underwriter and has been highly successful in the Insured Savings and Retirement fields. He has built a successful business, helping people understand how they can "pay *themselves.*" He says, "Throughout your lifetime you pay everybody else, and then reach retirement, only to find that you forgot to pay yourself." When Bennie ends his presentation, the question is a matter of how much you are going to pay yourself each month, not whether you are going to start a program. When a client says, "I just can't save that much," Bennie will ask, "How much do you want to have coming in monthly at age 72?" It is very difficult not to want to be set up for a comfortable retirement, so the

focus is on how much I will receive, not how much it will cost me *today*. Many times I have heard Bennie say, "If I could show you a way that you could have "X" amount of dollars in your mail box every month for as long as you live, even if you live to be 110, and I hope you do, would you be interested?" Very few say, "No."

Two Step Concept

The first step in determining the fear that is causing the block is to ask the question, "If I could show you a way ....would you be interested?" This moves the prospects from behind the *block* so that, in essence, they are asking, "Will you please show me a way that I can have that which I want and need."

Secondly, with the mind open, the prospect can hear your presentation, which allows you to build value in your product, based upon your client's value system. In a later chapter we will cover the *first close*. In that lesson, you will learn how to determine the prospect's values, wants and needs. You will then use that information to build value while the prospect has an open mind.

Most salespeople try to make a sales presentation while the prospect has a closed mind They make *strong* statements, give great *reasons* to buy, and many times they relate the presentation to the prospect's wants and needs, but with very little success. I have seen salespeople making a splendid presentation, telling the story so well that almost anyone would be interested in buying. And then, they get to the close, expecting the customer to be excited about the purchase, only to get many of the objections we have mentioned here. After the customer leaves they say, "I don't know what more I could have said to close that sale." And they are right. They said all the right things, but the prospect's mind was closed, and therefore, could not relate to one word of the sales presentation.

Make a Presentation Only to an Open Mind

Never, no never, start your presentation until you have created an open mind. Should the prospect's mind become closed during the presentation, you must *stop* and create *curiosity* thereby reopening the mind. Many sales are lost, and good, qualified prospects are turned into *suspects* who ultimately become some other salesperson's prospect! This occurs merely because the salesperson attempted to make a presentation to a person with a closed mind. It is a total waste of time and those salespeople are "casting their pearls before the swine," or in plain language, "throwing something precious into the manure pile."

Once again let me review the steps: **To make a successful presentation, you must first open the mind, remove the fear from the psychological block, and while the mind is open, build value based upon the prospect's value system, satisfying their wants and needs.** This will make you the "doctor of sales" and you will find success in every endeavor.

CHAPTER 8

THE FIRST CLOSE

☞ *A Closed Mind*
☞ *Frame of Reference*
☞ *Closing the Sale*
☞ *Losing the Sale*

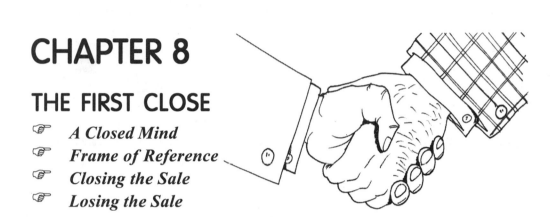

The *first close* occurs in the first five minutes of a sales presentation. So many salespeople tell me that the thing they dislike most about sales is "the close," or "closing the sale."

We come to the end of our presentation, knowing we have done a good job. We have shown all the diagrams, all the benefits, and all the things that are so great about our product, and finally we know in our mind that we *must* make the close. Our eyes roll back, our voice changes a little, and we begin to sweat.

In this case, we have allowed fear to control our thinking processes, and you can guess what happens. Our body chemistry then becomes negative, and our presence becomes negative. This unconsciously creates a negative response from our prospects who sense there is something wrong so they had better start setting up defense mechanisms. They then close their mind and now we have literally destroyed their ability to purchase our product and close the sale. It is like saying "Put up your defenses because here comes the close." The prospects do not know why all of a sudden, they feel this cold wave coming over them, or why they are losing rather than gaining interest. They do not even understand why they say, "I'd better sleep on it." They merely sense there is something wrong. The salesperson's fear is projected into the mind of the prospects, causing

them to set up defense mechanisms, and they begin suggesting objections. If you can understand that as a salesperson you should establish your position at the front end of the sales presentation, and create a relationship as "doctor of sales" to a customer, you are then in a position to close the sale even before you have made your presentation.

If I were to ask you the amount of your life insurance coverage, you possibly do not know for sure. Or, if I were to ask how much cash value is attached to your insurance policy, you probably would say you do not know. Even if you sell insurance, you might say an *approximate* amount, which means you do not know either. This is true almost always. However, if I were to ask you the name of your insurance agent, you would be able to tell me, which tells me you do not necessarily know what you bought, but you do know from whom you bought. So, what did you really buy? You bought the agent. My insurance agent is the doctor of sales, and the "doctor" is taking care of me. All I have to do is pay the premium. Bill Graber has been our family insurance agent for many years. He handled all of my dad's car insurance and he has done a great job for me and my children. I have no idea what my coverage is, because I trust Bill to take care of that for me. It does not matter what field you represent, because when I believe in you and have bought you as my supplier, I do not worry about the details. You are my "doctor" when you create enough value in your product or service that I enjoy your product more than any other product of its kind. Part of your responsibility as the doctor of sales is to create so much value in your product that I must have it, regardless of cost. When you *clerk* houses, insurance, or whatever your product might be, then you are depriving the *joy of ownership* from your customers. Therefore, you will not enjoy repeat and referral business; because that only comes from selling value, and establishing a relationship in which you are the doctor of sales.

It is important to know that the *first close* takes all the pressure off of the *final close*. When it is time to close the sale, all you should have to do is ask the customer to "make your check payable to....(your company." Isn't that an easy close? If you are successful in the first close, you will have established a sales relationship, the prospect will trust you and believe the value of your product. You can then relate your presentation to their *needs* and the customers believe they are "making a wise buying decision."

At the beginning of a sales presentation, the prospect's mind is open. They have not passed judgment on you and they have not bought or rejected you. Their mind is completely open. This can last for a maximum of *five minutes*. Within five minutes, the prospects will either accept or reject you. They will believe in you as a professional who can be trusted, and will establish a psychological block to protect that relationship, or they will have doubts and fears, and set up defense mechanisms to protect their interests. Then as a sales professional, you are in trouble because you are working from a situation where you are not in a sales position.

Only Five Minutes to a Closed Mind!

There was a study conducted recently with professional interviewers. These people were hired and asked to keep an *open mind* while interviewing people for management positions. In this particular study, one-half of the college graduates who came in for the interview were instructed to give *correct* answers to the questions asked during the first five minutes. Likewise, they were instructed to give *incorrect* answers for fifty-five minutes of a one-hour interview. The other half of the graduates were instructed in the reverse; five minutes of *incorrect* answers, followed by fifty-five minutes of *correct* answers. The *professional interviewers*, who prided themselves in having an open mind, and having the ability to scout out and hire the perfect prospective managers for corporations, all suggested hiring interviewees who gave five minutes of correct answers and fifty-five minutes of incorrect answers. When the study was completed, the interviews were played back for the interviewers. They could not believe what they had done. What had happened was, once they had made a decision, and set up a psychological block, all the incorrect answers made no difference The psychological block was blocking out the negative side. They were astounded to find that for 55 minutes they were rationalizing that these interviewees were qualified. On the other hand, when the interviewee gave wrong answers for five minutes, the interviewer started making decisions that this person was not qualified. The interviewer would then act as if the person got *lucky* when they *did* give the right answers.

This study tells us that in five minutes you are going to make a decision. In fact, all of your life you have made decisions in five minutes or less. Many people make decisions and then after making the decision, they make the decision right. It is difficult to make a *right* decision, because if you *have* to make a decision at all, you do not have the information available to you to make that decision. If you had all the information you needed to make a decision, there would not be a decision to be made. You would see the outcome and there would be only one way to go. Any time you are in a decision-making process, it is merely because you do not have all the information you need to make an accurate decision. If I make a decision, then I must justify that decision. If I choose to dislike you, I can give you a hundred reasons why. Likewise, if I choose to like you, I can give you a hundred reasons why I do. In either case, I would be right. That is, at least in my mind I would be right, and that is what matters. It does not matter what your prospect's background might be, or what their needs are, they are going to make a decision about you in five minutes or less. The *first close* is selling yourself in five minutes or less.

Making sure that the prospect's *mind is open* to you before you try selling yourself will put you in a position to be the doctor of sales and create value. In those first five minutes you must cause the prospect to trust you as a professional. You cannot do that by describing how great you are, or why your product or service is the best, or even how long your company has been in business. Remember from the previous chapter, *curiosity* opens the prospect's mind. Asking personal questions will cause them to relax and not feel pushed. An interest in the customer's wants, needs, and desires creates the sense of trust necessary to ensure an open mind.

A light sense of humor helps relax the prospect. If you can get your prospect to smile, or chuckle a little, that is even better. One of the best brokers I have witnessed at doing this is Anna Pusz, a highly successful Realtor in southwest Florida. Anna has an infectious laugh. When she laughs you cannot help but join her. Anna will find something to laugh about within a very short time of meeting a prospect. This is not something she does on purpose, it is a part of her personality. I think it comes merely from enjoying her profession. She has fun, and the prospects relax with her lightness. Make sure you keep the first five minutes light and positive, with no pressure. Remember, it is just "get acquainted" time.

I want to share with you some stories I have collected over the years which illustrate this concept in action. I receive many letters from people who have attended my seminars, and who relate to me experiences they had in using what they have learned. I trust you will be able to relate your business to some of these.

A stock broker, Brenda Conwell, met Rich and Barbara Denson at the front desk of her office and discovered they were interested in hearing about available investments that might build a financial base for their future. She had not met them before, and soon discovered they had come in as a result of an ad in the Yellow Pages. She took them to her private office and began the *first close,* or, the first five minutes.

Brenda said, "Mr. Denson, please sit down right here, and I'll ask your wife to sit here next to me." The very act of telling them where to sit was the first step toward being in total control of their sales relationship. She continued, "We have found that if we get to know our clients, we can better help them make wise investments. I can show you everything that is in the market place today, but the more I know *you,* the better I can meet your needs. Now, first, I want to be sure I have the correct spelling of your name. Is your name Richard or Rich?" Rich answered, "It's Richard, but I prefer to be called, Rich." "Okay," says Brenda, "And, your name is Barbara? "Yes," his wife answered, "but you can call me Barbara or Barb." Now Brenda was on a first name basis with the Densons, and was able to use their names in their most acceptable form. She then used her clipboard, with an information sheet attached, to ask the questions which would begin building a relationship of trust. Brenda asked for their address and telephone number, to which Rich replied with a nearby address and local telephone number.

When prospects give you their telephone number, they are indicating an interest in a continuing relationship. After Rich gave her this general information, Brenda was then in a position to delve further into their personal life. She asked if they had children and Barb responded: "Yes we do. Richie is now seven and Tammy is fourteen months." In a later lesson, we will cover what a person's choice of words tells us about values, wants, needs and desires. In this instance, however, Brenda is getting far more information about the Densons than just the obvious. Brenda responded to each answer with words of acceptance. She said, "Seven and fourteen months! That's quite an age difference. But, at least you got to enjoy Richie a little bit before Tammy came along." By using the children's names, Brenda had become a part of the Densons' world. Children are the most important people in the world to the parents; therefore, if you call them by name, even if you were just given their names, they will feel more comfortable with you. After Brenda had related to their home life, she then asked about their professional life. She asked Rich about his line of work, and he gave her the company name, "I work for Central Control Systems." Brenda further asked what Rich's position was with that company, to which he replied: "I'm the Vice President in charge of personnel and operations." At this Barb interrupted Rich and said, "And employee problems! People are calling our house all hours of the day and night." Brenda now is getting more than she asked for, which is a further indication of trust, and adds, "I can just imagine. Barb, do you work?" She replied, "Housework, if you want to call that work!" Brenda said, "I call that work." It is very important to respond to each comment made by both persons. When you respond to their comments, no matter how small, it means you are listening and are interested in them as individuals. Now Brenda can ask about Rich's annual income and he feels comfortable giving her his annual salary. She is now the "doctor of sales" and you *always* answer the doctor's questions! Once again, she is getting more information than she asked for, which is a very positive sign that the *first close* is moving in the right direction. If she were to get *questions* rather than answers she would know the *trust* was not there. And if that were the case (I will illustrate this later), she would have to work at conquering the fear that was creating the block. Brenda went on to ask Rich how long he had been with his company and he replied, "It's been three years now. Seems longer than that, but it has only been three years." Brenda keeps it light by adding, "You know what they say, time flies...et cetera." Now, that is not a "funny" statement, but it is "light" and might bring a smile or positive response from the prospect. Light humor is important in the development stages of a sales relationship. By now, Brenda feels she has everything she needs, so she asks the Densons to look over the information to be sure everything is correct. She then asks Rich and Barb to sign their names so that her broker would know the information is correct. She has created a relationship in which she has sufficient knowledge of her new clients that she can proceed with her presentation. The Densons feel comfortable with her, because she has not tried selling them anything, but has been interested in getting to know them. This method has been used effectively with a wide range of sales  organizations, and for most salespeople who work with *walk-in* prospects, or salespeople who call on prospects in their homes, it is a great way to control the *first close*.

Earlier I mentioned the medical doctor in the examination room, and how effectively he uses a clipboard. He asks us all kinds of medical questions, and after answering the questions, we feel like *we* know the doctor. Really, the doctor knows *us* because he is the one asking the questions.

Brenda was doing the same thing here as a stock broker. She was getting answers to questions that she needed in order to make her presentation relevant to their needs. In the process of asking the questions, they felt like they knew her. She became their stock broker or their *stock "doctor."* To make it even stronger, after she had all that information, Connie gave the clipboard to the customers to verify the information. When they signed, they literally signed a contract between themselves and Brenda, their stock broker.

Once you have made your first signature, you don't mind signing other things. Have you ever noticed that after you read all the fine print on the front page of a contract, and sign it, you rarely read the second page, or anything that follows. You will then sign the check and the obligation note and the resistance to signing is gone. So when it came time for Brenda to present another clipboard saying they should buy the stock she was offering, the Densons didn't mind signing that either. The fear of signing was past, and the resistance was gone. So, in the first five minutes, she established that she was their doctor of sales. And once in that position, she was able to help them find the investments they were searching. They trusted her opinions and suggestions.

If you are in a sales field which requires you to call on prospects in their homes, let me walk you through the same five-minute interval, sitting at the prospect's dining room table.

Jim is a distributor in a multi-level marketing company and his success has come by being able to present his business opportunity so well that his prospects can see themselves being successful in this field. In this scenario, he is with the Cooks, in their dining room, and he is playing the "doctor" role.

The one difference here is that the other illustration was in an office, and this is in a home. Jim opened by mentioning his appreciation of the opportunity to share a program with them which he thought would excite them, as it had him. He began by asking Mr. Cook, "How long have you lived in this area? Mr. Cook's reply was, "In this house or in this city?" Jim said, "Both. I'm interested in knowing if we might have some mutual friends." They began to relax with Jim, and Mrs. Cook continued, "Well, we have lived most of our lives in this area, but in this house....it will be three years in August. I remember so well because it was the time my husband was promoted to manager." Jim responded immediately, "That's right. Don told me you are the manager of the store now. How do you like the added responsibilities." He replied, "I don't mind the responsibility, that's why I receive the added salary!" Jim now knows that *added income* is important to Mr. Cook. It is important for Jim to know this because he is there to show him how he can add more income to the family, by having his own part time business. "I understand you have two lovely children. What are their ages?" Mrs. Cook said, "Well, Arty is five; he is the busybody and never stops running. And there is 'Toad.' Cindy is her real name, but she loves little crawling things like toads, so we named her after her "best friends." She is three-and-a-half. They're a good bunch." Mr. Cook added, "When you have to keep them in clothes, bunch *is* the correct word."

Can you recognize the positive feedback? If Jim had immediately started showing the Cooks a bunch of circles, and telling them how they could make money on a part-time basis, he would never have gotten this information, which will give direction in his presentation. Now he knows a few of their *hot buttons* (wants and needs) and can use some related material in his presentation to make it relevant to the Cooks. Jim finally said, "Well, you really have a lot to be proud of, and I know you are." He immediately continued, "Now, I want to show you something that will add new dimensions to every area of your life, and help you pay for some of those things your family wants and needs." Jim can say this because he has *established a relationship.* He is now the doctor, and he is going to attempt to be the answer to their problems.

The Cooks enjoyed talking about their children, and as you will see later in the book, when you talk about your children, you really are not talking about the children, but rather, how you relate to your children. So, these two people were actually telling Jim a lot about themselves in talking about their children. You will understand this concept more fully as we later get into the *motivations of life.*

One situation real estate brokers face a lot is "open houses." I think open houses are interesting. As you walk through the door, there is a real-estate agent with a stack of business cards on the table and a sign saying, "Take one." That is a sad situation, because when the real estate agent merely gives away business cards, that agent gives up a position of authority. The customers are put into the position of *calling back* should they decide to buy the house.

In fact, in many cases, the salesperson does not even get the prospect's name. They are merely playing the role of a *clerk.* Then, later in the day when leaving the house, the agent finds that the gutter is filled with business cards. The prospect walks out after seeing the home and immediately gets rid of the business card because they have no interest in doing business with that agent. Why? The salesperson was a clerk -- just showing people through the house -- and not a doctor of sales. Rather than giving a business card to prospects, we want to get *their* names so that we are in a position of control. When we talk about *establishing sales authority* we must have the name of the prospects. The *clerk gives away* business cards, but the *doctor collects* business cards, or takes names, addresses and telephone numbers, so that they can make future contact with the customer. This is not a difficult thing to do in an open house.

Let me illustrate how Hazel Hansen holds an open house. When prospects walk into a home she is showing, they are greeted at the door with a smile, and,"Have you visited this home before?" Most salespeople ask ridiculous questions like, "May I help you?" or even more ridiculous, "Can I show you this lovely home?" I am always tempted to say, "No, I just need to use the bathroom." I wonder what the agent would do! Leonard Llewellyn, the broker/consultant I mentioned earlier, instructs his salespeople to *take a step backward* when you first meet a prospect and not be the first to offer a name. He has found that the best way for him to know when the prospects have *bought* him is when they ask for *his* name. Then when he gives his name he says, "Thanks for asking." Your name is not nearly as important as getting your prospect's name.

When Hazel met the Sampsons at an open house, she said: "Hello. Welcome to our open house. I'm so glad you could stop by." Mr. Sampson, being a polite man, responded with, "Hi. I'm Al Sampson, and this is my lovely wife, Lynn." Now Hazel is already on a *first name basis* with this couple. Normally, this is the fashion in which we greet people in our society, *except* in a sales situation. Then, for some unknown reason, we seem to get stiff and business-like, and in the process, miss some of the valuable input, such as a person's first name. If you remember that your first job is getting to know your prospect, rather than the prospect getting to know you, you will do a lot of listening rather than too much talking in that critical first five-minute time frame.

Now that Hazel has their first names, there is no resistance to signing the guest book, which, by the way, also requires their address and phone number. Hazel says, "Would you please sign our guest book for our free drawing? Then you will be on our mailing list, and when our new models are available, I will give you a call." She gives them a reason for signing the book (the free drawing) and then says she will give them a call later, which is a reason for them to give their phone number. She then asks, "Have you lived in this area long, Al?" While Lynn is signing the guest book, Hazel keeps a conversation going with Al. He replies, "No, but we would like to eventually find something in this part of town. That's why we decided to stop when we saw the open house sign. We thought we might get an idea of cost."

Lynn has now signed the guest book and responds, "We have no idea of the cost or conditions of the homes in this area." Hazel added, "Would it be closer to work?" This question can tell her several things about the Sampsons. "Yes," he replied, "it would be closer for both of us. I manage the First National Bank over on 23rd

Street and Lynn's office is also in the Bank Building." Lynn continued, "It would also be closer to the school for our two boys. They attend the private school just down the street."

Now Hazel is ready to show the house. She has knowledge of their work, and their children, she knows that they are school age, and that they attend a private school nearby. She has learned a lot about the Sampsons, and best of all, she has used the *first close* to establish a relationship. She kept in total control without being pushy. Now, what if they say they do not like the house? In a normal situation, the real estate agent is finished!! However, Hazel is in the position to call them, and arrange to show another house, possibly more to their liking or perhaps more in their price range.

The doctor of sales lets the prospect do all the talking in the front end. On the other hand, however, the *clerk* does most of the talking in the front end of a conversation. Clerks do not get to know the customers so they do not know how to fill their needs. In fact, in many cases, clerks sell the way they would want to be sold. The problem arises when the customer does not like the same things as the clerk. This happens a lot because most people sell like they would want to be sold, rather than the way the prospect needs to be sold. How do you know what their needs are? By knowing how to ask questions and then knowing when to shut up. The temptation is to jump on a statement as soon as it is uttered. The problem is, one variable is not enough information on which to base a sale. So, you should ask questions and remain quiet.

In the first five minutes, you ask simple questions about their children, where they live, and their job -- short questions requiring long answers, and at the end of that five minutes, the customers feel they know you, and that makes you the doctor of sales. Actually, they do not know you at all.

What would you think of your doctor if he or she came into the examination room and the first words uttered were: "Guess what I've been doing today?" And for the next five minutes he talks about his day. If so, by the time the doctor gets around to examining you, you are ready to leave. You do not want a doctor to tell you all of his problems. In fact, you do not even want to believe your doctor *has* problems.

Salespeople do it all the time. They get so caught up in their own world that they think everyone will be interested.

You, as the doctor of sales, must get interested in your customer's world and let them talk about themselves. Everything they tell you is exactly what you need to know to be in a position of authority and control, and to be in the position to build value in your product, service or opportunity.

No matter what you are selling, you can build value based upon your client's *frame of reference,* if you will keep your mouth closed and listen to your prospect. When you do that, you are truly the doctor of sales, and you are successful.

Your closing rate will increase, as well as your repeat and referral business, and you will smile a lot. And I think that is good. **If you are successful in the *first close,* you will have a client rather than a prospect and you will see how great it is to sell when you have first established a sales relationship.**

CHAPTER 9

BEING THE DOCTOR OF SALES

☞ *Projecting Acceptance*
☞ *Buying the Salesperson*
☞ *Taking Control*
☞ *Dr. of Sales vs. Clerk*

This is a *fun* lesson. I have a good time with it because I believe it says a lot, but also because it is just fun material. Be prepared to read something that is going to assist you in being an authority in the field of sales.

The greatest salespeople in the world today are *medical doctors*. They are great salespeople. In fact, they have a one hundred percent closing ratio, and that is not just a pun, it is the truth. They never miss! When you visit a medical doctor, the doctor is *always* "The Doctor." They have a tremendous position of authority in our society. You do not argue with your doctors. In fact, when you go into a doctor's office, you find that the entire structure is designed to make you respect the person you have an *appointment* to see —your doctor.

The "Medical" Doctor

The Doctor's Office is designed so that the first thing you see when you enter is a sliding glass window, and behind that window is a person who acknowledges your presence with, "May I help you?" You tell her you have an appointment and she tells you to sit down. Have you ever told the receptionist that you would rather stand? Of course not! You sit right where she tells you to sit, and you stay in that position for a half-hour or so. This, by the way, is the reason you are called "the patient."

Finally, a nurse comes into the waiting room, wearing a little white hat (that's how you know it is the nurse) and tells you to go back into a little room, and *disrobe.* Now, you do not take off your clothes for just anybody, but you *do* for this person because it is the *nurse,* and it is a *doctor's* office. You do what you are told to do in the doctor's office. You are back in a little room wearing no clothes, sitting on a table covered with toilet paper, and you hear other people walking up and down the hall. Did you ever wonder if the wrong person might walk into the wrong room at the wrong time, and there you would be sitting, in all your splendor and glory?

Finally, the door opens and you sigh with relief. Not because of the person who walks in the room, but because of the thing hanging around the person's neck -- a *stethoscope!* Immediately, you recognize this person as the doctor. I have often thought it would be interesting to go to a doctor's office, put on a stethoscope and check out a few rooms!!

The doctor picks up the clipboard and asks you some very general questions. When it is time for a *personal* question, the doctor will not look you in the eye, but rather will look at the clipboard. They will ask your *weight* and you will tell them. Have you ever lied to the doctor? Then the doctor will look you in the eye and ask a few general questions such as whether you have had chicken pox or the measles, and when he glances back at the clipboard, he will ask another personal question, "Your age?" Why do they lose eye contact when they ask personal questions? We will answer a personal question more honestly if there is not eye contact.

After about five minutes, the doctor begins poking around on your nude body with a cold instrument. Now you do not let just *anybody* do this, but you let this person, because it is the "doctor." The doctor will tell you to do strange things, such as, "Bend over," or "Turn your head and cough." The doctor looks where no one else has ever looked, and touches what no one else is allowed to touch. You allow this because the doctor has established the position of "*The Doctor.*"

Do you realize you *must* be the doctor of sales, if you are to be successful. Let us consider the differences between a *doctor of sales* and a *clerk.* The doctor of sales establishes a position, determines the needs of the prospect, and directs the sales presentation based on those needs. The doctor of sales then sells the decision: "This is what I want you to think," or "This is what I want you to do." Clerks wait for customers to come to them, show a variety of products to sell one, and then put the decision-making responsibility on the shoulders of the prospect. The problem is, the only thing prospects know is that they have a need. The salesperson is the one who has all the information and knowledge regarding this product or service. The prospects do not want to make a decision. They are looking for a doctor to help them make a "wise buying decision."

What would you think of a dentist who asked, "Would you like them pulled or filled?" You want the dentist to know what to do! Or, what would you think of a medical doctor who asked: "How would you like an operation on Thursday morning?"

When you meet your prospects *you* are the doctor of sales. You tell me what I should think and what I should do. You have all the knowledge. I have not been trained as you have to know the benefits of your product, service or opportunity. The sad thing is that our society has very few real salespeople, but lot of clerks who are saying: "What do you think?"

Few Meet the "Doctor of Suits"

The gentlemen, especially, will appreciate this illustration and most likely relate well to the story.

The time has come to purchase a new suit and as you enter the men's clothing store you are met by a clerk who says, "May I help you? Now I personally believe that is a *dumb* question. I would not have entered the store had I not wanted to be *helped.* However, you do have to answer the question, because the clerk will just look at you until you answer: "Yes, I would like to look at some suits." The clerk will ask, "What size suit do you wear," and "What price range do you have in mind?" So you give them a size and an approximate price range. Now, you might not have purchased a suit for a couple of years, and there is no way you could know the latest style, price, or possibly your current size. The clerk then takes you to a rack of suits and points out the suits in your size and price range, and tells you to make your choices. There are probably six or seven suits on the rack that look good to you and the clerk says, "Would you like to try them on?"

You go into that little closet that was designed just a bit too small, so that as you lift your leg to put on the pants, you bump into the wall and fall out through the curtain! And, of course, that just happens to be the moment that everyone in the place is in that corner of the store, looking your way. Also, have you noticed that the curtain in changing closets always hangs a little crooked, so that there is a gap? You have an instant flashback of that day in the fourth grade when the photographer was taking your picture and said, "If you can see me, I can see you!"

A sales situation with a clerk is never a comfortable situation. You come out wearing a suit and stand in front of the mirror and the clerk asks: "How do you like this suit? I think it looks very good!" You are not quite sure so the clerk says, "Would you like to try the next one?" So, back into the closet, and once again, standing in front of the mirror, the clerk says, "Oh, I like that one too. What do you think?" When you have tried all the suits and the clerk has told you they all look good, it is *decision-making* time.

Now the clerk says, "Of all the suits you tried, which do you prefer?" That was a "close," in case you did not recognize it! You tell the clerk which suit or suits you prefer, and he asks you if you would like to have the suits altered. When you return in several days and try on your new suit you wonder if that was the suit you really bought. It just does not look quite right. When you wear it you notice people looking at you a bit strange and you eventually put the suit in the back of the closet, where you only choose to wear it in dire emergencies. Why did this happen? Because it was *clerked* rather than *sold* by the doctor.

A doctor of sales will greet you at the door and say, "Hello, welcome to.....(store name), how are you today? The doctor of sales has genuine interest in people, and a positive presence will be projected that will draw people to, and cause them to believe in, that person.It is the law of *projection* and *attraction.Project* "acceptance" and you will be "accepted." *Project* "concern" for people and their needs, and they will have an open-minded approach toward purchasing your product or service.

The *suit doctor* will always know your size, and never ask your price range, because it is *assumed* you want to buy the best in the house. The suit doctor brings out three suits and carries to the dressing room the suit you should try first. When you stand in front of the mirror he says: "You know, the color of this suit picks up the color of your eyes and makes them look larger." You cannot believe it as you stand there—you have great big eyes. "It also makes your skin look more alive." You look, and sure enough, your skin is alive. "One more thing you will notice," he says, "It makes your hair shine." So there you stand with big eyes, your skin is alive and your hair shines, and you say, "I'll take it!" The suit doctor then says, "Try this one." You stand before the mirror again and he says, "Once again, we have the color that is best for you," and sure enough, your eyes are big, your skin is alive, and your hair is shining. He continues, "The tailoring of this suit makes your shoulders look broad and your waist look small." You say, "I'll take it!" But the doctor says, "Try this suit." Then he says, "The same things are true as in the other two suits, with one addition, "The vertical stripes in this suit, while subtle, make you look four or five inches taller." So, there you are with your eyes big, your hair shining, your skin alive, your shoulders are broad, your waist is small, and you look six-foot-five, and you say, "I'll take it!" Of course by now the "suit doctor" is already marking the cuff, because he knew from the beginning that this suit was the one for you.

Is it important for the *suit doctor* to know what colors flatter your skin tone? Of course. There is a science of colors and how your skin tone reacts to particular colors. The doctor will be aware of that information. Whatever field you choose, you must be the doctor of sales. You must have product knowledge and understanding and certainly you need to know what you are doing.

When I lived on the East Coast I had a "suit doctor" at Raleigh's in the Springfield Mall in the Washington, DC area. Tom would not sell me a suit, even if it was my choice, if he did not believe as the doctor that it was the best suit for me. I remember on one occasion attempting to purchase a "Johnny Carson" suit and Tom said, "You travel a great deal and you would not be happy with this suit. It wrinkles too easily and the wrinkles will not fall out when you remove it from your garment bag." I cannot remember how many suits I have bought from Tom, but I know several of my friends on the East Coast have purchased suits and coats from him. A "suit doctor" will always keep you informed of the current product line, and advise you of wise buying times. Then, you will probably purchase multiple items. Once you have found the doctor of sales in any field, you will not be comfortable buying from anyone else.

One of the fastest growing department stores in the United States today is the *Nordstrom* chain. The reason for this growth is not price or unique inventory. The success Nordstrom has enjoyed has been a result of their training program which teaches all of their employees to be "doctors of sales." Go to *any* department store and then visit a Nordstrom store and you will see the difference very quickly. A Nordstrom salesperson will make you feel relaxed, unhurried, and will make sure you are completely satisfied before they will wait on the next person. You know how important you are to them by the way they attend to you.

This is more of an attitude than a presentation or approach. If I believe you are an important person, that belief will dictate my relationship with you. I will take the time to get to know your wants, needs, and desires; and when you sense this, your fears will no longer hinder a strong working relationship, which eventually becomes a sales relationship.

Clerkink Fatalities

Let me describe how a real estate agent who is a clerk meets prospects, and you will see the down side or opposite of being the doctor of sales. A clerk is unaware of the prospect's wants and needs because they *are not* relationship-oriented.

Bill, a *clerk,* is in his sales office talking to a friend on the telephone and a couple enter. He has one foot on the desk and is engaged in a lengthy conversation. If you were the prospects standing beside Bill's desk, this is what you would have witnessed.

"Uh-huh. The game last Friday. Yeah. I know we have to do better if we are going to win the trophy. But how can we be consistent with Al on the team? Yes, I know. I don't know who in the world ever told him he was a bowler. You'd think he could see how badly he's hurting us. (Pause) Well, that's what I told Richard." He took a break from his conversation to recognize the customers: "Uh, you folks have a seat. I'll be with you in just a minute. Then he continued his telephone conversation. "Where was I? Oh, yeah. I was telling Richard that Art is a lot better. I tell you what! Why don't we make Art a regular and Al a sub? (Pause) Well, I think so too. Listen, I've got to go. I've got some people here." Turning to the waiting customers he said: "Hi, may I help you folks with something?"

I would like to be able to tell you that this is a *rare* happening, but, the fact is, I see it happening continually, and possibly you have, as well. It certainly makes one wonder why Bill was in a profession that requires meeting people. Would you buy from Bill? Most likely, you would exit quicker than you entered.

Have you ever walked into an office where two clerks were talking and it seemed they were unaware of your presence? Recently I was sitting in an office awaiting an appointment and observed this in action. Two salespeople were discussing deals each had put together recently and it appeared each was trying to outdo the

other. Finally, they looked at each other, shrugged their shoulders, and walked out. The most interesting part of this story is that the two salespersons never noticed that two customers had entered, and departed, and were unnoticed. They were so involved in their own conversation that they were not even aware of the prospect's presence. However, had either of these salespeople noticed the customer's presence they would not have been able to make a sale anyway. It would have taken a *master* doctor of sales to make these customers open to anything these people were selling.

The doctor of sales makes a decision for the prospect and then sells the decision. The clerk places the prospect in the decision-making process with limited information and knowledge.

I watched and listened to a real estate agent as he was talking to a couple to whom he had just shown some homes, and was ready to get their decision. He said, "Let's get comfortable here." As they sat down, he continued, "Well, we had quite a ride, didn't we? What do you think?" That question could lead anywhere, which means he definitely is not in control of the conversation. The wife replied, "Oh, I don't know." The agent said, "Well, out of the five houses we saw today, which one do you think you like the best?" Again she answered: "I like the green bathroom in the white house, but the living room was a little small. The brown house had a nice kitchen, but the location left something to be desired." The husband who was not quite as patient said, "I think we have a lot more looking around to do." The agent, being a *good clerk* said, "Well, I'd be glad to show you some more homes, I have a book that is *full* of nice homes." The man said, "That's a pretty thick book. I'm really not interested in looking at that many houses today! We'll look around on our own and let you know if we find something." And at this point he started toward the door. As he was walking out, the agent was muttering "I'm sure I could help you find what you're searching for. Here's my card. Be sure to call me if I can help you in any way."

I really felt sympathy for this agent. He was doing what he had been trained to do. He showed a variety of houses to sell *one*, and then asked questions that caused the prospects to be the decision-makers, and they *chose* not to make a decision! They were sure about one thing. They certainly did not want to see any more homes. They were so confused that they did not know which house had what, and when the husband started to leave, he really was saying: "Hey clerk, I want to find a doctor of sales who will take care of me." It was a *lost sale* and it was impossible to recoup their interest. This occurs when you put the decision-making process on the prospect rather than being the doctor of sales.

Also this happens in the real estate business when the salesperson allows the owner/seller to over-price property, which makes the house non-sellable. It becomes shop-worn from all of the traffic and eventually both the salespeople and the customers think there is something wrong with the property. That leads to the owner/seller getting negative toward the listing agent, which snowballs into a myriad of problems. Never allow the client, customer or prospect to be put in the position of making the decision.

Working with numerous multi-level marketing organizations, I have witnessed this same mistake being made over and over, in an attempt to sponsor distributors. The sponsor says, "The great thing about this business is that you can choose your own hours." So, at his convenience, the new distributor calls a few friends and they are not interested! When the sponsor calls to follow-up with the distributor, he finds that his new distributor has chosen to work "no" hours this week!

Likewise, if the "sponsor" in the multi-level marketing business had been the doctor of sales, he would originally have asked: "How many hours each week are you willing to invest in your own business?" When there is a commitment to invest a certain amount of hours each week, then, as a leader you can direct them toward the most profitable way to use those hours. I have witnessed *Amway* distributors become "Diamonds" in less than a year, when they became a doctor of sales, and *led* people into success.

The Doctor's Decision

Let us look at the doctor of sales working *floor duty* in a repeat of the situation we covered earlier. The salesperson is on the phone when a prospect walks in the door, and is saying, "Oh, I'm so glad. That's great. And if you have any problems at all, give me a call." As she is talking, a family enters and she interrupts the caller, "Just a minute," and to the customers, "Hello. I'll be right with you." She quickly ended her phone call, and immediately her full attention was placed on her customers. "Thanks for your patience." The husband replied, "I hope we didn't make you cut short your call!" If you show people courtesy it will be appreciated, and they will return the same. She replied, "Not at all, I was just ending my conversation." They exchanged pleasantries and then the sales associate asked, "Did you come in as a result of one of our ads, or did one of *our* friends send you?" With this

question she was picking up the *good will* of a referral, even if they had not come in as a *result* of a referral. "No," they answered, "We just saw your sign and decided to come in and ask what houses are selling for these days. We'd like to see if there's any way we could buy. We're tired of renting." This is excellent information, and it also indicates openness or trust. You want to be aware of statements such as this, because it tells you that a sales relationship is being formed and you can move ahead with your presentation. The associate's reply was, "Well, you've come to the right place. We specialize in getting people into their own homes. Why don't you come back to my office and let me get to know you a bit." She realized it was time to find some privacy so that they could tell her everything she needed to know to enable her to do a good job for them. That is how the doctor of sales meets a customer and turns a prospect into a client from the front end.

There is one final illustration to share regarding how the doctor of sales gets a *listing,* and lists the home at a price that will sell.

During the *walk-through* of the home, accompanied by the owners, this broker has established his position, and is now ready to make his close, or write the *listing agreement.* Sitting at the dining room table the broker says, "Well, I believe your home is very marketable. You won't have any trouble finding buyers looking for this type of home." Because these people are interested in selling their home, that is *good news* for them to hear. The wife said, "If you will call us before you come by with a customer, we will make it as presentable as we can." The contract had not yet been signed, and a price had not been set, but the owner was asking for a call prior to showing the home.

The agent agreed, "We always do that. I might say we do a better job if you're not around when the prospects walk through. The buyers feel more at ease, and don't think we're just saying nice things about the home because the owners are present." The doctor of sales *always* is in control, and it is far easier if the owners are not at home during showings. He was establishing this point in the listing process so that they understood from the beginning, but at the same time, it was creating a belief by the customer that the broker knew his business.

The husband said that made sense, and then asked his most important question, "What do you think a house like this is worth on the open market today?" The *big question* -- what can we get for our house? The broker said, "Well, it's easy to see that you've put some extra money into the home, and you've kept it in good condition, which is very important. I like to list houses at the top end of the price range. You can always come down a little if the need arises. According to our market analysis, and based on today's market, I would suggest listing the house at $210,000. Now I realize that is much more than you paid over four years ago, but that's its present value. And, of course, you reap that benefit!"

The wife replied, "Do you think someone would pay that price for this house?" and her husband quickly interjected, "Why not?" Look what it is costing us to build our new home. I'll tell you though, I was thinking of a higher price than that; but, I'm not in your business." This is recognition of his *professionalism.* The broker responded, "You can be sure that we want this house sold for as much as we can. What we don't want is to have people just "walking through." They agreed and the broker assured them, "Believe me, we *will sell* your home.

"If it is that easy, why aren't all salespeople doing it?" is the question I hear from salespeople everywhere. I have found in my research that about 20% of the salespeople play the role of *doctor of sales,* and the other 80% are *clerks,* standing around waiting for something to happen, and earning enough commissions to make a small car payment. The desperation and pressure felt by them is passed on to their customers, which creates a closed mind, with all kinds of *fear* pushing away the salesperson. In this case, the broker took charge, told the customers at what price the home would sell, what he could and would do for them, and why he believed it was the best thing for them.

It is important to *sell the benefits* as opposed to being in a reactionary state like a clerk, where people tell you what they do not like and you tell them why they should. This is true of any product or service. The doctor of sales is always in control, makes the decision, sells it, and creates enthusiasm about the services they offer.

This is important, because when you think of yourself as the *doctor* you will start acting as if you are one. You increase the value of the services you offer, and the value of your presence. People will begin treating you as the *doctor of sales* because you project that image.

You have everything you need to be the doctor of sales; you need only to believe it. When you believe it, you will act like it, and when you act like it, your sales will increase.

I want you to think of yourself as Doctor...(your name)..., and your prospects also will think of you as the *doctor of sales*.

CHAPTER 10

SELLING VALUES

☞ *Value of Time*
☞ *Negating Objections*
☞ *Building Value*
☞ *Establishing Sales Authority*

In Chapter four, I talked about *values* being the *basis* of our *principles*, which, in turn, becomes the basis of our behavior. Here I want to pull that into focus by *selling* values. It is very important that we create a *high* value in our product or service as well as in the company we represent. If we are able to create a high value in these areas, then we will be able to create a sales relationship. If, in the prospect's mind the value is low, we will actually create objections.

Over the years, sales trainers have taught *answers to objections*. In fact, for many years this has been one of the favorite subjects of sales trainers and motivational speakers. There have been books written, tapes recorded, and lectures given on the subject. I believe it is far better to create such high value in your product or service that there are *no objections*. By doing this, you do not have to work from the bottom up, but rather you will stay at the top from the beginning of the presentation to the close of the sale. And you have created a relationship in which the prospect's mind is open to your entire presentation. As you create value, you add dimension upon dimension of high-level beliefs or positive decisions so that ultimately you have the sale.

The "Clerk" Sells Cost

The clerk has a problem with this concept. A clerk will create, in the prospect's mind, a product or service that is worth its selling price, or use the formula, *"cost = value."* If cost equals value, you are in a clerking situation at best. In a grocery store, you do not find people in every aisle selling products, because that would be a clerking situation. As you go down the aisles, what are you searching? Most of us look for something that is worth its price. You might even look for something that is a little cheaper than it is worth, if you are a frugal shopper. I have often heard people in a clerking situation say, "It is really *worth* the price." In fact, when they find a good sale, they might even call someone and say, "I just had to let you know about this sale!" In a sales situation, your product must be more than "worth it," for me to invest. Your product or service must be of a *higher value than the cost* in order for us to be in a sales relationship. I do not need a salesperson to tell me something is selling at a price equal to its value. However, if the product or service is worth more than the asking price, I need a salesperson to explain its value.

Cost = 1/10 of value

In a sales situation we want cost to be about 1/10 of the value, so that the value is *far greater* than the cost. This is not only the cost of the product or service you offer, but also, how much time or inconvenience the customer will have to endure to obtain that product or service, or opportunity. If you are the best doctor in town, I do not mind sitting in your waiting room for a half hour or more. If I can purchase a high quality product for a great price, I will wait for it to be shipped to me, or even drive across town to buy it. But, in all cases, someone, and more specifically, a *doctor of sales,* must tell me why it is of that value.

Milk is priced identically at Roosevelt's Country Store near my home as it is in town at the big Super Market. So, why should I drive to town for milk? If I am looking for variety, fresh produce, or fruit, then I will drive the five miles to town, because the *value* is there.

My life is measured in time. How I invest or spend my *time* is of great importance to me. It carries a *high value* in my life. If you are offering me a business opportunity, the only real cost is time, *my* time. Is the time I put into a business going to be worth it? Unless you create enough value in this business opportunity I will say, "I just don't have time." For some time I have been associated with a product brokering company that offers fine jewelry through network marketing. The product offered by this company is well known, and it is the same jewelry that is offered in fine stores throughout the world. So where is the value of buying jewelry from a distributor, rather than a local store? The future success of each distributor will be dependent on how they answer that question.

What *value* does your product, service, or business opportunity offer me that will make me want to buy or use your service on a repeated basis?

Value of Time

Have you ever contacted someone by telephone, attempting to make an appointment and his or her response was, "I just don't have time right now." What he was *really* saying was that you did not create high enough value, and, therefore, he would not make time to hear the presentation of your product, service, or opportunity.

Personal Values

Values are based upon a person's *frame of reference.* If we believe something is valuable, we will spend the necessary time and money to obtain it. We need to know our customer's values and sell those values, as it relates to our product, service or opportunity.

A few years ago, while living in the Washington, DC area, I noticed three unusual toadstools growing in our backyard. These particular toadstools grew very fast. We would mow the lawn on Saturday morning, and by Monday afternoon, the three toadstools would be above the grass. When it was time to mow the lawn again, the toadstools would be ten inches high and the grass two inches! I was in the yard one day when a neighbor walked by and said, "Is that what I think it is?" I said, "Well, if you think it's a toadstool, you're right." He said it looked like a particularly rare and valuable variety of toadstools and that he had a friend at the Smithsonian Institution who was looking for my particular toadstool. I told him to bring his friend by to take a look.

What is the Value of a Toadstool?

His friend did come, and agreed that it was a very valuable type of toadstool. He said, "Do you realize that each of your toadstools are worth about $3,000?" I replied, "SOLD!" He indicated that this variety of toadstools had a very fast growth pattern. I replied that I already knew that because I mowed them every week. He advised that if I would let them grow, they would multiply. These three toadstools could populate a two-acre plot in one growing season. I thought to myself, $3,000 per toadstool -- two acres of toadstools -- the wheels began to turn! I asked if he knew where I could find a good plot of ground. He said it took a particular type of soil for the toadstools to grow, and that he would research it for me. He later told me, "As you know in the Washington, DC area, property is very valuable. The two acres I have found will cost about $100,000 each. However, within six months, you will be harvesting millions of dollars a week." My problem was that I did not have the $200,000. So, I offered him a proposition: "You put up the $200,000 and I'll put up the toadstools!

If this story was believable, is there anyone reading this book who could not raise $200,000 to participate in this business venture? You would get that $200,000 some way, because the value was so great. If you could earn $1 million a week, you would sell, beg, and borrow to get the money, because you know the cash flow will buy back whatever you lost or sold. The value is so great, that the cost is almost nothing. If you sold 99% of your share of the venture, you could still make $100,000 per week. That is pretty good money!

When value is high enough, cost is *never* a factor. When people say they do not have time or they are not interested, in most cases, the salesperson has failed to create high value, and did not relate their product or service to the prospect's values, so that they could see why they should make the purchase.

Keep Value High "After" the Sale

After you have made the sale, if you continue maintaining a high value in your product, service or opportunity, guess what happens? You have the advantage of *repeat* and *referral* business. Think about this for a moment. From whom would you buy a home today? The person who jumped into your mind would be the person who offered you the greatest service, with the highest value attached thereto. I have "my" doctor. I also should have my "*doctor of real estate,*" and my "*doctor of insurance*." You need to be that doctor. If you have created a high value in the services you offer, you have a legalized monopoly, and I can think of no one other than you when it comes time to buy that particular product or service. If you have been in sales more than five years, and you are not living on repeat and referral business, then you are not creating a high value in your product or service.

High Value Negates Objections

I want you to understand the importance of values because *objections* arise from values being too low. If cost *equals* value, then the prospect will object. If value is *greater* than cost, the prospect can hardly wait to buy. You have closed the sale by creating high value.

Let me illustrate this for you. Don, an insurance agent, has a customer in his office, and they have just completed the first five minutes, or as you learned earlier, the *first close*. Mrs. Robinson has told Don all he needs to know about herself *and* her financial situation. Don will use this information to create value in his services, his company, and in him as a doctor of sales. She told Don they had lived in their home for six years prior to her husband's death, and that the insurance policy he had with Don's company had paid off the mortgage. She said, "It is too much house for me now. I plan to sell it and find something a little smaller, perhaps a home with a small garden and a backyard. I don't know much about finances, and especially insurance, so I thought I would talk to you before I make a big mistake." Don told her that he appreciated the trust she had put in him and his company. Then he told her, "I have been your insurance agent for many years, and now you are in a position where I can be of service to you. I will help you find a good broker, to list and sell your home, who will make sure you get a fair price for it. We then can take the profit over what a new home will cost you, and place it in an

annuity that will build good interest for you. Then when you are ready for retirement you will have a lifetime income. Since you will be paying cash for your new home, you will not need a mortgage insurance policy. And, you have a life insurance policy now that will take care of all costs to your children at your death. It will all be very simple. So, I want you to *trust* me and I will continue to work on your behalf. Remember, I am here for you." Mrs. Robinson now feels she is in good hands because Don has proven the value of his service over the years, and now when she needs him, he is there for her. When Mrs. Robinson has a friend who needs insurance in the future, who do you think she will refer as an agent? Don created such high value in himself and his company, that he will enjoy repeat and referral business for years to come.

Building Value in Things

Real estate salespeople have an advantage over most salespeople in that they spend a lot of quality time with their customer, especially in automobiles. When you put your prospects into your automobile, they are *locked* in. You take them to see a house, or other property, and they cannot return to their car until you are ready to take them. You have a captured audience and it is a tremendous time to create value. The problem is, most salespeople talk about politics, the weather and all the problems of the world, while driving to their appointments. When you speak of negative things, it creates a negative *presence* which destroys the positive relationship you are trying to create. This causes the prospects to question whether they want to do business with you.

Most people have enough problems of their own. They certainly do not need a salesperson to create more problems in their mind, or to discuss circumstances over which they have no control. I have seen many salespeople take *good* prospects to look at property and when they return to the office, the prospects look as though they have been run over *by* the car, rather than riding *in* the car.

I want to show you how Carol, a doctor of sales, used her new Cadillac as a tool to create high value in her services, her company, *and* in the home she was selling.

As Carol and her prospects drove away from her office, she kept the conversation light, commented on, and moved through subjects *they* mentioned, and used the casual conversation to *build value.* She used the *first close* to get to know her prospects and then she selected the house that she believed best fit their wants, needs and desires. She did not show this couple a number of homes, hoping they would pick the one they liked most.

Their conversation generally followed this pattern. Carol said, "*Isn't it a lovely day?"* This *question* will be covered in a later lesson because it is one that can give you tremendous feedback on the *inner motivations* of your prospects. Carol asks this question *everyday,* even on rainy days. The wife replied, "It's very nice," and her husband said, "I understand it will be 82 degrees this afternoon." He continued, "This sure is a nice car. Business must be good!" Some salespeople might worry that a luxury car would *turn off* a prospect who could not afford one. The opposite is true. I don't want my physician, attorney, or dentist driving an old car that looks like it is on its last leg. That would tell me business is bad, or they must not be doing a good job. I want everyone who offers me services or products to be the most successful in their field. Then I know I am dealing with the best!

Your automobile, if it is used in your business, is a statement of how successful you are, *in the mind of the prospect.* Carol answered, "You know, I spend a lot of time in my car, and I think it's very important that my customers are comfortable. When you're getting in and out of a car most of your day, you could wear yourself out. This is my office on wheels."The wife replied, "It really is nice, but I'll bet it costs quite a bit to keep it on the road, doesn't it?" This concern for finances is excellent feedback. It told Carol that this couple watch closely howthey spend their money. Carol continued, "Well, I suppose it costs a little more to run than a small Honda "Civic" but I think *business* is always a good investment. And I certainly feel that being concerned about you, my customers, is a great investment." This statement built value in the relationship because she was showing concern for her customer's comfort. "The home we will be seeing today has been rated very highly by our company. We have a rating system that takes into consideration the pluses and minuses of a home. This particular house will sell very quickly because of the eye appeal and its excellent construction. And, it's in a very good neighborhood." The husband asked, "Does that mean this house is going to be on

the 'high end?'" There is the concern of cost again. Carol *must hear* these warnings and be prepared to *build value* so great that cost would not be a problem. "No, the actual price is one of the variables that is computed into the rating. If the price is too high, the rating of the house is lower, because it is priced where the market survey determines it will sell. The rating indicates that this home is listed *below* the market value. This could be because the owner needs a quick sale, or perhaps his move is being subsidized, but for whatever reason, you will find that this house is a great buy." Now she has handled one of their fears. "That's excellent," he replied. Carol continued, "I sold this house to this family two years ago, and they have really enjoyed living there. But he's being transferred to another city. And the great thing is, when it came time to sell, he could think of no other company to list his home."

The customer responded, "That really says a lot about your company." Carol said, "Yes, it really does. We've been in business in this area for over 23 years. Eighty percent of our business is repeat and referral. It's like this car. I really like this Cadillac. It's nice to drive, it's comfortable, and I enjoy driving a heavy car. However, I don't drive it for myself alone -- I drive it for my customers as well. I feel you're worth the investment. And, I *am* in the "people business." I live on repeat and referral business. I have to do it right."

Building Value in a Possibly Negative Situation

"Now I want you to put yourself into this picture." Carol told her customer. "You've just had a busy day at the office, with all the hustle and bustle of business, and you're on your way home, driving beside this river. As you cruise along, you feel yourself beginning to unwind, getting yourself in a frame of mind to enjoy your family when you arrive at home. And, it will help your family enjoy *you* a little bit!" The customer *then said,* "How far out of town *is* this house?" This question *could* be a problem, because the house is a bit of a drive from his office in the city. Carol has already built *value in the drive* as a time to unwind.

You must anticipate and build value higher than *price* of the negative, and in this case, it was the drive. Carol replied, "Well, this home is 15 miles from downtown. It's about a 30-minute drive. You can see today, that the traffic moves right along using this four-lane highway." He said, "That's not *too* bad, we definitely want to be *away* from the city." Carol already knew this because they had both mentioned the fact in their earlier interview, back at the office.

Every word and thought expressed by your prospect is important in building value. Do not allow yourself to get so caught up in making a sales presentation that you miss what your prospects are telling you about their values.

Carol continued, "I would imagine you have people in your office who might drive an *hour* to work." He agreed, "Yes, Harvey drives at least an hour every day, each way. He feels it's worth it because he lives out in the country." The customer's wife followed, "Yes, it is a long distance, but Harvey's wife, Sylvia, really loves the house. So, I guess that's the main thing." She was saying the value of living where they want to live, and in the home they like, has great value and is worth the inconvenience.

Building Value Based Upon Needs

As they drove into the neighborhood, Carol began building value based upon the *needs* of this family. She said, "This house on the right is owned by the Brenners. He's principal of the local high school. Right next door to the Brenners is Dr. Smalley, who is a professor at the local "med" school. There are really nice families in this community, which has a very active civic association that keeps things looking good in the neighborhood." The wife said, "You sure can tell. It's beautiful!"

In a later chapter covering *"The Motivations of Life,"* I will refer back to this story to help you understand the extent of the information Carol was getting from this couple, which was assisting her in making the sale. Let us continue as Carol presents the house. "Now, this is your drive. As we turn here, you will be able to see *your* home." The wife is sitting forward in her seat and says: "Wow, it's beautiful!" and he added, "I like it!" Carol said, "Your friends are going to be just as impressed as you are." How does she know that their friends will be impressed, and why would she make such a comment? Because the customer told Carol several times how important her friends are to her. And since Carol was not only *listening* to her customer, but *hearing* why she said it, she knew! And finally, the wife said, "I want to see inside. Could we?" Carol said, "Of course. I have the key and the owners were notified that we were coming today."

All Conversation Should Build Value

During this entire drive, Carol was selling *value* upon *value*. She used each subject that arose, including her car, because it was of interest to the customers. The husband spoke about what a terrific car it was, and Carol turned that statement around to say, "I bought it for you. You are such a valued customer that I want to carry you around in a valuable chariot."

Then, driving alongside the river, Connie showed how it would relax them, and make them feel more comfortable, so that when they arrived home they would enjoy their family more, and in turn, their family would enjoy *them* more. She sold the value of the drive. Rather than it being a negative 30-minute drive, Carol turned it into a beautiful time in preparation for a relaxing evening. She turned something that could have been *negative* into something of *high value*. And, finally, Carol *sold* the neighborhood. She talked about the people and activities of the community.

Product Knowledge Builds Value

Did Carol have to do a little research? Yes. You do not just pull something out of a book and ask what someone thinks. As a doctor of sales, you are *always* prepared. If you do not prepare yourself to be in a sales situation, you will never be in a position to create value. You must know your customer and your product equally well to create high value. For some reason, high school principals and doctors are the two most impressive neighbors, especially to *relaters*. (This will be covered later.) Relaters are impressed with certain *types* of people. In this case, Carol was selling to relaters. So, for some people, the neighbors are important, but for others, it might be *privacy*. You must know your customer in order to create value in your product or service, and turn the customer into a client.

Building Value in Ownership

Carol drove into the driveway and said, "Here is your home." So, the couple visualized it as being their home. They looked at *their* landscaping, *their* front yard, and *their* interior, because Carol had built such high value based upon their wants, needs and desires. Can you see why Carol sells over $6 million in real estate each year? She is a "doctor of sales."

Building Value at the Receptionist's Desk

One way your company can build value with a customer from the beginning of a relationship is by giving your receptionist the proper training. One of our three-hour seminars teaches receptionists how to build value in their company and its employees. The receptionist's voice is the first heard by your prospects, and is usually the first person they meet when they come to your office. We have covered extensively how *first* impressions are *lasting* impressions. Some receptionists are so poor at creating good first impressions that prospects and clients hang up, or walk away before the salesperson has an opportunity to meet them. I am sure you have experienced a time when you felt the receptionist was inconvenienced by your call.

I had the opportunity to observe a receptionist at a large real estate firm build value in the mind of every caller. She paved the way for a good sales relationship before the salespeople spoke to the customer. As she answered the telephone she built value in the company as well as the agent before she passed the call to the agent.

Establish a Position of Authority

There were two things she did to build value. She answered the phone by saying, "Good morning, this is Beth Brown with Reliance Realty."

Beth answered the telephone using her name. She is the voice of Reliance Realty. Here, Beth created a high value by giving her name, which established her position with the company. The customer said, "Hello, I need some information regarding one of your ads." Beth replied, "We would be happy to help you. To which ad are you referring?" The customer replied, "The one in today's paper. It read: 'Four bedrooms, two-and-a-half baths, fenced backyard, near a school.'" Beth said, "Are you referring to ad #209 in today's Post?" "Yes," he answered, "That's the one. Can you give me some information on that house, please?" Beth then said, "Let me connect you with Tom Betser. He is one of our *executive* sales associates. Your name is...?" She didn't ask, "Can I have your name?" because that *could* have been a "NO" question. The customer answered, "Marshall, Jim Marshall." "Fine, Mr. Marshall,"she replied, "I'll put Tom on the line."Beth had the ad immediately ready on her desk, so she *could have* answered his question. However, she is not the salesperson. She is the receptionist and knows her position. By filling that position well, she was able to create a higher value in the executive salesperson. Beth dialed Tom's office and said,"Mr. Jim Marshall is calling about ad #209 in today's Post." Tom thanked her and immediately responded to the caller: "Good morning, Mr. Marshall. If you will tell me what you're looking for in a home, I can tell you whether looking at this particular home is worth your time."

Establishing Sales Authority

The second thing Beth did was she put Tom in a position of authority. Since Beth took the call and was able to tell him what he needed to know, he was able to be prepared with product knowledge *before* he began his conversation. He also knew the prospect's name and interest, which placed him in control of the sales relationship, and built value in his professionalism. A receptionist can do a great job for you if well trained. A well trained receptionist can build *deference* which establishes your position and creates a higher value in the product, and in your sales presentation from the outset. That first five minutes is vitally important. When you build high value, you have created a sales relationship which ensures an open mind. You have the control, the ability, and the opportunity. You need only to *do it*. You must understand how to *sell value rather than cost*.

Creating Value Step-by-Step

Remember, value should be greater than cost by at least a multiple of ten. To create that level of value, you must understand the values you are building, or selling, within each area of sales. In an *approach* to a prospect on the telephone, you create a different value than in the actual sales presentation. You begin by creating value in the program, project, or product, so that the prospect wants to take a look at your offering.

Until I am at least interested in what you have to say, my mind will be closed, and I cannot hear a word you are saying. If you create value in your product or service, that will create *curiosity* so that my mind will be open, and I will want to hear or see more. With this concept in place, you are able to create value in your company, in you as the salesperson, and in the services and follow-up you provide. And, when my mind is open and I buy you, or believe in you and your company, I will then believe what you are saying. When I believe what you say as truth, then I will buy what you sell. It is a sequence of events in creating value. The mistake most salespeople make is that they focus on creating value in the product or service rather than curiosity in what the product will do for the prospect, which is where value must be created. You might be selling automobiles, and I might need one, but you have to create value in how your automobile will fill my needs in order for me to have an open mind. You do not want to tell me about trunk space, or how many horses are under the hood until you have first discovered where my values lie, and create *curiosity* in your product based upon *my wants and needs*.

Creating Value in the Appointment

If your business requires you to *set appointments* by telephone, it is important for you to know that you *do not sell* your product or service on the telephone. You *sell an appointment* to show what the product or service can do for the prospect. It is most difficult to learn the values of a prospect by telephone, so what you must do is sell the appointment, so that you can get to know the prospect's values, and *then* sell your product or service. Since you do not know the prospect's values, you must create curiosity with good questions. This will cause the prospects to place such a high value on the appointment that they will give you the time you need. Remember, you are selling time, not a product or service. You need to create value in the presentation so that they will be willing to give you some time.

What will your product or service do for this prospect? Will it help pay for a college education, retirement income, a new home, or car? That, then, is what the prospects will learn if they give you some time. Will it introduce to them a better product, a healthier lifestyle, or perhaps a business of their own? Then sell the *value of a few minutes* of time so they may learn about this.

I have observed numerous salespeople trying to sell their product or service over the telephone, without knowing the prospect's values and without establishing a sales relationship, and they lost a good prospect. "I am really not interested." How *can* they be interested when the salesperson was not relating to their wants, needs and desires. Create *curiosity* and *sell value of the appointment,* not the product or service.

I will show you through illustrations some ways that you can create value in each of these areas. In each illustration, I want you to think about the area of your presentation in which you need to build value. To help you more fully understand, I will use a wide variety of illustrations showing how to successfully build value. In each case, the salesperson is either *creating value* or playing the role of the *clerk* and not selling values. If you can plug what you are reading into your own situation, then this chapter will help you in one of the most important areas of *relationship selling -- creating value.* It will help you avoid objections, and create repeat and referral business.

High Value Creates Referrals

I mentioned earlier a young man in Southern California who walked into a real estate agency and said, "I'm here to see Mike Griffith." Mike was called to the front and met this young man, who said, "I was told I should buy a house from you!" He said he was moving into the area and was told that Mike was the best agent to help him buy a home. This was a referral from a client with whom Mike had established a great relationship. He had created such a high value in his services, that he was able to transfer that value into referral business. Remember the opening sentence we suggested, "Did you see one of our ads, or did one of our friends send you?" This question creates the value or goodwill of a referral and may be used when answering the telephone or when a prospect walks into your office. People only refer their friends to someone who can be trusted to do a good job. His friend had said, "Mike took good care of me and you can count on him to treat you right." Since his friend sent him, he would assume most of your business must come from referrals, which assures him you *must* do a good job. Also, it creates future referral business. When they walk out the door after buying from you, they will send their friends. You automatically set yourself up for referral business when you create value in relationships.

Value in the Relationship

Another statement that creates a high value at the beginning of a sales relationship is, "I would like to get to know you a little bit." One of the nicer things in life is when someone wants to get to know you. It is called *acceptance*. With that statement you indicate you have accepted that person as your customer. You are saying that you will be the *doctor of sales,* and that all the services you offer and the value you have created will be geared toward the customer's needs. This is establishing a relationship in a sales situation.

Value in Your Product or Service

An insurance agent had an appointment with a young couple on a Saturday afternoon. As he approached the house, a football came rolling up to him. A "pee wee" football player, all decked out in pads and helmet, came running after the ball. The agent picked up the ball, threw it to the boy, and he caught it. It was obvious that his dad had been working with him to encourage him in the sport of football.

After making his presentation to the parents, the agent said, "I'd like to tell you a story, if I may. I would like for you to visualize a typical fall day about twelve years from now. There's a chill in the air, the leaves are in their fall colors, and you're getting ready to watch the football game of the season on television. Richie is getting ready to go to the local supermarket where he boxes groceries to help pay for his college education."

Building Value Through Story-Telling

At this point the prospect said, "Wait a minute, I don't like your story." The agent responded "I didn't think you would. Now let me tell you the *real* story. It's a fall Saturday afternoon, about twelve years from now. You both have tickets on the fifty-yard line at your son's college football stadium. The news media tells us that Richie will make All-American today, no matter what he does. Just as you are leaving for the game, you reach into the mailbox and an envelope like this is waiting to be opened." At this point, he handed the prospect an envelope and said, "Go ahead and open it." Inside the envelope was a check made payable to Richie. The agent continued, "This is just a sample check, but a check like that is in the mailbox each month to guarantee Richie a college education, no matter what. Why? Because twelve years ago you decided to save money in Richie's name by investing in an insured savings program. That's the reason Richie doesn't have to work his way through college."

The value was not the insurance policy, so he did not try to sell one. The value in this case was a *college education, no matter what!* This particular agent always carries sample checks, regardless of the type of policy he is selling and it has worked for many years.

When you create enough value, cost is never a factor. When you can understand needs, you are understanding the highest levels of motivation in a person's life, thus you create value based upon the prospect's needs. Then you are in a position where you can sell value so great that cost is never a factor.

Value in a Business Opportunity

Earlier, we looked at a real estate agent using her automobile to build value with her customers. Let us go back to the car again, but use it this time to create value in a business opportunity or financial investments.

Jack has an appointment with the Andersons to show them a business opportunity. He picked them up in his car and drove them to the presentation. If he had set an appointment and asked them to meet him at a designated address, there could have been too many possibly negative variables. They could lose your directions and get lost, they could forget the time of the meeting, or they could just stay home! Jack picked them up so that he was in full control. Riding in the car to the meeting, he was able to create just enough curiosity that by the time the Andersons arrived they were ready to take a look at this business opportunity. They already were thinking about what they were going to do with their new earnings. They were *pre-sold*.

Now let us observe how Jack sells value as he is driving. He drives a luxury car for several reasons. He likes it, he can afford it, and he uses it in his business. His prospects said, "It's a pleasure to get into this car. You drive in style." Jack thanked him and continued, "You know, Jerry, we had a small car, and it felt very crowded.

So awhile back I realized my *family* was worth the investment." Mrs. Matthews said, "Yes, but don't you have to scrape to put gas in this car, and how about the insurance?" Jack answered, "Well, it does burn more gas, but the ride and safety of a big car make it worth the expense. I guess if money was a problem we would worry about gas consumption, but it is not, so we just enjoy the comfort and luxury."

Value of Financial Independence

Jerry added, "Business must be good." "It is," Jack replied, "and you are going to hear a story today that not only will expand your thinking, but could possibly put you behind the wheel of a car like this." Bev Matthews, having a little more fear than Jerry, said, "What is this program all about, anyway? It sounds like a 'get-rich-quick-scheme' to me." Jack immediately followed, "I can tell you this, I didn't get rich quick, but I did learn how to make wise use of my time and energy. The exciting thing is, it's just now beginning to pay big dividends. All of my tomorrows are more exciting than *each* today, and today is so much fun, I can hardly stand it!"

Value of Investing Time

Jerry said, "But, Jack, I don't have a lot of money to invest in a business. This might be too big for us." Jack assured him, "I wouldn't have invited you and Bev to be my guests if I didn't believe it was an opportunity that you could handle. Remember, I was in *your* shoes only a few months ago. I know where you're coming from." He was saying, "Don't worry, folks, you're in good hands. I'm not going to embarrass you by putting you in an uncomfortable position." Bev said, "I don't have very much business experience. I don't know if I would be much help." Jack asked, "Would you like to learn and earn at the same time? You can!" Jerry replied, "What can I expect to make in this venture, if I do get involved?" "Jerry," Jack replied, "that is something only you can determine. This opportunity is determined entirely by your initiative and ambition." Bev said, "Well, I'm sure curious," and Jerry added, "Yeah, you have sure whet our appetites. I hope we are not disappointed." This was when Jack knew his prospects had an open mind. Jack ended by saying, "Believe me, Jerry, this will be a day you will *always* remember."

High Value Creates an Open Mind

Jack actually handled every objection the Matthews might possibly have before they got to the presentation. Not only did he handle it, but he created such high value that they would not even think of objecting. The money angle, the uncertainty of succeeding, and everything else that might possibly be an objection was taken care of by *selling value*. It made the presentation much more fun, because the Matthews were listening with an *open mind*, accepting the role they were playing as customer, and accepting Jack as their doctor of sales. They chose to be a part of what he was doing because he was so confident and knew his subject well. All of a sudden it is a situation that looks very comfortable.

In sales, the customers should always feel comfortable. If they are not it will set up a chain reaction. Their fear motivations will cause resistance, which will set up psychological blocks, and ultimately, will destroy the sales situation. If, as a salesperson you are properly doing your job and are *selling value*, then the prospects are very comfortable. In fact, after they sign the contract and write you a check, they will *thank you*. That is quite different than being talked into something, or having buyer's remorse, which has caused our government to set up laws to give us three days to "cool off" and say "no."

Creating Value in a Product

For years, salesmanship was based upon developing good sales techniques. It was like a chess game where you put people in a position where they could no longer say "no." Salespeople were trained to use *pressure selling* as a way to close sales. In today's marketplace, however, you must know relationship techniques in order to close and hold on to a sale. If you create enough value, you not only will make the sale, but you will live off of repeat and referral business. Once the relationship is established, you can build value in your product or service because your prospects are now your clients. Their belief value is high, and you are in a position to lead them into a wise buying decision. A real estate agent was telling me how she builds value in the homes she shows. She makes sure there is a name on each bedroom door. This is only in the mind of the customer, you understand, but she has them place their furniture in each room and hang their clothes in the closets. You have to buy a house when all of your furniture, and *your children* are already living there! This is one of her stories.

Moving the Family into the Home

She was showing her customers their future home and she said, "Now, this is a large bedroom. Who's room would it be?" The wife said, "This is the perfect room for our Marty. I can see his bed right over there. I can put his dresser here and his desk next to the closet." The husband added, "Or, we could put his desk under the window so he would have more light." The agent said, "Oh, I can really see Marty will fit in here perfectly. He'll love it." How can she know that, she doesn't even know the boy? What she does know, however, is that the parents know the boy and she is echoing their excitement. "Let's go to the master bedroom," the agent said. "As you can see, this room is really spacious. I'll bet your bedroom furniture would look great in here." The lady said, "Yes, we have a king-size bed, and we could put our two dressers right along that wall." The agent added, "Did you notice the walk-in closet? And, of course, there are "his and hers" bathrooms with a shower big enough for *you,* Al!" He responded, "It *is* nice, and this carpet looks good. I bet it would feel good under my bare feet." Now, while she has this couple in the master bedroom, walking in their bare feet, subconsciously, of course, the agent says, "Let's put together an offer on *your* house and get you moved in. Come downstairs and we will talk through the possibilities." That was her *close.* It is not too difficult if you have built enough value.

Personalize the Presentation

Notice that the agent did not talk about "this house," or "the owner built this," but rather she talked about *your house.* As soon as the clients have put their son's name on the door of that room, and moved in his furniture, they will not let anyone else buy the house; especially with their son, Marty, sleeping in the bed. They had even moved their king-size bed into the master bedroom and placed her shoes in the closet. You *must* pay for that which you are enjoying.

So many of our decisions are controlled subconsciously, and in these customer's minds, they were *living* in the house. Closing the sale was no problem because the value of the house was so high. It became their dream home because a doctor of real estate created so much value in the product (the home in this case) that they could relate to it based upon their needs. You have to be able to relate your presentation to your prospect and to their wants and needs. Your ability to do this is your ability to create value which will *close the sale.*

Recognize the Prospect's Frame of Reference

Most salespeople sell from their own point of view or *frame of reference.* A salesperson might say, "This is the model I like best because it can do so much," and will try to sell that model, even when it is not what the prospect really wants. Or, they might try to sell a fund or stock investment, when the prospect or client had something totally different in mind as an investment. If you can get your prospects to talk and you *learn to listen,* they will tell you where their values lie. Once they tell you, then you can say, "Well, here is what we are offering," and surprisingly enough, everything they said interested them. It matched exactly what you were offering. How are you going to offer it, if you do not know the prospect's values?

In a later chapter, we are going to look at *inner motivations;* what causes people to do what they do and say what they say. The reason we want to understand inner motivations is because in understanding these motivations, we also understand needs, and when we understand needs, we understand values. I will refer back to this study when we get to that chapter.

Values Create Wants, Needs and Desires

The values of the prospect create their wants, needs and desires. Wants are normally very easy to understand, but needs and desires are more complex. As you understand your prospect's values and relate their values to your product or service, you will be able to satisfy their wants, needs, *and* desires. People will buy when the value is high, or if the value is based upon *their* value system. And, as the doctor of sales, it is your responsibility to *know their values.*

CHAPTER 11

ETABLISHING AUTHORITY

☞ *Telephone Authority*
☞ *Referral Authority*
☞ *Authority With Friends*
☞ *Setting Appointments*

We have talked about the "doctor of sales" in previous chapters, and how the medical doctor uses authority. Here we want to talk about *sales authority.* We will zero in on how to *establish your authority* as a salesperson. Without establishing your authority you cannot create a sales relationship, and you are really in a prospecting position.

I believe as you read this chapter you will discover that most salespeople whom you know, sell from a *prospecting position,* rather than a *sales position.* When I meet you at a social function or church gathering, we are merely two people meeting, and neither of us has sales authority. However, if you come to my home for dinner, I am the host and have authority. You are *my* guest. And, if you are a guest in *my* home, you do not have authority to sell. If you try selling in that situation, you will strike out. In my home I can tell you where to sit, and to clean up your peas or you will not get dessert! In all of the above cases I am, at best, in a prospecting position.

You must recognize when you *are* in a prospecting position and what you can do to create sales authority. If you want to talk about the product or service you offer, you *must* wait until you can revisit at a later date, with your authority already established as a salesperson. You can create some degree of curiosity about your offering, and tell me you will get back to me when we both have more time, but you cannot sell!

Telephone Authority

When I call you I have authority because I initiated the action and you are the recipient of my action. If you try selling something to me *on my dime*, I might say to you, "I didn't call you so you could sell me something!" Now you have not only lost the sale, but you have also created bad will, which you must overcome, if you will ever be able to sell me your product or service.

This becomes a challenge when placing ads in the newspaper. Customers call about the ad, and because *they dial* the number, they have the authority. Have you ever noticed how difficult it is to get someone's name when they telephone *you?* It is even more difficult to get their phone number, and it is nearly impossible to get their address. The reason is, you do not have authority. The caller is in control and they can hang up on you if they decide they do not like what you are saying. For years, salespeople have given away business cards, and said, "If you are interested, give me a call." The problem with this is that unless you know how to handle an incoming call, you are setting yourself up to lose the sale. When I call you, I have the authority and you do not, and you *cannot sell* without sales authority. In a sales situation, you must be in the position of dialing the phone, and not the recipient of the call. When *your customer* says "hello" you have the authority, but when *you* say "hello," the customer is in control of the conversation.

Authority in Referral Business

Later in the chapter we will cover *appointment setting*, and how to be effective in establishing your authority. Referrals give you great authority from the beginning. You are calling the prospect because a friend thought this person might be interested in your product, service or business opportunity. Bennie Harris, my life insurance agent, works primarily from referrals. He has built a large client base, who supply him with prospects who need tax sheltered retirement programs. I have observed him on a Saturday morning as he took a stack of preprinted referral cards and set up his appointments for the following week.

Saturday mornings are the most effective for appointment setting because people are relaxed. Next week seems far away, and most people are not under a time pressure. Bennie holds the referral card in his hand as he makes the call. The person who gave the referral signed the card so that the prospect would know they *were* a referral. Most often, the prospect will not see the card, but that signature is a commitment on the referral's part that if the prospect were to call the person who referred them, that person would be able to verify the referral. We need that *commitment,* because we do not want the person who referred us to say, "Well, I just did it to get rid of him." That would be a *weak* referral, and most likely your prospect would not keep the appointment.

When Bennie dials the phone, he says, "I'm holding in my hand a card with your name written on it, signed by your friend Dave Goodman." The fact is, when he is holding your name in his hand, he is *really* holding *you.* That puts him in a position of *authority* as a doctor of sales.

Establishing Authority on the Telephone

Let me illustrate this with a telephone conversation between myself and a referral, Bill Thomas:

Bill: *Hello.*
Orv: *Hello, is this Bill Thomas?*
Bill: *Yes it is.*
Orv: *Bill, this is Orv Owens calling. You don't know me, but I am holding in my hand a card with your name on it, signed by your friend, Dave Goodman. Dave suggested that I give you a call. You know Dave, don't you?*

This question will give some feedback on how strong the relationship is with Bill. I will have difficulty building a sales relationship any stronger than their personal relationship.

| Bill: | Yes, he's a good friend of mine. |
| Orv: | *A few days ago, I had a meeting with Dave, and shared with him a program that he found quite interesting. In fact, he was so impressed by the merits of the program that he decided to become involved. He mentioned your name to me and said that this program is something he felt would interest you as well. What I would like to do, Bill, is set a time when I can get together with you and your wife, Betty, and show you this exciting program. You may or may not be interested, but if you will allow me forty-two minutes of your time, I can give you enough information to determine your interest. When is the best time to catch both you and Betty at home?* |

All of the above must be said without a break. It establishes authority based upon the referral, it gives an escape clause to take pressure from the appointment, it sells only the appointment, and it asks for a convenient time.

| Bill: | *What kind of program is this?* |
| Orv: | *Basically, this is a business opportunity, and with forty-two minutes I can give you the entire story. I have some literature I can leave with you, which will explain this business in full detail. It would be impossible for me to make you understand fully on the telephone. Dave believed you were a person who would want to take a look at this program. And, as I said before, he didn't know if you would be interested, but he did think you would take a look. When is the best time to catch you both at home?* |

Ask for the appointment at the end of every question or statement.

| Bill: | *I guess Thursday night is the best time for us.* |
| Orv: | *Thursday night...Let me look at my calendar here. Hmm, Thursday...I do have a slot from 8:00 to 8:42. How does that sound to you?* |

At this point I have a commitment on the date, so all I need is the time.

> **Bill:** *That sounds pretty good.*
> **Orv:** *Great. I'm writing it in my calendar now, and I have your address as being 1422 S. 6th Street. Is that correct?*
> **Bill:** *That's right.*
> **Orv:** *Are there any special instructions on finding your home?*
> **Bill:** *No, it's easy to find.*
> **Orv:** *Okay. I will look forward to seeing you and Betty at 8:00 on Thursday evening. I believe you will be excited about what I will share with you.*
> **Bill:** *Thanks for calling.*

This may appear too easy, but I have used this approach with referrals for many years, and there are salespeople across the country using it just as effectively. Now, because I dialed the phone, Bill was on the receiving end. I used the referral to create value in my service. When he asked what it was, I could say it was none of his business right now, because I was in a position of authority. If I were not in *authority,* Bill would have had a stronger position, psychologically. But, because he was the recipient of my call and there was value created by the referral, he was not opposed to listening to what I had to say. With authority, I was the doctor of sales. The *forty-two minutes* is also important because when I say "forty-two minutes" it does not sound like I am going to take an entire evening for the presentation. It appears as if I am taking only forty-two minutes! If I had said one or two hours, he would think differently. He might have a favorite television program at 9:00 PM and could say he was just too busy to see me on Thursday, or any other day.

There is less resistance to a specific time. We will give forty-two minutes to anybody. Therefore, by setting a specific time, I made it easy for Bill to set an appointment. I wanted to make sure I had created a solid footing for my appointment, so that when I arrived he would have an *open mind* and be curious to hear about my program. And, by the way, I told his friend, Dave, not to discuss anything about the program with him prior to our meeting. It is important that you coach the client on what to say to the referral.

Position of Authority Must Be Established to Sell

In selling, you must be able to establish that position of authority. Without authority, you cannot create value, or ask the questions you need answered in order to determine your customer's wants and needs. Therefore, it is impossible to sell *without establishing authority.*

Establishing Authority with Friends

Audrey Harris and her husband were at one of their friend's home for dinner. Sometime during the dinner, the conversation turned to business and the cost of living. The hosts, Bob and Virginia, said they were hardly making ends meet, and that they were thinking about getting involved in a part-time earning situation.

It just so happened that Audrey was newly involved in a direct sales business which offered a great opportunity for extra income. The tendency would have been to say, "Wow! Do I have an answer for you!" But she did not have a position of authority from which to work because she was a guest. When they arrived earlier, Virginia had taken their coats, offered them a seat on the sofa, and when dinner was ready, she told them where to sit. As hostess, she had the authority. And, as a guest, Audrey had none.

The next morning, back in her own home, however, Audrey could dial the telephone and with *authority* she could say to Virginia, "In our conversation last night, I mentioned we had recently joined a new business opportunity, and you and Paul expressed an interest in what we are doing. I would like to set a time when we can get together and tell you all about it. I need about forty-two minutes of your time. When is the best time to catch both you and Paul at home?"

With her authority established, she could turn a friend into a prospect. She set the appointment, and when she returned to their home to present her program *she* made the decisions. From the time she entered, she was the doctor of sales. She then could *sell* in her friend's home the same as she would at any other place, because she entered their house having *authority.*

Never try setting an appointment when you have not first established a position of authority. This *is* hard to do, and it takes a lot of self-discipline, but it will pay off with much greater success. The tendency is to jump right in and "spill all of your goodies" before you even know your prospect's level of interest.

Establishing Authority When Receiving Telephone Calls

In a sales office, answering the telephone can create a problem in establishing a position of authority. The best way is to have a receptionist who can establish authority *for* the salesperson.

The receptionist's job is to get the name and other pertinent information for the salesperson so that when they go on line, they are in control.

Let me illustrate this with Beth, the receptionist at Reliance Realty, taking an *ad* call-in.

"Good afternoon, this is Beth with Reliance Realty." The caller responded, "Good afternoon, I need some information on the house you listed in today's paper." "Sir, to which ad are you referring," asked Beth. He replied, "It's this three bedroom with two baths -- you know, the handy-man special. What's the address of that house? I just want to drive by and see it."

"Well sir, I don't have that information," Beth said, "but let me put Mary Jo on the line. She is one of our sales representatives, and I am sure she can help you. She is the associate who listed that particular house. Could I have your name, please." He adamantly responded, "I'm not interested in talking to anybody! I just want to drive by. You *must* have the address there." "Sir," she answered, "I am the receptionist. I am here to make sure you reach the salesperson who can do the best job for you. In this case, that would be Mary Jo. She *is* in the office this afternoon and I'm sure she can answer all of your questions. Can I have your name, please?" He reluctantly responded, "This is Pete...Pete McIntyre." She said, "Thank you, Pete. I will put Mary Jo on the line."

Name Responsibility

Beth refused to give information to the caller or to turn the call over to the salesperson until she had his name. Now, the salesperson comes on the line with all the information she needed to establish authority. It is better to let the prospects hang up and possibly lose them, than to lose them by giving them the address and risking Pete harassing the owners when he goes to see the house. When you know your prospect's name he or she will act and react differently, because they take on a sense of responsibility when the salespeople know their name. This is more difficult when you do not have a receptionist.

One option that has worked for many salespeople is to ask the prospects if you can call them back. Once you know the caller's interest you can say, "Let me get right back to you, if I may. I am busy at the moment, but as soon as I am free, I will be happy to give you all of the pertinent information on this particular house. May I have your number?" In less than fifteen minutes you need to call the person back, and your authority will be established. This technique keeps you in a control position, and allows you to prepare yourself with the necessary information to satisfy the caller.

Calling VIP's

An obstacle that is sometimes difficult to overcome in sales is getting directly to the decision-maker, because most VIP's have someone screening their calls. Try this. Give the receptionist your name before you are asked, and use the VIP's first name when asking to speak to him. This will give you a greater chance of getting through. When you give your name, the receptionist is now *responding* to you, which is somewhat of a *switch* in authority.

Calling for Sale by Owners

If you are in a sales field that requires you to call on prospects who are selling their own personal property and your sales job is to convince the owner that you can do a better job with their property than they can, you have a good challenge. My good friend, Lee Johnson, has a lot on which he sells used cars, travel trailers and mobile homes. His job is to convince his prospects that it is in their best interest to let him sell their vehicle or mobile home. The problem he must face is, each of these people have made the decision that they can clear more money from the sale if they sell it personally. The owner has kept the authority to sell and Lee now is calling with the purpose of *stealing* that authority. If this sounds like a basis for a *fight* you are correct, and that creates a no-win situation.

If Lee is to be successful, he *must* create so much value in the advantages he offers that are not readily available to the seller, that the seller will choose to give him the authority.

Some advantages could be the possibility of a quicker sale because Lee's lot is on a busy street; advertising and promotion would be paid for by Lee; there is ready financing for the buyer who cannot pay cash; there are trained salespeople on duty all day; and there is a service department that can fix anything that needsrepair. Lee has a lot to offer, but he *must* open the seller's mind with the question, "If I could show you a way that you could get a quicker sale for your travel trailer, would you be interested?" If the answer is "yes," Lee then has the authority to tell his story, open the prospect's mind, and then sell the value of allowing *him* to market the property. If Lee tries to sell before the seller gives him the authority, he will be in a "word war" or the seller will simply say, "Not interested," and end the conversation.

Real estate agents face the same problem when they call on people who have placed a "For Sale By Owner" ad in the local newspaper. I conducted a survey which revealed that 80% of the phone calls the seller receives on an ad are from real estate agents asking to list the property. Can you see that the seller might build up a little sales resistance after a few calls? If you are a real estate agent, let me give you a mind opener that has worked for some of the top listing agents in the country.

Remember, when you call the seller, *you* have authority because *you* dialed the phone. You will only have this authority for your opening statement, so you need to take advantage of the opportunity.

Getting a Listing

The seller answers your call and you respond with *your name* and ask with whom you are speaking? The seller gives *his name* and asks why you are calling. When he gives his name you are then in a position of authority. The seller is responding to your request, and since you gave your name he will not hesitate to give his name. Your response to why you are calling could be, "I wanted to speak to the person whose house is in today's paper. Is that *you? Always* end with a question.

The seller responds, "Yes it is. Are you interested in my house?" With this question he is trying to establish his authority. You answer, "Howard, (Always use the seller's name because it is a step toward creating a sales relationship) I am with ABC Realty, and if your house is as nice as your ad says it is, (a positive statement) I have several people who would be interested in seeing it. Have you had a good response on this ad?" End with a question.

He has to answer your question. "Yes, we've had quite a few calls, and several people are coming by. As a result, I don't think we'll need any help from your firm, but thanks for calling anyway. (A closing statement)

The sales agent replied: "Well, Howard, if I could show you three things you could do to sell your home more quickly, would you be interested?" When you ask this question, you *must* be *love-motivated*, because in order for it to work for you, you must be willing to give the seller three creative ideas that will make his home more attractive to a buyer, even if you do not get the listing.

Howard replied, "I'm not interested in listing my home with *any* real estate company." (another close)

And the response, "Oh, I guess you misunderstood me. I said, if I could give you three ideas that *you* can use to make your house more attractive to a buyer, would you be interested? I *understand* you are not interested in listing." Now you are *giving* without expecting anything in return.

He said, "Why would you want to do that?" Or, in other words, he was asking, "What's in it for you?"

"Howard, I've been in real estate long enough to know that if I can offer my services to people, I never have to worry about having enough clients. I'm sure you know people who, sometime in the future, might be looking for a professional real estate agent, or if and when it comes time for you to buy or sell in the future, perhaps you will remember me if I have offered good service. Here's what I would like to do. If you will show me your home as you would show it to a prospect, I will give you three ideas you could use to make a quicker sale. When is the best time to catch you at home?" End with a question.

The seller, still being apprehensive said, "Well, as long as you understand I am not listing this home. . . . "

And, he might not. On the other hand, I have found when you come into his home with the authority of a professional, in most cases you either will list the home right then, or within a week to ten days you will get a call from the sellers saying they think you might do a better job than them in selling their home. This has happened in my own real estate experience and I have observed it over and over with other salespeople who have attended my sales seminars over the years.

The Best Time for an Appointment

The phrase, "When is the best time to catch you at home," is a very important line. Most sales trainers teach, "Is Wednesday good or is Thursday better?" That is a *"No"* question, and you *never* want to ask *"No"* questions because they close the prospect's mind. If you ask for the best time to catch prospects at home, they will normally give you one or two times, and you *maintain* a position of authority.

Using the Prospect's Name

In the illustration above, we covered getting on a first-name basis with sellers from the front end of the conversation because you are working toward *establishing* a sales relationship. If you know and can use their name, they feel like you know them, and that makes them comfortable with you. You also learned in this illustration that you ask questions that create curiosity in the seller's mind, which, in turn, creates a higher value in the service you offer. Therefore, you *could* say, "You owe it to yourself to see what I can do for you." The seller has to respond, *if* you have established your position of authority, created value, and have asked for an appointment.

Place High Value on Your Time

The only *commitment* the prospect made when an appointment was set was to give you some time. This is *all* you want at this time, but that *time* must have a high value in the prospect's mind or you might be "stood up." When you ask, "What is the best time for you," you are saying, "I have a high respect for your time." When you tell the prospect that you are writing the date and time in your book, you are placing high value on your own time. By doing these two things you create value in your time *and* a respect for the prospect's time. When I ask for forty-two minutes of your time, I am recognizing that your time is very valuable, as is mine.

When your prospects believe your time is valuable, they will make sure they are there at the precise time of the appointment. On the other hand, if you say, "I have the whole week open. When is the best time for you?," you have placed a low value on your time and you will not have established a strong position of authority. Therefore, your prospects possibly will not keep the appointment.

When you create a high value in your services, you will do it because you first established your authority, and when you had a position established, you were truly in a sales relationship. Establish your authority *first,* then set the appointment. And, when you have done that, you *will* enjoy greater success.

Establishing Authority in the Presentation

We have concentrated on establishing your authority on the telephone, and now we want to discuss the area of face-to-face confrontation—how to establish your position of authority when you are with a prospect.

Selling Door-to-Door

Some reading this book might be in a position that requires you to call on customers, door-to-door. It is an area that has created fear in many salespeople for as many years. You need to understand that if you are knocking on doors, or you are not expected, you are in a prospecting position rather than in a sales position. When you knock on your prospect's doors, they are the host or hostess. Even though *you* are doing the knocking, *they* are in a position of authority, because *they* are *inside the castle.* Until you can turn around that situation, and you are given *authority* inside their castle, you are *not* in a sales relationship.

Often sales people drop by our office, peddling everything from office machines to wall art. Some of these salespeople come barging in and before we can voice an objection they lay out their wares and jump into their sales pitch, not even asking if we have time to listen. These are the old door-to-door salespeople who are disliked by most people, because they do not establish a relationship. They have "no clue" as to our wants or needs, and appear pushy and rude. Therefore, most salespeople, who are required to make *cold calls,* have that image in their mind and dislike that part of the business.

Good Cause - Poor Presentation

A man representing a very good organization dropped by our office, uninvited. Normally, I will not see anyone unless they have an appointment because I have found that people who do not set appointments do not value my time and, obviously, they have a low value of their *own* time.

However, since this man was representing this particular organization for which I have great respect, I opened the door to him. Once he was in my office, I found that he only was using that name as an entrance to me, and was not connected with that organization at all. He was *selling* a product *endorsed by* that company.

His sales techniques were so bad, and so forceful, that we got rid of him as fast as we could. But, before he got out the door, he tried to make us look stupid for not purchasing his product. That caused me to want to lock the door when a salesperson walked down the hallway.

I understand what that salesperson was doing, so we can guess what the homeowner or the person behind the door thinks when a salesperson with an attaché case knocks on the door. They quickly say, "I'm not interested!" and the door slams in the salesperson's face. The mind is *closed* before the door is *opened.*

Setting Authority in
Door-to-Door Sales

It becomes important if you are in the position of calling on people door-to-door that you understand you must establish your authority *before* you can begin to establish a sales relationship. Until then, you are only prospecting, at best.

If you are in this type of sales, we recommend that you leave a card, and possibly a small useful gift -- a ball point pen or a calendar -- along with a brochure or other promotional material, that states you will call again later. That is *almost* an appointment, because by *taking* what you have offered, the person gives consent for you to call again. The prospect has *received* from you, and in receiving they gave you permission to call. Remember, in door-to-door sales, you *do not sell* with your initial knock on the door. You sell when you come back and *establish your authority*. The Fuller Brush Company salespeople were always welcomed at the door because they operated on this principle.

Establishing Authority in Cold Calls

In many sales fields you must knock on a few doors to find out what is happening in your territory -- make a few cold calls in person or by telephone. You need to *first* establish your authority and then you will become the professional in your field to your customers.

Allied Plywood is an *employee-owned* company operating in several eastern states that offers "wood" products to the construction industry. They have *clients* who will not buy from anyone else, and they have *customers* who *sometimes* buy from other suppliers. Salespeople at Allied must make cold calls daily to the contractors in their territory because there is always new construction; and, to companies they have not supplied previously.

Their unique approach to cold calls is to ask the contractor, "How would you like to personally deal with one of the *owners* of a company that will supply *all* of your lumber needs?" How is that for establishing authority? You may not be able to enjoy that approach, but whatever your product or service, you must create value in that which you offer, if you expect your prospect to give you the authority you need to be in a sales relationship.

Establishing Authority in the Prospect's Home

If you go into a prospect's home or office, you must be in a position of authority so that the customer will recognize you as the *doctor of sales*. You will *know* when this has been achieved, because they will ask questions such as, "Where do you want us to sit," or, "Do you need a table for your presentation?" He will say to his prospects, "Before we get started, I want you to know that the material I will be sharing with you in the next 18 minutes is so valuable that I do not 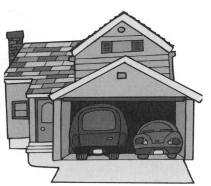 want you to miss anything. So, I'm going to make the phone busy." He goes to the telephone and dials the customer's number, which causes it to ring busy, and leaves it "off the hook" during his presentation.

You must have *strong authority* to be able to do this. I do not necessarily recommend that you try this approach, but it *has* worked for him for a number of years.

Controlling the Authority

When you are showing your product or service in the home, you have several variables to control, or you may lose your authority. Small children can *destroy* your sales position very quickly. If they should happen to fall down the stairs, the sales presentation is *over*! If it occurs just when you are ready to *close the sale*, you have two options.

First, you can do whatever you can to help should the child be injured, and then excuse yourself by saying, "I will call you later to set a time when we can get back together." If the child is not hurt, the mother will still need to settle down the child, which will mean she will not be open to your presentation. In this situation a wife or husband might say, "Why don't you just continue your presentation to my (spouse) and he/she can fill me in later." Do not do this!! If you do, you have given *your* authority to the spouse, who cannot tell your story as you can, and who has *no* answers to questions. Then when you call back to reset the appointment, you will find they have made a decision. And, since you were not there at decision-making time, that decision will usually be, "We have decided we want to wait a while. We will call you when we're ready to buy." Can you see who has the authority *now*? When the prospects tell you what they are going to do and when they are going to do it, *you* have most definitely *lost your authority*. The best thing to do in this situation is say, "I want to be able to answer any questions either of you may have, so I will call you and set a new time to get together."

Secondly, you can wait a short time and see if the child gets settled down. If the parents are *back to normal* and you sense that their minds are open, you can proceed with your presentation. However, be over-sensitive to their state of mind. If there is *any* concern for the child, *reset* the appointment. They may *think* they are ready to listen, but their minds will not be open.

Getting Children to Bed

If you have an evening appointment and the children are still up when you arrive, you can do what Neil Davis does in that situation. He will say to the wife, "I see you haven't had an opportunity to get the children ready for bed. Maybe you could get them comfortable while I chat with your husband for a little while." In most cases the couple appreciates the concern for the children and say, "Fine. It will take just a moment." During this time, he can ask some *first five minutes* questions that will give him greater insight into their wants, needs, and desires.

Eliminate the Television

The television can be a distraction if it is left on during your presentation. Neil handles that situation this way. "Do you mind if I turn the television volume down a bit so you can hear my presentation?" In most cases they say, "Sure, why don't you just turn it off." Neil has total control by *avoiding circumstances* that may possibly interfere with his presentation. He will not begin until he has that control. The reasoning for this is that a "news flash" could come on announcing that the president has been shot, or that terrorists have just blown up a building, or that there is an earthquake somewhere in the world! These types of occurrences have great impact on all of us when they are witnessed or televised and, therefore, *everything* in our world comes to a halt. You never know what is going to come across the "tube." This can also be true with radios. You are not even safe with soft music in the background, because that also can be interrupted by news flashes. To be in a position *of control*, you need to have all variables *under control*.

Physicians will not examine you in the reception area. I am sure you are happy about that. And, they will not, in most cases, examine you in your own home. Why? Because in your home, they do not have the control they need to complete the best possible examination.

This is also true for you as a salesperson. Sales people get into impossible situations. When the television is blaring, the children are playing around on the floor, and the phone is ringing off the hook, there is no way Neil can make a presentation which can keep their prospect's attention and concentration. If they cannot concentrate, how are they going to buy? It is very difficult to compete with *anything* in a sales situation.

Remember, the mind can think only one thought at a time. The prospects either will think about what is going on around them, or about what you are saying. Every time something distracts their thinking, they will tune you out, and it is as if they block out your entire presentation. Suddenly, you find that you are wasting *your time* and *theirs,* because you have lost your authority to sell.

Losing Authority

It is easy to lose the position of authority in a sales relationship, and often it is the salesperson who literally gives it away. When you are in a home or office and *accept* a cup of coffee, or let your prospects buy your lunch, you have become the guest. Because *you* are now the *guest*, the prospect has authority to tell *you* what is going to happen next.

Paul Waas, who sells Mutual Funds and other investments, was in the middle of a presentation in his prospect's home when the wife said, "Can I get you a cup of coffee?" Paul, not wanting to offend said, "Sure, that sounds great." As she left the room, Paul continued to sell the husband. "Now what I want you and your wife to see today is what this can mean to you in earnings." The husband said, "I'm always interested in making money." As the wife returned, carrying a tray of cookies, a pot of coffee, and three cups she said, "Money? Did I hear the magic word? Let's take a break and have a cup of coffee. Good idea?" Paul answered, "Sure. This sure hits the spot." *Bad* news!!

Now the *prospect* is asking the questions, selling cookies and coffee, and Paul is the guest, responding to their questions. He did not realize it, but he had *lost his authority* to sell. The husband then said, "Paul, getting back to business, you know I'm involved in several things myself and they look very good. You might want to take a look at what I'm doing!" Paul responded, "I might just do that." Now the prospect is selling Paul an investment and the tables are totally turned. It was at this point that the wife, playing the role of hostess, said, "Is that all you men ever talk about -- business?" The husband responded, "Well, there *is* a football game on today." As host and hostess, they can change the situation to whatever is of greatest interest to them.

This was a long way from where Paul started. He was making a sale when she entered with refreshments and he then became the guest. As soon as he accepted a cup of coffee from the hostess, Paul no longer had a position of authority. The wife was now in that position and she turned the business meeting into a social affair. Because she was in control, the husband felt comfortable talking about *his* investment opportunity. Paul then became the prospect to the husband, when it was he who had set the appointment. He totally lost his authority, and experienced complete role reversal, simply by accepting a cup of coffee.

If you are in the type of sales where you *must* work in a home situation, you must keep in mind that *anytime* you *accept* any type of refreshments from your prospects, you have *lost your position.* You may ask, "How can I refuse a glass of iced tea on a hot summer day?" As good as it sounds, when you allow yourself to take from the prospect, you have lost your position, and are no longer in a sales relationship.

I realize this is not a popular teaching, and you can tell me about times you have done this and still made the sale. I would just suggest that you try this technique for six months, and see what it will do for your closing ratio.

You need all the authority you can possibly get, so *guard* and *value* it. Then, *after* you have closed the sale, the check has been written, they have given you four or five referrals, and they have thanked you for helping them -- *then* you can eat their cookies, drink their coffee, and let them play host and hostess the remainder of the time you are in their home or office.

Authority in the Office

Refreshments *can be served* in an office situation, but if they *are* served, it is because you or your secretary served them. You then remain in the position of authority, and host or hostess. If you take the prospects out to dinner and pay the tab, you are in authority. You must *always* be in a position of control, if you are to maintain your sales authority.

Authority in a Restaurant Setting

If you like to have appointments in restaurants, I suggest that you arrive before your prospects. This will enable you to select your table and meet your waiter. Explain to the waiter that you are having an *important* business appointment, and that once the meal is finished, there are to be *"NO"* interruptions until you leave. I also suggest tipping the waiter in advance, making it sizable enough that they will cater to you. It builds great *deference* for you, when the waiter knows you and treats you with special respect.

The Devil's Advocate

Now let us deal with a situation that is *most* difficult -- when a *third party* shows up at an appointment. It might be a favorite uncle, mother or father, mother-in-law, or a good friend. Anytime there is a person who is not a part of the decision-making, and who was not included in the appointment setting, that person or persons will usually play the role of "devil's advocate." You can count on it! It does not

matter what you are selling, it will be "picked apart." Understand, they are not trying to be negative, they are merely protecting their "loved ones" from being taken advantage of. The reason they have license to do this is because you do not have authority over them, since your appointment was not with them. This can be very difficult since you do not want to upset the third person by telling them to leave. Then they really will become negative and will make sure you lose your authority.

Two for the Price of One!

Some salespeople have thought, "Great, two prospects!" That is, until they get into their presentation and begin hearing the third party's negative questions and suggestions, such as, "I think you should look around a little," or "I think you could do better than this."

You have two choices in this situation. First, you can reset the appointment. The reason must be logical. "Our company has a policy of presenting our services or products to just one customer at a time. That way we can relate to our customer's specific needs." In real estate, I suggest you say, "We are under contract with the home owners to only bring interested buyers into their homes. Once this couple has decided which home best fits their needs, then the seller would welcome you into their home as well."

Dropping in Unannounced

I discussed earlier a situation in which salespeople unexpectedly dropped by the prospect's office. When you "drop in" on a prospect (without an appointment) you have *no* authority; therefore, it is virtually *impossible* to establish a sales relationship. And, most importantly, you can destroy future business if you interrupt your prospect at a busy time.

In this illustration, Jim Lane dropped in on Jerry Matthews, at Jerry's office. Jim had made a presentation to Jerry at an earlier date, and was making a "call-back." The problem was he failed to call and set an appointment with Jerry. Jim stuck his head in the door of Jerry's office and said, "Hi, Mr. Matthews. I'm sorry to interrupt you, sir, but I was in the building and thought I would drop by to see if you have just a minute to talk." Anytime you feel you must *apologize,* you must be in the "wrong." Jerry answered, "Well, I am really busy. You caught me at a bad time." He was saying, "I cannot give you sales authority at this time. The problem was that Jim was *not listening* and he continued, "There is no denying that. I can see you are a busy man. But this is going to take just a minute. May I sit down?" He sat down before Jerry could answer him. Jerry, becoming agitated said, "Jim, I haven't had an opportunity to look at your proposal as yet, and to tell you the truth, I haven't even *thought about it.*" This should have been enough feedback for Jim to *know* he should excuse himself and get out of there. Not Jim! He continued, "Well, I can appreciate that. Let me encourage you to take a little time to look this over, because I know you will see what a good deal this really is." Jerry replied, "Well, Jim, I am sure you *think* it is a good deal, and I know that you *believe* in this offer, but I am just not prepared to do anything right now. I will, however, give you a call as soon as I make a decision." Now Jerry has taken *total control* and authority and Jim is in a *clerking* position, with no authority to build value, create curiosity, or try to close the sale. Jim thanked Jerry and said he would wait for his call.

That call will *never* come, and should Jim drop by again, he will find the receptionist has been instructed not to let him in. If he calls on the telephone, Jerry will be too busy to receive his call. And, in fact, the proposal will find its way to "File 13."

The sad ending of this story is that Jerry *will buy* Jim's product. He just will not buy it from Jim. Jim might even have the *best product* of its kind, and the *best price*, but Jerry is so turned off that he will no longer consider a proposal from Jim. The strange thing to me is that this happens over and over again, and many salespeople just think the "turn downs" are a part of being in sales.

You Keep the Authority - They Buy!

You often will buy a product or a service for a price higher than that of the competition because of the professionalism of the salesperson. What really happened was that the sales person established position as a *doctor of sales*, and established a position of authority, which caused you to be comfortable. This caused you to believe your needs were being met. You were not being sold something you did not need, but rather the salesperson was relating to your area of need by creating a high value for the product or service. This could be done *after* the salesperson's position of authority had been established as the doctor of sales.

Sales Authority is a "Must"

Let us review this. If you try making a presentation without first establishing your position, you are in a prospecting position at best. It becomes impossible to build value and very difficult to maintain a high closing ratio. You might be a good *clerk,* and persistent, so that you do sell. Or you might be selling something so great, that in spite of all your mistakes, people will buy from you anyway.

I would tell you that you can have a *higher closing ratio* and enjoy *more repeat* and *referral business*, if you will make this simple correction in your approach to your prospects. Have you ever purchased something *in spite of* the clerk? I have tried getting away from that as much as possible, but it is difficult to find *real* salespeople today. There are many clerks, but few salespeople. You always are comfortable with "real" salespeople because they take care of you. They maintain their position of authority, and they help you make a wise buying decision. A true doctor of sales makes a decision and then sells that decision, and you say, "Thank you."

I took a group of salespeople to a busy downtown intersection and asked them to stand back and observe something about human behavior. I stepped to the street corner where a crowd of people were waiting to cross the street. As the light turned green, I jumped out ahead of the crowd and shouted, "Stop right where you are!" Everyone froze! You could see amazement in their faces. I am sure they were thinking, "I don't know what *he* knows, but I'm not going to take a chance he's wrong." I then turned and walked across the street. When I got to the other side, I said, "OK, now you can come across." They all stepped off the curb and walked across the street. Not one person stepped off the curb until I told them they could. The most interesting thing is that as they walked past me, not one person asked why I had stopped them. They just smiled and nodded as they passed. In fact, the last person to cross the street was an elderly woman, and as she passed me she said, "Thank you."

People in our world want to be told what to do by someone who knows what he or she is doing -- someone with *authority*. When you are the "doctor of sales" you create that kind of sales authority, and you will develop true sales relationships which will multiply your closing ratio. If your prospects are *ready, willing* and *able*, you should be closing 95% -- if you are the doctor of sales. Establishing sales authority will help you do that.

CHAPTER 12

VARIABLES OF SUCCESS

☞ *Friend vs. Customer*
☞ *Give Acceptance and Interest*
☞ *Manager's Deference*
☞ *Enthusiasm*

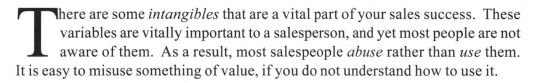

There are some *intangibles* that are a vital part of your sales success. These variables are vitally important to a salesperson, and yet most people are not aware of them. As a result, most salespeople *abuse* rather than *use* them. It is easy to misuse something of value, if you do not understand how to use it.

Deference x Enthusiasm = Productivity

The variables are tied together in what we call a *formula for success;* and that formula is: **D x E = P**, or Deference, multiplied by Enthusiasm, equals Productivity.

Deference is one of those words that speaks of an emotional happening, but very seldom do we understand how to use it properly, so that it works for us, not against us. Deference is a measurement of knowledge, experience, and ability between you and your prospect, in the prospect's mind. We could say it this way: "Deference is how much the prospect respects you as a sales professional, or how much you are a 'doctor of sales' to that prospect." If you are just old "so-and-so" there is not much deference. With this in mind, it is easy to understand why your friends and relatives are the hardest people in the world to sell on something. They know you so well and have seen most of the mistakes you have made. They remember the last sales "thing" you got into, and how it faltered and failed.

A doctor once said to me at a seminar, "Man, have you ever made me understand my problem! Awhile back, my sister called and told me her son had fallen down the stairs and injured his leg. She asked if I could suggest a good doctor who would see him. You know, I've been practicing medicine in this city for over twelve years, and she asked me to refer her to a good doctor. The part that really confused me is that she has sent a lot of her friends to me over the years. But, when it came time to take her son to a doctor, she wanted a 'real doctor.'" What she was saying was that he was just her kid brother who fell down the stairs himself when he was a kid. She has known him all her life, and in her mind, he is still her little brother. You probably have found the same thing true in your own business. The hardest people to sell are your friends and relatives, because they have the most doubts and objections.

I have heard sales trainers say, "What you need to do to be successful in sales is establish a friendship with your prospect." Or, "you have to be able to find common ground -- find the things you have in common, and then build a strong friendship." This chapter will not be your *favorite* in this book. In fact, as I teach this material, this is the one area that most salespeople have trouble accepting. If I am buying a product or service from you, I will be more comfortable if I believe you are the *doctor of sales*. I need to believe that all you do, everyday, is help people like myself make wise buying decisions.

You need to be the most knowledgeable person in my world regarding your product or service. However, if I get to know you personally, I will start seeing your weak areas -- your feet of clay. It does not help me if I hear about your problems and bad days. In fact, I will question your ability to give me good direction and correct answers to my questions. There is a thin line between being *friendly* or being *a good friend*.

A Sales Relationship or a Friendship

There are salespeople who enjoy socializing with their customers, and, if everybody likes them, it appears to be highly productive. Our research has shown, however, that the salespeople who are the most consistent, year after year, and keep a strong customer base with repeat and referral business *are not* the ones who socialize, but rather, the ones who are held as the *professionals* in their fields. You need to be the *friendliest* person in your profession, but *not a close friend.* We want our professionals to be *exactly* that.

What would you think if you were sitting in an examination room, *naked,* and the doctor breezed into the room wearing coveralls? And when he entered he said, "Hi, I'm a full-time plumber and a doctor part-time. I'll be with you as soon as I get into my "doctoring clothes." Most likely by the time he got into his doctoring clothes, you would be in *your* clothes and long gone. You do not want a *plumber* looking at your *plumbing*! You want a doctor who is "full-time."

Some of you are in part-time sales. As soon as you tell your customers that you are in part-time sales, you are telling them that you are not very good at what you do. You are saying you cannot make a full-time living at it, so you are doing it on a part-time basis in your spare time, which gives you another source of income for living expenses; this is merely a plaything for you.

I do not want to buy from someone who is *playing around* with the product. When do doctors work? In our minds, doctors work whenever we need them. We expect our doctors to drop everything they are doing when we have a need, because they are *our* doctors. What if the doctor is delivering someone else's baby? Too bad! That is *my* doctor. This is also true with my sales person. I expect my salesperson to be a *professional.* I also expect my salesperson to have direction, be an *authority* in his or her field, and be concerned about taking care of me, as relates to their product or service.

For you who are in *direct sales*, you will find that most people will "call in" orders right at dinner time. Why? Because you are the doctor of sales, and *your time* is *their time.* Incidentally, if they call you at weird hours, it is a pretty good sign that they see you as their doctor of sales. So, rather than being irritated, you should feel complimented. They really are saying that they believe in you. You must be the doctor of sales -- a professional. When I believe you are just like *me*, I have no reason to respect you or to look up to you.

When you establish a relationship with a prospect in a sales situation, you create *deference.* If you *close a sale*, you have established deference, and there is only one person who can destroy your deference with that client, and that person is *you.*

Finding Common Ground

There are a few things you might have heard over the years that you might believe to be true. In fact, you might have made them work for you on occasion. Let us look at the *common ground* theory.

You, my prospect, have a hobby of photography. I am the salesperson, and my hobby also is photography. We have an appointment to discuss the product I am offering. During the *first close* (first five minutes) I discover that you are a photography bug. So, I tell you I am a photographer, as well. Then you begin to talk about your photographic equipment, and comparing yours with mine. We go on for 30 minutes about photography. When I attempt to get back on the subject of my product or service, you want to talk more about photography. My position is now lost as well as my deference, and I am just plain old Orv, fellow photographer. I literally shot myself down!

You do not want to find a *common interest* with your prospects, but rather, determine your prospect's hobbies and compliment them on that interest. They should never know that you like photography, and that your equipment might be even better than their equipment. Show interest in their hobby, and let the discussion revolve around them.

Give Acceptance and Interest

Let us take another look at that situation. I determine you are a photographer and I say, "That's very interesting. Tell me a little about your hobby." You might say, "Well, I have a darkroom downstairs, and I have one of the best enlargers on the market today." You tell me the name of the enlarger, and I *know* you are incorrect because I know there are better enlargers on the market. The tendency would be to point this out, but when I do that, I have established *common ground.* So, you see the darkroom, let your prospects get it out of their system, and then compliment your customers on their photography. When I accept you based upon your interests, you accept me.

When the doctor examines you and asks all his personal questions, you feel like you *know* the doctor. I have often asked people their doctor's first name. About 50% do not know the answer to that question. Here is the question of the ages: "Where did your doctor receive his degree?" Would you not think that would be important? But it is not! Why? Because the doctor, in asking you questions, makes you feel like you *know* the doctor.

What would you think if you visited the doctor's office having chest pains and the doctor said, "You know, I've been having pains in that area myself. I wonder what is is." The doctor would lose a little *deference.* Or, how about a doctor who examines you and talks about his personal marital problems. In fact, all through the examination, the doctor talks about personal matters. Would you ever return to that doctor? Of course not. Do you realize that medical doctors have very little instruction in counseling, and yet they are constantly put in a position of *counselor* by their patients. We talk to our doctor about things they are not even trained to handle, simply because they are the doctor and we believe they are an authority on just about everything. People continually discuss personal problems with the doctor, yet, if the doctor tells us all of his problems, he loses *deference,* and thus, loses his position. He no longer is *your* doctor, and you begin at once to search for a doctor without problems. Our doctors have to be *perfect* in order for them to be "our doctors." If our doctors cannot handle their family situations, how are they going to *diagnose* or perhaps *operate* on us. There really is *no relationship, except in our mind.* Yet it is strong enough that we select our doctors, lawyers, dentists, ministers, and sales professionals, based upon their ability to maintain *deference.*

137

For many years, ministers had to be perfect to stand behind a pulpit and deliver a sermon. It is just in recent years that people have discovered that ministers are also human beings. They do not have wings beneath their robes.

There is quite often news about malpractice suits. This lets us know that some people *are* doubting their doctor's ability to be perfect. I want you to understand this fact. In a sales situation, as the doctor of sales, you have the same authority the medical doctor has in the examination room, *unless* you destroy your *deference*. And you can destroy your deference simply by getting on *common ground* with your prospect.

There is a story that is all too common which will bring this to light. Linda Piazza is a real estate agent, and some time back she met John and Ginny Phillips and showed them a few houses. In the process of doing this, they became friends, and of course, in the process of becoming friends, she lost her deference.

One day they came into Linda's office with some news. Ginny said, "Boy are we ever excited!" And John said, "We have some *great* news for you." Jenny added, "*And* some bad news." Quickly, Linda said, "Well, tell me the bad news first, and then the good news." Jenny continued: "Well, the bad news is that we won't be able to make our bridge game this week." Linda said, "Oh, no. We've had so much fun playing together. You guys haven't missed a night in three or four months." John said, "What do you mean, three or four months? It's been more like seven or eight." Jenny said, "It seems like just last week you showed us that first house, and then the second, and on, and on.... If we hadn't started playing bridge together, we never would have done anything. We must have been your worst prospects." Linda said, "Well, we haven't put any deals together, but we sure have become good friends." John added, "That's true, Linda, and that's the part we're really excited about." Jenny said, "That's right. I really am sorry we can't get together this week." Linda asked, "What's the problem? Why can't you make it?" John said, "Oh, that's the good news... Jenny interrupted, "Let me tell her about it." Linda knew this must be good news and said, "Come on, out with it!"

"We were driving down a very nice street," Jenny said, "and we saw this man putting a "For Sale By Owner" sign in the yard. So, we stopped and looked at the house. It had everything we've ever wanted in a home." John added, "Just wait until you see it. You'll love it. We bought it right on the spot. That's why we can't play bridge this week." Then John continued, "But, here's the best part. Since we bought it from the owner, we *don't have to pay any real estate commissions.*" And Jenny said, "And *you know* how much *that* saved us." Linda knew all right -- it was *her* commission.

Why would they think Linda would be happy that they were saving the real estate commission? Because they are friends, of course. You do not make money off of your friends, you give things to *them*. She lost her position and her deference, and now she was their friend rather than their real estate agent, the doctor of sales. It is so easy to do, and so very tempting.

You may be in a management or leadership role, and in that position, you must maintain your deference with your sales force as you would a salesperson with a prospect. If you lose your deference with your sales team, you have lost your ability to motivate, discipline, or to manage those people. In an office setting, especially if you have a small staff, it is very difficult to maintain deference.

I arrived early for a sales seminar sponsored by a well-known real estate franchise and observed the following conversation between the manager/broker and a sales associate.

Manager's Deference

A salesperson entered the lounge, fixed himself a cup of coffee, and a donut, and said to the broker: "Hello, boss lady, how are sales this month?" The manager said, "Not bad, but we could use more production from you." He said, "Aw, come on, it's coffee-break time. Relax! You can chew me out later." The manager replied, "What to you mean, chew you out? You've never had it so good, and you know it." He laughed and replied, "Well, that's true. You *are* a lot of *fun* to work with. Say, by the way, how's Jimmy doing?"

Does that not sound good -- his interest in her son? However, the son has very little to do with his low production. She answered, "You mean in school?" He said, "Yeah, are his grades getting any better?" She replied, "Not very much, I'm afraid. I don't know what to do with him. He's not dumb -- he just acts like it. I can't get him to work." The salesperson said, "Well, don't feel bad, you're not alone. I have a friend whose son just got kicked out of school. At least Jimmy's still in school." She said, "More or less! I don't think he's learning anything, so what good is it doing him? I don't know what to do. Do you have any advice to give me?"

That was a major role reversal. She has made the salesperson her counselor. She continued, "Ever since the ninth grade he's been a problem. I just feel like throwing up my hands." The salesperson gave her some great advice, "Just hang in there, baby, everything will work out in time. Just hang in there." By now, her deference is *totally gone*, because she is no longer the sales manager, but rather, she is a person with a problem and he is her counselor. At this point she tried shifting gears back to her management role with, "I don't know, I really don't.....Well, it's time for you to get back to the phones. You need to set some appointments to make some money." The salesperson said, "Yeah, yeah. Well, right now it's time to relax. The phones will still be there later." The manager said, "Seriously, you do need to be making more phone calls." Without deference the manager could no longer motivate or discipline. "Come on, don't push. It's not like you. I'll get with it, just don't push," said the salesperson. The manager shot back, "I'm not pushing you, but I've got to have some production from you." He replied, "You don't call that pushing? Every time you are upset with your son, you come up here and push the sales staff around. I mean it, back off a little bit." The manager said, "I'm sorry, I don't mean to push." It was clear this was not the first time he had played the role of counselor.

Lost Deference is Lost Opportunity

It was also clear that she no longer had power to lead because her deference was gone. She was sorry she had lost her deference, and could no longer lead this salesperson to a higher level of productivity. She needed to apologize, because this salesman will fail; and the sad thing was that as a manager without *deference,* there was nothing she could do about it.

The manager, in turning the situation around, transformed her sales agent into her counselor, rather than her employee. You will notice several things here. First, the sales agent brought up the subject. He started the conversation regarding her son. Then she turned the table and asked advice from him. He had no answers, so in desperation, he told her to "hang in there." As her counselor, he has authority, and with that authority, he has moved *above* her in the relationship. Now who has deference? He has more *deference* than she. As her counselor, he does not have to listen to her anymore as a manager. Therefore, when she tries to get some production out of him, he accuses her of taking her personal frustrations out on her employees.

The manager was not upset about her son when the salesperson walked in the door. The salesperson had created a problem for her, and it was a serious one because she lost her deference as well as her authority with him. It is a very easy thing to do.

As a manager, she did not have the luxury of having a bad day, or a problem. Everyone has bad days, but you do not take your personal *or* business problems to your subordinates or customers. If you do have a problem, always take it to your *upward relationship* -- never go down. This is a principle for *every* area of your life. Take problems *up,* and solutions *down.* That is why there are managers and vice presidents. You go *up* to them with your problems, and you go *down* with the answers. As soon as you make your customer or employee your counselor, there is no longer a customer relationship or employee relationship, because you have lost your *deference.*

Be Friendly, Not Friends

A high percentage of salespeople are *relaters,* who like to develop friendships with everyone they meet. Relaters have great people skills, but it can also cause a *loss of deference.* They like to sit around for hours, drinking coffee, eating donuts and talking about problems. Then, when time comes to sell, they have such a negative attitude that they project a negative presence, and their prospects are turned off and close their minds, which ultimately means they cannot buy from them. Then the salesperson returns to the office, cries some more, and wipes out the positive attitude of the rest of the sales force.

If you are having a bad day, you need to correct the problem before you allow it to destroy your sales ability and become a negative for everyone else in your world. That is what the seed list is all about.

Remember, anything that is bothering you is based on a fear-motivation. Attack the fear, whatever it is, and you will develop a positive attitude. If you are dealing with and correcting the problems, then you are not carrying that load and you can keep your deference.

Instability Destroys Deference

Mike Hutchings is in a sales field which offers products to families, so he is required to set his appointments to fit the prospect's schedules. This often requires evening appointments.

On one particular evening he was presenting his service to a husband and wife, and his answers destroyed his deference. Mike was saying, "....and you can see why we are so excited about this program." The wife interjected, "Mike do you work a lot at night?" And he said, "Well, yes, to catch people at home, I have to work *every* night." The husband said, "Isn't that a little hard on family life, Mike?" Mike replied, "Well, yes, as a matter of fact it is. My wife has been pushing me to quit this job. I can't really blame her, though. She just sees me coming and going. I'm never at home." The wife agreed, "I wouldn't like that, either." "How long have you been doing this?" the husband asked? Mike answered, "Eight *long* months. But you do what you have to do, you know." She said, "Don't lose your family over a job." Mike said, "Well, I won't, I would quit first."

Then he attempted to resume his presentation with, "I was telling you what we could do for you, and I am sure you can see what this program can mean to you." The man said, "I'll tell you something Mike, we think the program is great, and it's interesting, but we'd like to sit on it a while. Maybe in a couple of months...." And the wife continued, "Yes, give us a call back later, won't you? I'm sure we'll do something."

All of a sudden, fear caused this couple to back off. Do you know why they want to sit on it for a couple of months? They want to see if he is still around then. I am not going to buy from someone who is not going to be around. I might have a problem with the product and *then* who would I go to. I do not know anyone else in the company except Mike, the salesman. In fact, I do not even buy the product, I buy the salesperson. If the salesperson is that shaky and possibly will not be in the business two months from now, I had better not buy until I find out if he will be there.

There was interest in the program, and in *everything* he said except for that one thing -- Mike's deference was gone when he made them his counselor. As soon as his deference was gone, they began questioning whether or not they should purchase from Mike.

We go back to the doctor who says, "I have the same problem." I will not allow that doctor to operate on *me,* and I question whether I should ever again let him examine me.

I want a doctor or a salesperson who knows and loves what they are doing, and are dedicated, twenty-four hours a day, seven days a week. If you are not that kind of doctor of sales, I am afraid to buy from you. You are the only contact I have. I do not have a sales relationship with the president of the company, or your sales manager. You are it! You carry on your business card the name of your company, and with that is your name. I put the two names together as being one. If the company is not going to be around in two months, I am not going to buy a chunk of it today.

Lost Deference is a Lost Sale

Mike lost his deference, *and* he lost the sale. Deference is a *fragile* thing, easily lost and very difficult to regain. It is a precious "tool" and you must guard it with your very life, because it *is* your life as a salesperson.

You need to understand that your ability to keep the relationship in proper order with proper authority is based upon your ability to keep your deference. Understand that I am not talking about being standoffish and unfriendly; you should be the *friendliest* person in town. But *never* tell your customers and prospects your problems. Go to them with *answers,* and when they believe you *are* the doctor of sales they will *want* to buy from you. They will, in turn, send their friends to buy from you, and when it is time for them to buy again, it will be a *repeat* sale. Keep your deference, and you will keep a high sales volume.

Enthusiasm

Enthusiasm is one of those words, like "love," that has been abused over the years. We have always thought enthusiasm was jumping up and down and yelling and screaming a lot. In fact, I heard one motivator teaching that when you arrive at an appointment, and before you get out of your car, you sound out three warhoops. The idea is that with each warhoop, you create a bit of enthusiasm. I also heard a motivator teach a sales organization to take three laps around the car before entering the prospect's home. Supposedly, it will get the adrenaline flowing.

I was speaking for a state sales conference in El Paso, and while I waited to be introduced backstage, a man came by and said, "What a lousy day!" He told me it was a day where nothing had gone right. Then he sighed and asked me how I would like to be introduced. I am sure you remember "presence" from a previous lesson; so, how would you like to be introduced by someone who is having a lousy day? I replied, "Well, if you're having a bad day, I would rather you just "point" to me and I will introduce myself." He told me "not to worry" -- he could get himself *up* for it. Then he took three deep breaths and went running onto the stage. You would not believe what I saw and heard for the next fifteen minutes. He was all over that stage, and he had the audience yelling and screaming. He was a cheerleader. He introduced me, and I was given a standing ovation. I would call that *excitement,* not *enthusiasm.*

I have often been introduced as a motivator, but I do not consider myself a motivator because to be a *good* motivator, one must tell a funny story at least every five minutes and be able to "spit and hit" the first three rows in the audience while speaking. I have never been able to develop that ability! It *is* my intention, however, that the material I teach motivates people to a higher level of productivity.

Motivational speakers are exciting and very entertaining. The real measurement of effectiveness, however, is how much of what you heard can be applied in your life the following day. The ability to use instruction to grow and become more productive is the most important measurement of value. I like to think that the material I am sharing with you is material that you can apply on a day-to-day basis. I do not want it just to "jack you up," but rather to give you some understanding in dealing with people and being more of a professional in your field of sales. If I can accomplish that in this book, then this has been time well spent for you *and* me.

Enthusiasm vs. Excitement

I want to concentrate on *enthusiasm* rather than *excitement*. Everything I have described thus far has been excitement. Enthusiasm and excitement appear to be the same, but one is very loud, and the other is very solid and consistent. The best way to describe enthusiasm is to have you visualize a circle which we will call, *our world*. We choose to live in our world either from the *inside-out* or the *outside-in*. Excitement *always* comes from the outside-in. Motivators can get us excited because they are outside our world, feeding us exciting information and humor.

A closed sale or a raise in pay will get us excited because that is an outside source feeding information in. We *need* excitement in our life. It brings us happiness and it feels good. Also, it can help us forget some of our problems for a time, and we need to do that occasionally.

Living *outside-in* can also cause the opposite reaction. If the opposite were to occur, such as someone saying something negative, a lost sale, or any negative happening, our excitement could be wiped out. When we are living outside-in, we are at the mercy of the things that happen outside our world, over which we have little control.

Enthusiasm is living inside-out. It begins on the inside of us and flows outward. We control our enthusiasm because it comes from within us. Enthusiasm is determined by our decisions or what we choose to think about any circumstance or situation that touches our life -- and most of all, the person we are.

If you can understand this concept, you will be continually and consistently enthusiastic, whereas with excitement, you are up and down like a yo-yo.

Who Are You?

There are two factors that determine your enthusiasm. The number one factor is knowing *who you are*. If you know who you are, you are enthusiastic. You may ask, "Who am I?" That is what your *seed list* is all about. If you will read it aloud to yourself ten times every day, and begin to believe all the wonderful things you are putting into your subconscious mind, they will automatically begin to be true. This is the basis, or cause of your enthusiasm.

Here are some further examples of *seeds* you could add to your list:

"I believe I'm strong in the close."
"When I talk to customers on the telephone they want to listen."
"I'm a top sales producer."
"I have the ability to establish relationships with anyone."
*"I have the ability to know people, and recognize how to relate
 to their need structure."*
"I have great enthusiasm for my work."

Source of Power

The second factor in enthusiasm is knowing your *source of power*. I believe personally that my real power comes from God. So, it is part of my daily self-talk. In a working situation, your power comes from your corporate headquarters. Therefore, if you have a good relationship with your boss, you have the power to do your job. For those reading this book who have been in sales for many years, I have a few questions for you. Have you ever worked for someone you did not like? What kind of sales volume did you produce in that sales position? Have you ever had a manager with whom you could not get along, or worked for a manager in whom you had no belief level? What was your closing ratio? As you answer these questions, it will help you understand this concept. It is difficult to be successful in sales if you do not have a good upward relationship, because your *power* in sales comes from the top down. Most turnover in personnel in the sales force is caused by poor upward relationships (with management) rather than low sales volume. So, sales managers, if you do not have a good relationship with your salespeople, correct it, or suggest they find other employment. That person will never be successful in sales without a good relationship with you, the manager. Your function and responsibility as a manager is to do the best job you can for your salespeople. When you are doing a good job, you are establishing a good

relationship with that salesperson, and making sure that salesperson has a good relationship with you. *You* are their *source of power*, and their power keeps their enthusiasm high.

Use Your Upward Relationship

Salespeople, if you don't have a good relationship with your sales manager, *develop one*! If there is something about that person that you do not like, go to your manager and make it right, because you will not be successful in sales until you do. It's impossible, emotionally and psychologically, to be *successful downward* unless you're first *successful upward.* You will not have power, and therefore, you will not have enthusiasm. Enthusiasm is very contagious in sales. When you're around people who are enthusiastic, you become enthusiastic as well. It's a chain reaction because when you enter a sales situation with great enthusiasm, it passes on to your prospect.

Living Inside-Out

With these two variables working for you, you can live inside-out consistently. Will there still be bad days? Of course, but your bad days will be higher than most people's good days. So, the majority of your world will never know you are having a bad day. You will be consistently more positive. Remember, the only thing that puts you below the line is fear, and fear is not real. Do not say that you have bad days and there is nothing you can do about it. You *can* make the decision that the bad things *are not* so bad. When you accept things in your world as being bad, then you are in trouble, because when you choose to live a negative lifestyle, that choice will destroy your enthusiasm.

Living from inside-out causes you to control your own thinking. When you know *who you* are, you can conquer *any* problem that comes along. The things you cannot conquer because you have no control over them, are the things you should forget. Why get concerned over things you cannot change, such as the weather? Can you change the weather by being concerned about it?

People also like to complain about the government. Many do not even vote, but they complain. Be concerned only about things you can change and forget about the things over which you have no control. If you can do that, then you will be consistently enthusiastic.

Productivity

Productivity is the third part of the equation. You are paid for your productivity. Sales volume is productivity. Repeat and referral business is productivity. There are five variables of productivity that I want you to remember. This probably will be different from what you might expect, because most people equate productivity directly to income. I believe income is a result of being productive, but is not necessarily productivity in itself. When you are productive, you have cash flow. Let us get to that level of productivity, then we can enjoy the cash flow.

1. Love of Position

If you are a productive person, which is the result of having deference and enthusiasm, then you also love your work and your position. You think selling what you sell is the greatest thing in the world. You can hardly wait to get to work, and you enjoy your day. Salespeople who are very productive love their work; people who do not like their work will never be productive. They destroy their deference when they walk into the room and there is no enthusiasm. Some people are habitual complainers. They complain to their fellow car-poolers all the way to the office. They continue complaining all day, and especially on coffee and lunch breaks. Then, they ruin the emotional environment of their car-poolers on the ride back home, who wish they could leave that person on the street corner the next morning. Finally, they arrive home and complain to their spouses and children the remainder of the evening. When you love your job, you wonder where the time goes, and if you must be with people in the evening, it is a fun occasion because you are enthusiastic.

2. Pride in Your Work

When you have pride in your work, you do the extra special things to be *proficient* in your job. The fact that you are reading this book tells me that you *do* take pride in your occupation. Most people will not take time to develop their own abilities to a higher level. They have no real concern about their personal growth. That is why only 5% of our sales population rise to the top and become the *doctors of sale*. Those salespeople who take pride in their work are the ones who do everything possible to develop themselves to a higher level of productivity.

3. Assume Responsibility

You will find a love-motivated person assumes responsibility wherever they can find it. They go farther out on a limb than is necessary to satisfy their prospect's wants and needs. They work longer hours because the "project" must be finished that day! They make sure applications are filled out completely and correctly to avoid losing time making corrections. In other words, they do the extra things because they enjoy assuming *responsibility* in their job.

4. Loyalty

Loyalty *always* comes from the *top down.* That means your clients or customers will only be as *loyal to you* as you *are to them.* How do you speak of your customers or employees when they are not in the room? That will tell me how well they speak of you when you are not in the room. Life gives us what we deserve. How loyal are you to your company? I have news for you: that is the level of loyalty your customers will give to you. When you talk with your prospects about a weak person on your management team, your clients, in turn, will peg you as a *shaky* salesperson. Again, understand that loyalty comes from the top down, not the bottom up. You will not be *enthusiastic,* you will not keep *deference,* and you will not be *productive* unless you are *loyal.*

5. Consistency

When you are consistent you maintain a high level of professionalism at all times. You are always where you need to be at the appointed hour and you make the number of calls you need to make in order to reach your sales appointment goals in a timely manner. You need consistency even in areas such as sending greeting cards to your customers and clients.

I know an insurance agent who not only sends birthday greetings to the entire family, but also sends anniversary cards of the date they were issued their insurance policy. If you will do *little things,* consistently, you will build a solid relationship with your customers and clients, and that is *productivity.* When customers can depend on people to do what they are supposed to do, they will feel very comfortable with them. The customer then, is in a position with the salesperson that they are confident all the details will be taken care of.

149

To summarize, when you are *consistent* with your distributors, clients or customers, there is *no way* you will lose them to a competitor. *You* are the only salesperson in the world selling that particular product, in their mind. Is that *valuable* to you?

Using Your Seed List Effectively

Does it take a little work to be consistent? Absolutely! Remember, self-discipline is making yourself do something that you do not feel like doing. It is either *not* doing what you want to do, *or* doing something you do not want to do. Let me tell you where self-discipline *really* works. Do you realize if you have the right kind of *seed list*, and you read it consistently every day, all of your other disciplines will be automatic? For example, when you believe you are a runner, you get up in the morning and run, and, you *enjoy* it. When you believe you are a thin person, you only eat foods that are healthy.

One couple I met lost weight consistently without dieting. He lost about 18 pounds and she lost 12 pounds in eight weeks. They ate everything they felt like eating. The only variable was that they added their desired weight to their seed list. Of course, they actually weighed much more than what they read on the scale, but by telling *themselves* everyday that they weighed their goal weight, the subconscious mind would tell them they were no longer hungry when their body had taken in enough food.

Did you know that your appetite is controlled by your subconscious mind? By adding to your seed-list things such as, "I am enthusiastic," "I am energetic," "I have great *deference,*" "People know me and love me," and, "I am successful in sales," you will put this *formula* into action in your life. You will have *deference, enthusiasm,* and you will feel *productive.*

You will be happy as well. So, from this day forward, *discipline* yourself to do your "seed list" *every day*, and by so doing, these other variables will fall into place, automatically. You will be successful, and be known as a successful leader in the sales field. And to your best customers and clients, you will be known as the Doctor of Sales, which is exactly what you want to be!

CHAPTER 13

FIRST IMPRESSIONS

☞ *Wardrobe and Jewelry*
☞ *Personal Hygiene*
☞ *Automobile and Image*
☞ *Posture*

Within thirty seconds of the time I first meet you, you tell me what to think about *you!*. You do this with your *presence,* and your *personality,* which are projections of your attitude, along with your *physical appearance.* Many sales managers and salespeople have told me that this part of my teaching is very important; others have said it is a waste of time. Those who feel it is a waste of their time usually need it most; and those who tell me it is good material hope the others, who think it is a waste of time, are listening. So, you might want to breeze over this chapter, or maybe you should take a strong look at yourself as you read it. The material I will cover here is just *common sense* and *good personal hygiene.*

In sales, you are the "company" to your customers, and in many cases they never see your office; they see only you. And often they see you far before they see a product or service. What they *really* are buying is *you*. Therefore, you need to be packaged as well as possible. It is a lot like a courting situation. When you have a very important date, you do certain things in preparation for that date. The same is true in a sales situation. As a professional salesperson, you need to do everything you can to yourself, and surround yourself with as much glamour as possible, in order to make your best presentation. There are some things you cannot change, but you *can* work with certain parts of your anatomy and dress to make the best possible appearance. *First impressions* are highly important, because your prospect's first impression of you will be a lasting one. It is important that you do everything you can with what you have to work with, in order to make that *first impression* as positive as possible.

Top Ten List

There are many things of importance to consider in preparation for making a good impression.

Bathe

This should not need to be on a list like this, but all of us know someone who needs to be reminded. Some people enter a room before they *physically* get there. A man came into my office selling copy machines, and as he walked through the door, I knew someone was entering. Not only did I hear his footsteps coming down the hallway, but his odor preceded him into my office. He was very heavy, and fatty tissues have a tendency to produce more perspiration. His glands were definitely overworked. He filled my room, not only with his physical presence, but with his offensive body odor. Perspiration stains had discolored his shirt and he was quite disheveled.

He said to me, "I've got a problem -- it's my boss! He was OK when he first hired me, but he has changed over the years, and it has become very hard to work for him. Do you have any suggestions on how I can straighten him out?" I once had a Sunday School teacher who taught me this lesson; if you point a finger at someone, you have three fingers pointing back at yourself. If you blame someone else for your problem, usually *you* are the problem.

Commercials say that your friends will be the first to know, but the last to tell you when you have a problem, such as, *needing a bath.* On warm days, it might require taking a bath twice a day. You will find your skin does not really wash off.

When you enter my home for our appointment, I do not care what you have done all day. I do not care if you have had to crawl over fences and around dirty basements. When you enter, I will have a *first impression* of you. So, you had better be as fresh as you were at eight o'clock in the morning. That might mean taking a shower prior to your *evening* appointments, even though you took one before your *morning* appointments. It is most important. These are things no one will ever tell you, but you will not close the sale, and you will wonder why.

Shave

Some people need to shave more than once a day. Have you ever heard of "bluebeard?" I knew a man whom everyone called "bluebeard," and it was years later that I learned it was because he always looked as though he needed a *shave.* If you have a beard or mustache, keep it well-trimmed, so that it does not draw attention to itself. However, that is not the point I am making here. I am talking about when you *really* need a shave. We have difficulty trusting people who need a shave. It is a totally subconscious response.

If you have difficulty keeping yourself in good appearance, I will have difficulty trusting *you* with my business. This is true with both sexes. If you are from a different culture than we have in the United States, you might not agree with this, but in the American society, we believe that women should shave their legs as well as under their arms.

I was having lunch with a young lady in Washington, DC, and as you know it is quite warm and humid in that area on a summer day. This particular day she was wearing a sleeveless blouse, and as she pointed at something, hair fell out from underneath her arms. I never even looked at whatever she saw! The hair looked long enough to braid. I totally lost the point she was making. Have you ever seen a woman cross her legs, and hairs were sticking through her panty-hose? You subconsciously are thinking that it must hurt when she removes her hosiery.

It is very difficult for the prospect to listen to what you are saying when you project poor personal hygiene. I want you to know that in our society you *can* lose a sale if you need a shave. Be conscious of that.

Wardrobe

I believe that in sales we have a tremendous opportunity to make unlimited income with very little investment, other than time. However, I do urge you to make an investment in clothing. Most salespeople do not have to purchase or furnish an office; the company does that. The salesperson's major expense is probably personal wardrobe. Therefore, I feel it is vitally important that you put money into your clothing and grooming. I know a man who buys a new suit every time he loses a sale. That purchase motivates him to make a sale, because those credit card bills come due eventually.

I also believe you should make a *sizable* investment *in* your wardrobe. You may be thinking, who would ever know how much I spend on my clothes, and the answer is simple -- *you will!* You stand, walk, and talk differently in a new outfit that cost you more than any clothing you have ever purchased. You stand a little taller, and you have more confidence, because you know you are well-dressed.

Secondly, expensive clothes still look good when they are cleaned. They will always outlast the less expensive clothes, so you end up getting your money's worth, many times over. When those clothes are two years old, they still look very good, whereas the less expensive clothing begins to look worn.

Third, if you are dealing with people who are knowledgeable about clothing and current styles, they will recognize an expensive outfit. If you dress expensively, that tells the prospect that you are prosperous and the reason you are prosperous is because you do a good job.

Therefore, I am interested in you being my *doctor of sales*. It is like walking into a doctor's office and finding no one in the waiting room. You feel as though this doctor must be either killing off his patients or chasing them away. Either way, you do not want to go to visit *that* doctor again. We want a doctor with a busy waiting room. We assume that if there are a lot of people waiting, then this doctor must be one of the best in town.

If my doctor came to work wearing jeans and a tee shirt, I would worry a lot about that doctor; because I expect my doctor to dress in the uniform of the day. As a doctor of sales, your uniform is the most current style of the day. You are worth it, and you will feel good when you are dressed for success.

Your clothing should be well-pressed and neat. Have you seen people, who by the end of the day have such wrinkled clothes that it looks like they have been sleeping in them? There are many things you can do to make sure you are still looking sharp in the afternoon and evening. It is important that your clothing not draw away the prospect's attention, nor do you want to distract from your presentation. That can happen by being so current that you are the first one in town to wear the latest style, or the last. Either way, it does basically the same damage.

Colors are very important because there are many bright colors today, both in men's and women's clothing. Always be color-coordinated! I saw one salesperson wearing a red shirt and an orange tie. If you are *color-blind,* then ask someone who loves you to help you get dressed before an appointment. Wearing clothing that has not been color-coordinated will often turn people off. One prospect anonymously called a real estate office and told the receptionist that someone should teach a certain agent how to dress, or buy him a book on professional dress, and then hung up. You may never know, but it *can lose sales.*

Over age 30!

You have no control over being past age 30, but you need to understand that people place a higher trust and belief in people who are over 30, because they have greater deference. They have been around longer and should have more experience. Therefore, they receive our trust.

Have you ever noticed how on a television ad you often see a head shot of a mature man, leaning into the camera. He usually is wearing dark rimmed glasses, has graying temples, and a receding hairline, and says, "Are you suffering from faulty elimination?" What do you know about this guy? He must be a doctor -- right? Wrong! He has a product he wants to sell, and is trying to project the image of a doctor. Some men with a receding hairline are not too proud of them, but it is *good for sales!*

So, if you are under age 30, you need to understand that you should dress a little more conservatively, and speak more conservatively. You need to wear the uniform of the day, or that which is acceptable to the prospect. Remember the customer is king, and you are dressing for the customer. You must understand that you are playing the role of doctor of sales, and if you stay on the conservative side, you will be more effective.

Automobile

This is not a popular topic but it needs to be addressed. The best automobiles to use in sales today are luxury cars which are less than two years old. If the automobile is more than two years old, the customer will think business is bad. Also, it must be clean, inside and out, including the trunk. I am sure no one looks inside your trunk, but you do, and that subconsciously affects your attitude.

Personal Hygiene

You have to take good care of yourself. Deodorant and toothpaste are not optional -- they are a must. Be aware also that perfume or cologne should be used sparingly because it can be distracting; especially if the prospect is allergic to ingredients contained in the formula.

Hairstyle

A hairstyle should never attract attention to itself. You do not want to be remembered as the salesperson with the "hairdo."

"No" Smoking

If you are a smoker, *never* smoke in a sales situation, even if the customers are smoking. Sometimes they are trying to cut back, and your smoking may tempt them to pick up a cigarette. If they are non-smokers, long after you leave, you are still in their presence, and they will lock the door when they see you coming again. Location does not matter. Just *never* smoke in a sales situation, period!

Jewelry

If it attracts attention to itself, jewelry is not good. Earrings so large that when you make a right turn you knock someone out are "too much." The only lapel jewelry you should wear is jewelry that has something to do with your field of business. Do not wear your Lodge Pin, or Sunday School pin. I have known people who have lost sales because the prospect had been in that particular organization earlier, got upset about  something in the organization and left! When they see you wearing the badge of that organization, there is a negative reaction. There is nothing wrong with those organizations, but do not wear any emblem when you are in a sales situation.

Posture

Try to stand tall with your shoulders back. When you slouch, it appears you have a poor self-concept, and that you do not believe in yourself. When you are in a sales situation, practice good posture. It feels better anyway. You will feel *more confident* when you are sitting or standing erect.

One other thing to mention is to never wear *white socks* with a *dark suit!* Have you even seen a man in a dark suit cross his legs and you cannot help but stare at his crew socks? His deference has just disappeared.

All of the "little things" mentioned above will help you keep your deference. And abusing any one of these suggestions may destroy your deference *and* productivity.

You can understand from what I have shared that appearance is very important. You have only one opportunity to make a good *first impression;* so make sure that *impression* is *favorable.* The client will then see you as a successful salesperson -- a doctor of sales. Not only does their opinion count, but *yours* does as well. When you feel confident and look in the mirror, you are proud of what you see. And when you know you have done the best you can with what you have to work with, you can hold your head up high and feel good. That is being the *doctor of sales.*

CHAPTER 14

SALES INTERVIEW

☞ *Office Structure and Decor*
☞ *Seating Positions*
☞ *Privacy*
☞ *A Qualified Prospect*

O ver the years, the *sales interview* has been the focus of sales training, ore than any other one subject. If you have been in the sales field for a period of time, you have been taught

the approach, the presentation, and the close, many times and many ways. I want to introduce to you ten elements of a sales interview that will assist you in effectively telling your story.

When all ten of these elements are in force in your sales presentation, you have the best chance of closing the sale. If you begin removing any of these elements, you are lessening your chance of success, and objections (fears) increase. That does not mean that you must have all ten elements in every presentation to make a sale. In fact, you might find that some sales people *never* have *any* of the ten going for them, and yet they still sell, simply because their presence or charisma is so strong.

However, if you can understand these ten elements, there is no reason why you cannot have as many of them as possible in your favor at every sales interview, thus lessening your chances of failure and increasing your chances of success. I believe it is most important to do everything we can to be as successful as possible. If you are planning a presentation, make sure that *everything* is focused toward your goal, so that you can get maximum results from the presentation.

Office Structure

Some of you sell in situations where you do not have an office, so this will not apply to you. But even if you are making a presentation in your prospect's home or office, you can create a positive structure, provided you are aware of room conditions. I will describe for you the best and the weakest structure for your presentation. You never want to make your presentation across a desk or table. The desk or table becomes a divider between you and your prospect, and can lessen your ability to establish a sales relationship. Some salespeople are more comfortable with something between them and their prospect, which could be a defense mechanism, caused by their fears. The prospects will sense this and it can create feelings of distance or staying at arm's length, which, ultimately, can cause the customers to set up resistance.

The second problem with this is that it sets up a face-to-face confrontation, where you and your prospect are on opposite sides of the table, and in a debating or negotiating position; and *that* is a negative sales structure. If you *use* a table for your presentation, you should be at the end of the table, and your prospects both on one side. This allows you to make your presentation with your material in front of you *and* the prospects, rather than it being awkwardly upside down for you. If the presentation is set before both you and your prospects, you are moving together toward the common goal of understanding the value

of that which you are offering. There is no resistance when you are moving in the same direction.

In the perfect setting, you want a four-walled, private office, where no one can interrupt or distract your prospects by walking by, talking loudly on the phone, or overhearing other salespeople talking.

A sales presentation room should create as little distraction as possible. When that door is closed, no one interrupts. The receptionist is told to hold all calls, and the other salespeople are trained that when the door is closed, they stay away.

When I am making a presentation, my secretary knows if the building catches fire she is to knock on my door just before the building collapses. I want the office staff to know that there must be a major emergency in order to interrupt my sales presentation.

Can you imagine yourself as a customer sitting at a desk with a salesperson, and another person walks into the office and throws a piece of paper on the salesperson's desk? You would probably wonder what was on that paper. In a real estate situation, this can create a real problem, because if they just happen to give you the latest listings, and your prospects are ready to close the sale, guess what runs through their minds? They think there may be something new on the list that is better than what they have decided to buy. That is when you hear, "Maybe we should look around a little more before we sign this contract."

This cannot happen if you have created a closing room with proper structure that everyone understands. I have visited offices where there are rows of desks and the noise was unbelievable. You could hear laughter at one desk, someone signing a contract at another, someone making an approach at another, and someone on the phone at the other end of the room. When you hear all of this going on at the same time, it is confusing. Even the cubicles that divide you from the next desk are distracting; they work as an echo chamber. And, of course, your prospects are sure that if they can hear the person in the next cubicle, then that person can hear them.

We want a closed office where there is privacy, and it is structured so that the prospects know they are alone with the salesperson. In this sales situation, you have the best chance of holding attention, and controlling the interview.

Office Decor

When your prospects enter your office, they will have a first impression of you and your company. Your reception area should make a statement about you. It should look professional, classy, clean and uncluttered. I recently had an appointment with a real estate broker and when I walked into his office I could not believe what I saw. The reception area had business cards of the past clients stapled to one of the walls. The remainder of the walls were covered with snapshots of houses, and pictures of the broker with his friends. Some were pictures of him fishing, others were of just small groups of  people, but none of them were of people I would know. It was like walking into a museum. The first impression for a prospect would be clutter and confusion.

In your closing room or conference room, the walls should be clear of anything that may distract from your presentation. Plaques and trophies, or maps and posters with neat slogans, all will attract the eye of the prospect and be a distraction from your presentation. Try sitting in the chair that the prospect would occupy and determine what that person would be seeing during your presentation. Keep the wall behind you as simple as possible.

You will recall that the eye gate takes in 72,000 characters per minute and your mind can only think one thought at a time. Therefore, you should always position yourself so that the wall behind you is very plain. You do not want your prospect studying a map while you are making your presentation. Also, if you make presentations in your client's office or home, keep this in mind, because they can be just as distracted in that setting as in your office.

Seating Positions

There are some seating positions that can create sales resistance and some that will ensure a good sales situation. I mentioned earlier that you do not want to work across a table or desk; a face-to-face presentation will cause your prospect to have sales resistance without ever knowing or understanding why. You want to have good eye-contact with both prospects at all times. This works well if you are sitting at the end of the table and your prospects are at one side. If you do not maintain good eye contact with both people, you can lose a prospect without knowing it. Sitting between two prospects will cause you to always have one of them looking at your back, and then you have lost the eye contact you need.

At a presentation in your prospect's home, you may be most comfortable sitting on the sofa. In that case, you should sit at one end with the prospect's wife in the middle, and the husband on the other end. This is because the husband is usually larger than the wife, and it makes it easier for both to see what you are offering. A sofa is a piece of furniture that creates relaxation in most homes. You will sometimes find people will be more relaxed sitting on a sofa than sitting at a table, and relaxed means their minds are open.

Another area of extreme importance is the best seating arrangements if you are driving your prospects to a presentation or to see a home. Driving is an excellent time to establish a relationship with the prospect, unless one of the prospects is in the back seat. You need to be the doctor of sales and tell them where to sit. Again, you do not want one of your prospects in the back seat because you lose eye contact. It is difficult to hear what the person in the back seat is saying; and it is a divider between you and one of your prospects. The best situation is to put both of them in the front seat, with the wife in the middle. It is easier to have good conversation and you can hear better as well. You can make eye contact, and even though it is slight, it is enough to keep control of the situation, because you have better communication from the salesperson to the prospect and vice-versa.

Privacy

Privacy simply means that I can talk to you, and you can talk to me, without anyone else eavesdropping. I do not like discussing financial matters with other people around. Many of you are in a position where you do group sales presentations, or there are other salespeople with prospects in the same room with you. You must be able to isolate yourself and your prospects to the point that you have privacy. Then personal questions can be asked.

If you are the doctor of sales, I will feel very comfortable with you. I will ask you things I will not ask anyone else, and I will tell you things I will not tell anyone else. I want you to hear me, so that you can take care of my needs. You will never hear those things if other people can hear what I am saying.

When you cannot get a prospect to talk, it is often because you are lacking privacy.

Physical Comfort

Do not seat your prospect near the heater or air conditioning vents, where the prospects either will freeze or roast. Also, you do not want your prospects in a position where they are squinting because the lights are too bright or too dim. You need comfort, which includes comfortable chairs. Physical comforts will build a sales situation, whereas discomfort causes the mind to wander, and then you may have lost the prospect's attention. Be aware of what your prospect is feeling and seeing throughout your presentation, because when it gets to be a level of discomfort, you will lose them. They will not say they do not want what you are selling, but you will lose their attention, and when you lose that, you have lost communication. When you have lost communication, you are no longer selling, but rather, you are talking to yourself, and the prospect can no longer hear a word you say. These things will help you keep a sales situation clean. I call it clean when it is uninterrupted. When you have settled the need for physical comfort, you have their full attention, you have a sales relationship going, and good communication from the salesperson to the prospect and back.

Qualified Prospect

Some salespeople (clerks, actually) are so hungry for a sale that they will start selling their product or service to anyone who will stand in one position for a few minutes. When you meet this type of salesperson at a social gathering, he or she will make a presentation to you whether or not you are interested.

I enjoy singing. I have been a part of several singing groups over the years. If I am walking down the street and see some people awaiting the bus, I will stop and sing them a song, just because it is a captive audience!

I know they have to listen to me sing or miss the bus. However, that will not work in sales because if you make a presentation to unqualified prospects you are wasting your time. You are also discouraging yourself and you are planting in your subconscious mind that since you are not closing sales, you are not a very good salesperson. However, the fact is that it is impossible to close a sale, if you do not have a qualified prospect.

It does not matter how great a sales person you are, you will not sell if the prospect is not qualified.

There are four important "beliefs" to help you qualify a buyer. We covered them in an earlier chapter but not in this context. The first belief is a belief in the "teacher." When I qualify a prospect, I have to know that the prospect believes in me, and until I can establish a relationship wherein prospects believe in me, I will not make a presentation. I might have to talk 30 minutes or more before I open my presentation book. If the prospects are not in accord with me, they will not hear what I am saying anyway. If I cannot get them in tune with me in the amount of time I have allotted, I will say, "It was nice talking to you today. Maybe we can get together again in the near future," and then I leave. I will not make a presentation to someone who is not a prospect. If you are a real estate agent and you see your prospect has a closed mind, you must realize that you are taking them on a tour of homes only. You cannot start selling until you have established a sales relationship in which they believe you are their doctor of sales.

My friend, Leonard, believes that time has arrived when your prospects ask for your name. When they say, "I didn't catch your name," you know they now have accepted you as the doctor of sales. They are not prospects unless they are qualified, and the first step of qualifying is establishing a relationship. If you do not have a relationship, you will not get the sale. You have to be the "teacher" (the doctor of sales) to that person in order to have a qualified prospect.

Secondly, the prospects have to believe that what you say is "true." If they are continually questioning the things you are saying, the prospects are telling you that they have intense fears and psychological blocks. Until you get rid of those blocks, you will not make an acceptable presentation. If your prospect is questioning the truth of your statements then that is feedback that you have a suspect whose mind is closed, rather than a prospect. When you can open their minds you will have qualified prospects.

Third, we must have prospects who believe they "need" the product, service or opportunity that we are offering. If I have no need for what you are selling, I will not buy. As you will recall, needs are based upon values, and if I do not need it, I will not value it. Why should I pay for something that is worthless? So, make sure the prospect sees a need for your product. If you cannot create "need" you do not have a prospect.

And fourth, the prospect has to believe they can "use" your product, service or opportunity. If you are talking to me about a sales opportunity, and in my mind I am thinking that I cannot sell anything to anybody, then I am not a prospect. I have to believe that I can use, or in this case sell, before I am a prospect.

So many salespeople talk from their own beliefs; "Boy, can you use this!" or "You will be excited about this." Without knowing the prospect's wants, needs and desires, they make statements from their own frame of reference, not really knowing the prospect. The prospect might tell the salesperson that they "will think about it," but they really are thinking that they cannot use the product. I have to believe that I can use what you are offering, whether it is a product, service, or opportunity. Have you noticed, I have not mentioned financial status? If you, in qualifying a prospect try to determine whether or not your prospect has the financial ability to be a serious buyer, you will chase a lot of good prospects away. If your prospects sense that you are judging rather than accepting them, you have lost them. If they are qualified prospects and you are a good salesperson, based on what I have outlined above, you will find a way to help them solve any financial problems. If you have learned how to listen, your prospects will tell you what they can and cannot afford in the beginning of your sales relationship.

For Sale By Owner

A large part of real estate business comes from talking to homeowners and convincing them you can sell their homes for them. When I, as a homeowner, believe that I can sell my own home and save the commission, then I do not need you, and I do not want to use your services. In order to have qualified prospects, you must convince your prospects that they can use, and in fact, need to use, your product. If you follow these "four beliefs" in qualifying a prospect, you will truly be in a sales situation; but if not, you are dealing with a suspect rather than a prospect.

Appointments

If you are not working from appointments, you are clerking. Without an appointment, you have no authority, you have no deference, and the prospect has a closed mind.

It is important to understand that, from a psychological standpoint, the best time to call a prospect to set an appointment is between the hours of 8:00 a.m. and 11:00 a.m. on Saturday. On Saturday morning I am relaxed, I am unshaven, and my heaviest thoughts are about what I want to do on my days off. If you call me at 9:00 a.m. on Saturday and say, "Orv, I have a great new program you must see," and you build some curiosity and value in my mind and then add, "When is the best time to catch you and your spouse at home?" I will probably respond, "Well, we are normally home on Tuesday and Friday evenings." In my relaxed state of mind, at the beginning of the weekend, those two days might sound like a long time away, so I am open to seeing what you have to offer. As you tell me you are entering the date and time on your calendar, I mark it on mine. I am relaxed, my mind is open, and there are no defense mechanisms. Saturday mornings are great!

If you cannot reach clients on Saturday mornings because of your type of business, the second best time is Friday morning between 9:00 a.m. and 11:00 a.m. We stop calling at 11:00 because at that time, the prospects begin to think about where they are going for lunch, and their mind is focused on their afternoon. We need their undivided attention in order to be effective in setting an appointment. From Saturday, we count backwards to Tuesday; and when we get to Tuesday, we stop. Monday morning is not a good time to call because it is "getting back to work time." We then switch to afternoons or evenings, from 4:30 p.m. to 7:00 p.m., Monday through Saturday. This is the dinner hour and I know people do not like to be interrupted at dinner. I am not saying this is the best time; remember we are moving down our list of best times. One positive thing about calling at the dinner hour, however, is that you normally catch people at home, and they are usually anxious to get back to the dinner table, so they will be quicker to set an appointment. There are some dangers, of course. Sometimes they will hang up on you to avoid having their dinner get cold. Or, they possibly will agree to an appointment, then forget about it later, because they were anxious to get back to dinner. You definitely want to apologize for disturbing them at dinner time and say that you will take only a minute of their time. Next we move from Monday through Saturday during the evening from 7:00 p.m. to 9:00 p.m. This is far down the list because in our society, television has become a major part of most families' evenings. If you happen to call me right at the crucial climax of my favorite program, I will get rid of you as quickly as I can and will not hear a word you say. I'm probably watching television while I am speaking with you. So, you may get the appointment, but once again, I will probably forget all about it.

The final time to call, and this is the weakest time, is Monday through Saturday from 11:00 a.m. to 5:00 p.m. Afternoons are not good because shortly after noontime, your prospects start getting a little uptight. They may be yelling at their secretary, or yelling at their spouse on the telephone, and maybe yelling at themselves. So, when you get them on the telephone, they will probably yell at you as well. If at all possible, stay with the strong times.

Allow Sufficient Time

Always make sure that you allow sufficient time for your full presentation, answer any questions your prospects might have, and have time to close the sale. Many salespeople schedule themselves right out of prospects by saying things like, "I have to run because I have another appointment," and then they hurry out the door. Then, the next prospect stands them up, and now they have lost two customers. Or, they possibly set the appointment but do not verify that the prospect had enough time for a full presentation. It is vitally important that you allow sufficient time for your total presentation, and completion of the sale, without feeling rushed. Make sure that the prospect does the same.

The Presentation

I believe it is also important that you direct your presentation to the definite need of your prospects. To accomplish this, you must discover as much information as possible about the prospect before you begin any presentation. Then you determine how your product or service best fits that prospect's needs.

I have worked with a firm in southern California that shows a maximum of three houses to a prospect, and then sells one home, rather than showing fifteen and picking one from the group. That saves so much time, money and gasoline, and most importantly, you can see many more people. As the doctor of sales, if you really know your customers' needs and understand their values, you can select the house that best suits them. This Company shows a home that is on the high end of the prospects' needs, one that is on the low end, and then they will sell the one in the middle to the prospect. It sounds a little like the story of the "three bears" but it works for them.

If you are talking insurance, you need to determine whether the customers want protection, retirement benefits, or college education for their children. Your presentation will be the same, but you will emphasize the area that is most valuable to the client.

If you are showing a business opportunity, selling stock or any kind of an investment, you must find their area of need in the investment and emphasize that area. It is the same sales track, and the same presentation, but it will appear to be entirely different when you listen and hear it, because it is geared toward the person you are now addressing. I am sure that you have found over the years that you have never made the same presentation twice, and yet you run through the same presentation every time. This is the fun part of sales because it does not get boring. That keeps it interesting for you, which keeps you enthusiastic. That, then, helps the prospect be able to relate better to you and the presentation.

Business Card

Part of the presentation is how you present yourself. I have talked about your car, your appearance and your clothing, but I want to talk a bit about how you present yourself with your business card. Your business card is you, and when I look at it, I should see you as much as when I see your office. I was speaking in Dallas when a man approached me and said how much he had enjoyed my speech. He then gave me his business card and it read, "My Card." That was the entire imprint! While he was still standing there he said, "Oh, incidentally, here is "Your Card." He pulled that from his pocket and handed it to me. Then he added, "While we are talking about it, here is "Our Card." He does this to everyone. Can you imagine the value of those cards, if you were to have this

imprinted on the reverse side of your business cards. Do you think those cards would ever be thrown away? Every time your customer pulls out that little "conversation piece," they will be reading your name.

Do you know the real purpose of business cards? To be thrown away! About once every two months, you go through your wallet or desk and throw away all of the business cards you will not need. Before long it gets filled again with more cards. Hopefully before you throw this card away, you will read it one more time. Work on creating a business card that will not get thrown away. If it is creative, your customers will show them to other people, but they will keep your card when they throw others away, because it is valuable to them. Then, when it comes time to purchase your type or product or service, they will think of you. Create a unique, or humorous business card.

Controlled Emotional Environment

Finally, it is important that you stay positive because you project presence, and the presence you project as a salesperson will determine the atmosphere in the room. If you are having a bad day, you will create fears and a bad day for your prospect.

Remember the outflow of your thinking is your personality, performance and presence. You are in control of the environment of a room because you have the sales authority. If you are having a bad day, you will set up defense mechanisms in your clients. It is better to cancel an appointment, and reschedule it for a later date, than to call on a prospect when you are having a bad day.

The best thing is never to have a bad day! You can accomplish this by doing your seed list daily. That will keep your emotional environment positive, and cause you to project a positive environment, which, in turn, causes people to relax in your presence. That is controlling your emotional environment.

As a salesperson, you will control your emotional environment either positively or negatively, by your own thinking and atmosphere. Be the doctor of sales and be in control. Control your world and you will be successful in sales. When all ten elements are working for you, you are the doctor of sales, and that is success.

CHAPTER 15

PERSONAL AIR SPACE

☞ *Touching*
☞ *Socializing*
☞ *Breathing Room*
☞ *Resisntance*

Personal air space is a fun subject to cover because we are discussing the physical "you" which has some emotional nerve endings that reach out farther than you can believe!

People respond or react to us many ways, psychologically. One area of concern to salespeople is the value of touching — a "touchy" subject!

A medical doctor touches you anywhere and everywhere. I recently had a dentist stick his whole arm down my throat — it seemed! There are certain positions in life wherein the person filling that position has authority to touch you as much and as often as they want to, and you let them.

We place tremendous trust in the people who have to touch us as a part of their service. Our dentist, doctor, hair stylist or barber all have great authority and very little resistance when they touch us.

I spoke to a group of managers for one of the largest chains of hair salons in the country, and informed them that their stylists are in a great sales position because their hands are all over the customer's head and face. Customers are very open to the stylists. How do we know this? Because customers allow them to put their head in a sink, get it "all wet," and see them at their very worst. Then they allow them to use a very sharp instrument around their face, ears and throat, and do many other demeaning things. And when they have gone through this trying situation the customers pay for it. With that much power, they should be selling far more shampoo, conditioners, brushes, combs and other personal care products. The problem is, most hair stylists are satisfied with a tip, and never present the value of the products offered in their salon. When you want to buy some of their products, you must ask for them, and that is clerking.

You do not have to touch a person, physically, to enter into their personal air space. Personal air space is that area around you that reaches out a little less than arm's length, and creates emotional responses when another person enters into that zone. It can be a touch, such as a hand shake, or merely eye contact. You will automatically be influenced, either negatively or positively.

We covered in an earlier chapter the subject of face-to-face confrontations, or sitting in the right or wrong positions, and the impact that can have in creating an open or closed mind. In this position we are not necessarily touching, but the impact is as if we are. When we are approached face-on, we may feel under attack, and therefore, will set up resistance. This is why we often meet people who will not make eye contact with us until they feel secure. When they trust us, they will begin looking us in the eye.

I am told that dangerous wild animals will only attack us if we are staring directly into their eyes; and that if we avoid looking at them directly they will wander off. The reason is that eye contact or face-to-face, is confrontation to an animal. I also have heard, that if you carry a torch, wild animals will not attack you. I asked a man who has done much hunting in Africa if this was true, and he answered, "It is, if you carry it fast enough!"

If you meet people in a face-to-face confrontation, you may be violating their private air space, which will cause them to feel you are attacking them, and that, in turn, will cause defense mechanisms to arise. We want to move with people, and show them how we will help them meet their goals. We are working toward their goals together, and what one of us cannot do alone, the two of us can manage to do together. It is projection of a good attitude, and so the prospect will sense it and respond positively.

Touching

Here is a good illustration of the power of our personal air space and how we respond to most people who enter it. Select a person of the opposite sex, (not a close friend or spouse) and stand shoulder to shoulder, with both of you facing the same direction. As long as the two of you are facing ahead, both remain very comfortable. Now in that same position, pretend that the two feet (yours and theirs) closest together are nailed to the floor. With that in mind, you will both pivot toward each other, not moving the "nailed foot" so that you are face-to-face, and try not to step back. As you can see and feel, it is very difficult to remain that close, because you are penetrating each other's private air space.

To be comfortable, you must each take a half step backward. Then, in that position, shake hands. Your new position should be at a perfect handshaking distance. You can make eye contact, and you can touch that person (the handshake) even though it might be the first time you have ever met, because you are not violating their personal air space. Try this at your next sales meeting, and allow your salespeople to experience your same feelings.

When you are in a sales field which requires you to take your customers to a presentation, you have opportunity to open doors for them, help them in and out of the automobile, and put your hand on their back as you usher them through a door. All of this touching is acceptable. As you help a person of the opposite sex through a doorway, do not make eye contact. All of this is subtle touching, but it can cause the prospect to feel comfortable with you and create trust. You must be totally comfortable using this or in fact, it will create a negative, rather than a positive response.

The best handshake for you is a simple vertical handshake. I learned from politicians in Washington, DC, who do a great amount of handshaking, that if you will slip your hand all the way into the recipient's hand so that the area between the thumb and the index finger is touching, you will never crush their hand or injure their fingers, especially if they are wearing rings. Make sure you get that little extra surge, and if you miss, try it again. Be up front with people and say, "Let's try that again," and you will be surprised at how relaxed people will be if you attempt to correct a poor handshake.

To be effective in creating a sales relationship with your prospects, you must make sure that you do not violate their private air space, and you should use eye contact, a touch, closeness, and a smile, as often as possible to establish your authority. It will break barriers and the prospect will feel more comfortable with you.

Body Language

I am sure you are familiar with the study of body language. How you sit, how you stand, and the gestures you make, all are indicators of what you are thinking. I can glance at my audience and know by their body language whether or not they are with me. The following are just a few obvious indicators that will assist you in being aware of what your client is telling you. There are many books available on this subject, so I do not want to go into a lengthy study on the subject, but if you are able to relate more effectively to the fears, wants, needs and desires of your customers by understanding body language, it is worth your efforts.

When prospect's arms are folded, their legs are crossed or their chin is down, that is a sign of a closed mind. The higher the arms are folded, the more closed the mind, and the lower the arms are folded, the more open the mind. If you see all three of the above you need to stop your presentation and begin asking curiosity-raising questions, which we discussed in an earlier chapter. If you continue your presentation it will fall on deaf ears. You will see a physical change as you begin to open your prospects minds. Their arms will open, their chins will come up, and they will lean forward or move their body toward you as their mind becomes open.

There is such a thing in body language as a sentence or a paragraph. It is a series of positions that each say something such as the three mentioned above. You cannot isolate just one and say that person's mind is closed because of crossed arms. But, if they make a series of gestures, you can get a better feeling of the person's state of mind.

There are several physical signs that tell you the mind is open and ready to hear your presentation. When the prospect's arms are folded with one hand to the face and a finger extending upward, it means that person is evaluating, and it is an open-minded situation. The finger pointing upward normally indicates consideration and evaluation, or an open mind. That is a very positive sign, and you should at once start presenting the information you want your prospect to hear.

Stroking the chin means basically the same thing as does pulling at the mustache or upper lip. People with mustaches sometimes do this out of habit; but in a general sense, it means they are considering what you are saying. Sitting forward in a chair, or leaning toward the information, is a positive, open-minded stance. When people move forward in their seat, they are moving with you. With this degree of open-mindedness in your prospects, you are in a position of authority, you have deference, and they have accepted you as the "doctor of sales."

There are a few gestures that will help you better understand how your prospects are responding without verbal communication. People tell you what you need to know, if you are aware of what to look for. The problem is, most salespeople are so concerned with their presentation that they are not aware of what the prospect is saying back to them, either by verbal or nonverbal communication.

This is extremely important to salespeople because prospects will tell them so much that the entire presentation can be directed toward relating to the prospect's frame of reference, wants, needs, and desires. You may need to move along quicker, or slow up a bit. It might be time to close the sale, or maybe give a little more information to build higher value in order to close the sale.

Your head is probably swimming by now, and you are not sure if you can do all these things. You will not do them all in one day; but if you will review this chapter again and again, you will realize that each time you will find something you missed. The more exposure you get to body language the more it will help you. If you feel you need more information on this subject, write to me and I will be glad to refer to you some printed studies on this subject. It is important that you read this over and over, take notes, and read other related materials. If you want to be the doctor of sales, you will do the little things it takes to be successful.

It is fun to be in a social situation and know what people are thinking about you, or whether or not they are comfortable with you. It puts you in a better position of control in every area of your life, and since God gave you total control of your thinking, you may as well control your thinking to the point where you can control your life.

We call it being the doctor of sales, but you might as well be the doctor of "living" in every area of your world. **If you will be aware of what people are saying to you with their body language, you will be in the position to be more successful as the doctor of sales.**

CHAPTER 16

TELEPHONE SUCCESS

☞ *Smile*
☞ *Humor*
☞ *Voice Tones and Inflections*
☞ *Relationships*

The telephone is probably the greatest instrument ever created by man to help the salesperson. I know a close rival would be the automobile, but the telephone saves hours of driving time and hundreds of miles in wasted trips, if it is used properly. It allows us to set bona fide appointments, create a sales relationship, create sales authority, value, and curiosity before we ever see our prospect face-to-face. It is a fantastic instrument.

At the same time, however, if there was ever an instrument created by man that has destroyed more sales than a telephone, I do not know what it is. It has destroyed sales relationships, deference, authority, and curiosity; and, in fact, it can literally wipe out sales in general. Needless to say, an instrument like the telephone cannot do all that by itself. Therefore, it is a result of its use by the person holding the receiver in hand. There is a proper use of the telephone to help us be more effective in our telephone work. Perhaps you will be able to relate to this from your own experience.

Prospecting By Phone

First of all, realize that the telephone is a prospecting tool, not a sales tool. You cannot sell over the telephone. The only thing you can possibly sell over the telephone is an appointment, which is actually an act of prospecting.

There are salespeople who make their living by telephone solicitation, but that is not the type of sales we are considering here. We are talking about a sales relationship in which the salesperson takes the responsibility to relate a product or service to a prospect's wants, needs and desires. This takes a face-to-face relationship with a great deal of insight into the prospect's life because their decision to purchase is based upon the value in what has been offered. I do not believe this can be accomplished on the telephone. It is merely a prospecting tool. If you keep that thought in proper perspective in your mind, you will use the telephone correctly. You know, of course, that the check cannot be written or the contract signed by telephone.

We need to use the telephone so that it creates the strongest possible sales relationship with a prospect, by creating authority, value, deference, and curiosity, thereby establishing a bona fide appointment, which turns a prospect into a "qualified" prospect. There is a difference. Everyone is a prospect, but not everyone is a "qualified" prospect.

Take a close look at your telephone. If you look inside, you will find a microphone. It is not a high-quality microphone, but it does the job it was invented to do.

Voice Projection

We do not sound our best on the telephone. I imagine that is why you never hear of singers recording on a telephone!! To make matters worse, not only is it probably the worst microphone in the world, but if you opened the opposite end, you would find a one-sided "stereo" speaker. Put that in your home entertainment center and listen to the quality of sound you get from it. The telephone has a very small speaker; therefore, the quality is

not all that great. Yet, when you call me, the first thing I hear is your voice tone, and that will be my first impression of you. So, it is important that you use it properly.

The proper use of the telephone is to put the microphone just below your lower lip. This will give you the highest quality and eliminate the "popping" sounds when we use "P's" and "T's." The speaker also is not good, so we need to speak in easy-listening tones. Practice getting the most out of your voice. Some people have high squeaky voices, and others have low rumbling voices. Have you ever recorded your voice on tape and could not believe it was you? That is almost exactly what I hear when I talk to you by telephone.

This is an exercise you can do by yourself to determine the effectiveness of your voice, using a small cassette recorder that has a separate or extension microphone.

First: Speak into the microphone, and as you speak, move it around, from above your eyebrows down to your Adam's apple. You will hear the differences in tone just by moving the microphone, and you will discover that your best tone and sound is when the microphone is just below your lower lip.

Second: Speak a little slower than your normal speed and hear how much easier it is to understand you, and in addition, you will sound more relaxed.

Third: Add a little air to your tone. As you add air, your voice softens. You can add so much air that your voice sounds a bit breathy. You are talking just as loud, but with more air, so it softens the tone. If you use less air the

179

sound is more driven or projective. When you are speaking on the phone, you do not need to drive your voice. Talking on the telephone is the most intimate you will get with a prospect, because your lips are right against their ear. Think about that the next time you talk to people on the phone!

Fourth: As you speak, enunciate each word. It is important that you do not run words together. On the phone this can cause your prospect to misunderstand what you have said, and can create real problems. If you will concentrate on speaking each word clearly, you can avoid misunderstandings that can lead to incorrect dates, times and places for an appointment. It is more pleasant listening to you on the telephone if you will talk a little slower, use a little more air, and enunciate a little better. You should adopt a "telephone voice" and a "regular voice," and they are not necessarily the same. You may question why you should do this.

As a speaker for many years, it has been important that every person in the audience hear and understand every word that is spoken. You are as much a speaker as I am, because you make your living by talking to people. Why not hone your tools a little and professionalize your approach. I think it would be very wise for every salesperson to take at least one semester of lessons in voice; either singing lessons, or speech, taught at a local community college. You will be surprised that you can learn so much in one semester that can be used in your everyday sales to be a more effective communicator. Many high schools offer adult education classes on this subject. It does not matter whether or not the school is accredited; it will still result in money in your pocket and enhance a very effective tool — your voice.

Successful people do what unsuccessful people fail to do — the little things, not the big. When you talk to me and your voice sounds pleasant, I feel comfortable with you and I am drawn to you. Then I want to see the person who goes with that voice. So, I will set an appointment just to see to whom the voice belongs; on the other hand, if the voice is unpleasant, I will become less interested in what you are offering or in meeting you. You might ask, "Do people really pay that much attention to a person's voice," and the answer is, "not consciously." However, studies have shown that our impressions of a person on the telephone will determine whether we are willing to invest time (an appointment) with that person. You may have the greatest product in the world, but if I cannot buy your voice, you will have a difficult time setting an appointment with me.

The bathtub or shower is a great place to practice your voice, because that is when you sound the best. You can practice speaking in lower tones. Some individuals are monotones; they speak in an even tone with very little voice inflection and sometimes put you to sleep. If you are a monotone, you probably do not know it, but let me give you a clue on how to determine if you are. If, the last time you sang with a church congregation, the people sitting next to you moved to another pew, you are probably a monotone!!

Develop voice inflections: some highs and some lows. I am not saying to scream high or growl low, but merely let your voice inflections go up and down. It is more enjoyable listening to you when you are not a monotone.

Have you ever noticed that people tend to speak differently on an answering machine than they do on the telephone? When we talk on the phone, we sound excited, but if we hear our voice on a machine, we sound as if our voice is coming from a robot. I am sure most people do not listen to their own recordings. That is why when some say they are out for lunch, it sounds like they are out to lunch! Answering machines are very useful if used properly. But you know what happens when we hear a bad recording; we think if they sound that bad, think how bad we are going to sound, and we hang up. We do not want to sound that bad to anyone.

I sometimes answer the phone as if it is a recorded message. I am not recommending this, but it is fun just for laughs. Messages should be a little humorous. When you do this, you will probably get a humorous response. Also, people will have more of a tendency to leave a message if the original message sounds normal and has a little humor.

If I were to take a microphone and hold it just below my bottom lip, my P's and T's would not pop and my voice would sound full. However, if I raise the microphone, my voice will begin to thin out. I could be talking in exactly the same voice tone, but it would not sound the same because you would be hearing the high end of my voice. Likewise, if I move the microphone downward, you would begin to hear the low end of my voice range, and it would sound a bit muffled.

Have you ever noticed in an apartment building that the people living above you play nothing but bass drums and the people below play saxophones and trumpets? You are hearing all the highs from above and all the lows from below. That is because low tones go down and high tones go up. The lows do not make me sound better, nor do the highs, but if I can get both, it rounds out to give me a full tone in my voice.

You may think these are unnecessary topics; or it may seem like a silly game, but I want you to know that many a salesperson has never seen the person on the other end of the line, merely because of that person's voice. Why lose appointments over something so simple to correct? Keep the microphone right below the bottom lip and you will get the maximum out of the microphone and the speaker.

When you use the telephone, remember it is a prospecting tool, and you are calling for one reason only — to set appointments. If you must set appointments by telephone you want to have a telephone approach that will cause people to want to meet you personally. There are four factors you need to keep in mind while using the telephone.

Smile

A smiling tone is a pleasant tone. It makes your voice appear warm and you can easily tell whether people are smiling or frowning. I try to smile a lot, because I want pleasant tones to reach the other end. Some offices have mirrors in front of all their salespeople, and on the bottom of the mirror is written, "Smile." They are looking at themselves and smiling, but the receiver of the call thinks the salesperson is smiling at him or her. Maybe you think you have nothing to smile about, but you can smile at the fact that you are going to set an appointment, meet new people, and be productive.

Many salespeople dial a number and as they are dialing they are saying to themselves, "I hope no one is at home," and then they wonder why they did not want anyone to be home! The answer is strictly fear. When you have conquered that fear by using your seed list daily, that will never again be a problem for you.

Some years back I produced a series of Sleep Tapes helping both children and adults conquer the fears they carry on a subconscious level. A very successful Amway distributor who lives in Maine, told me that our sleep tape on salesmanship helped him conquer fear of the telephone. He was at one time literally afraid of the phone; he actually hated it! We all know that to be successful in sales we must use the telephone. Now, he is quite comfortable and relaxed on the telephone. He conquered his fear of rejection, which was not only fear of the telephone, but fear of the close, and all the other fears tied in with a sales interview.

Humor

We need a sense of humor in dealing with people. Life can be funny, if we keep it light. We all enjoy being around people who have a sense of humor. If we call someone and in the first thirty seconds we laugh a little, people will tend to listen to us. It is difficult to listen to people laugh without smiling. We cannot smile without being positive, and we cannot be positive without being open. By laughing, we literally create an open mind in our prospect. A line I like to use is, "Are you working hard or hardly working?" This is not really funny, but it has enough humor to make the person smile a little bit. I enjoy talking to operators, and especially long distance operators. I get them to tell me things they should not tell anyone, such as unlisted numbers. I have even had them ring the unlisted numbers for me. To do this, you simply establish a relationship with the operator. When they are laughing and having fun at their work, they will do all kinds of things.

I mentioned my friend, Anna, in the chapter on the first close. I have so often watched her work with her prospects who walk into her office, and as always, as she is getting to know them she will laugh at something they say or she says. A little while later she laughs again, and by now, the prospects are laughing with her. Anna is very successful, not just because she has a great laugh, and people laugh with her, but I do believe her laugh causes people to relax and feel comfortable with her, and that creates a sales relationship.

Voice Tones

If you take a speech or vocal music course, one of the first things you will learn is how to breathe correctly to create the best voice tones. When you take a deep breath, your shoulders and chest should not move. You should breathe through the diaphragm. When your chest moves, your voice thins out, but when you breathe from the diaphragm, the tone broadens because you have more of a foundation from which to speak. You never see singers' or speakers' chests move when they breathe. I learned a breathing lesson from my voice teacher many years ago that helped me achieve this.

Every night as you go to bed, put your hands on the small of your back, bend over as far as you can and take ten deep breaths, making your hands move every time. Then, bring your body up one notch and do that same exercise again. Continue four times, with the final time being in a straight up position. Within a week, your voice will change. It is not puberty, it is breath control.

Another exercise you can do right now is to put your index fingers on the joint of the jawbone, right on the hinge, and then yawn. Notice how your jaw dropped down? That is called an open jaw which creates an open voice tone. If you were a speech major or music major in college, one of the required subjects was one of the Romance Languages: French, Spanish, or Italian. The vowels in those languages require an open jaw. In speaking and in singing you learn to use the romance vowels. Learn a little Spanish. You will be surprised at how much it helps your telephone voice.

Voice Inflections

You do not want to talk like a monotone, nor do you want to go up and down like an elevator. Practice speaking in the shower, or on a recorder, and keep practicing until it comes naturally to you. Football players practice many hours before they play a game, pianists practice hours before a concert, and we should practice as professionals in our field.

If we are to be the doctor of sales, we will practice in private and perform in public. Too many salespeople practice on the prospects and lose sales.

As the doctor of sales, you will have a higher closing ratio on the telephone (setting appointments), and suddenly the telephone will become more fun. Practice, again and again, what I have shared with you in this chapter, and it will help you be more effective in sales, and especially in establishing relationships on the telephone.

CHAPTER 17

MOTIVATIONS OF LIFE

☞ *Fatalist*
☞ *Exasperator*
☞ *Appraiser*
☞ *Relater*

This chapter is a study of all the people in your world to whom you must relate if you are to be successful in sales. Most of the earlier chapters have focused on you becoming the doctor of sales by overcoming debilitating fears, establishing a sales relationship, establishing deference, and using your authority. Now let us look at your clients' and prospects' actions and reactions, and learn why they say what they say and do what they do.

As we enter this study, describing inner motivations and the behavior the motivations cause, you will recognize many people. I want to ask you to do a couple things. First, realize as we go through the motivations of life that we are not talking about people, but rather personality traits and inner motivations.

You will remember that subconscious attitudinal beliefs, or inner motivations, create personality, performance and presence. The easiest way to understand a

185

person's inner motivations is to recognize personality traits, which are the outward expression of inner motivations. We call it behavior. You cannot label people because no one person is a specific personality type at all times, but you can recognize that this person has an inner motivation that is causing a certain type of behavior.

The value to you in sales in understanding the motivations of your prospects or clients is that their motivations determine their need structure which, in turn, determines their values. We will discuss the preferred types of employment each of these motivations pursue. I am not saying all people who do the kind of work mentioned are that type of person; I am saying that a person with that motivation likes to do that type of work.

I want to warn you, however, that this is very personal information; therefore, if you recognize someone who might have any of these traits, do not tell them. In most cases they will be offended, and that is not what we want to accomplish with this study. This study is to give you a better understanding of people so that you can relate to them, based upon their frame of reference.

We will look at five motivations; four are fear-based motivations, each having a different degree of intensity, and the fifth is a love-motivation. As we move through these you will recognize that everyone, including you and me, have all five of these motivations. Our behavior day to day is based on having a high, medium and low motivation. The final two motivations manifest themselves in certain situations, but most of the time our top three will determine our actions and reactions, our wants, needs and desires, as well as our values.

The Fatalist

This individual is motivated by the fear of failure. The fear of failure is a fear of making a mistake which, in turn, causes fear of responsibility. There are five indications to help you understand the fatalist motivation and the effect it has on a person.

Fear of failure

This fear will cause a person to stay on a job until placed in a position of responsibility. When the boss gives more authority to the fatalists they usually get sick and quit the job, or they will use old excuses, such as a bad back or an old football injury, to get them out of that position of responsibility.

A personnel interviewer for a corporation shared this story with me. He hired a young man for a position beginning the following Monday. When Monday came around, the boy did not show up for work. Tuesday and Wednesday he still did not come to work. Finally, on Thursday he arrived promptly at 8:00 a.m. Of course the manager asked him where he had been. He replied, "I got into my car on Monday morning, and the engine sounded bad, so I thought I might as well overhaul the engine before I get started on a new job." He did not try to ride the bus to work, or even bother to call in. He just stayed home and overhauled his engine. He felt no responsibility because this fear will cause a person not to assume responsibility. It is as if they cannot even conceive what responsibility is, because of their deep and intense fear of failure.

Futile

Fatalists think, "Why try? I'm going to fail anyway." They feel trying is a waste of effort. You may be thinking that this sounds like your teenager! Parents everywhere want to know how to motivate their teenagers. It is very simple. Begin telling them how great they are, rather than pointing out the number of mistakes they make, and they will start stretching to meet your expectations. If you begin building their self-value, they will not be afraid of failure. Realize that a fatalist has developed this fear over a period of years by trying and failing, and being put down because of that failure. So, why try anymore? Any time people say, "Why bother, I'll just fail anyway," they are being controlled by the fatalistic-motivation.

Faulty

It is the fatalist's belief that everything he or she tries turns sour. Everything they touch turns to mud while everything that "other people" touch turns to gold. Individuals who believe this, will unconsciously make sure it happens. They will break and destroy things just because they believe they are accident prone. They think, "I'm the kind of person who just can't quite cut it," and they tend to prove it so in most areas of their lives.

Feeble

The fatalist-motivation will cause a person to suffer from various sicknesses. According to the American Medical Association, a high percentage of all sickness today is psychosomatic. The fatalist would say, "If I'm sick, you cannot put responsibility on me! You can't blame me...I had a headache." Understand this person did not say, "If I pretend to have a headache, I can get out of this." They really do have a headache and they can take an aspirin and get rid of it. The fatalist can create a physical problem, unconsciously, because that is a relief of responsibility.

Fabricate

This motivation causes people to develop a tremendous ability to create a "story" to get rid of a position of responsibility. You will actually believe their story because it is so believable. You will probably say, "I guess you're right."

The fear of failure causes people to run from responsibility; therefore, they are very difficult to deal with in sales. They stand you up on appointments, and their credit is usually bad, because they have difficulty in holding a job. The type of occupation that most appeals to fatalists is non-creative work. They want something that is routine, such as production-line work. They don't mind working hard, but they do not want to be expected to assume too much responsibility.

We can't put people down who have this fear, because it is common to all of us. In any given situation, the fear of failure can manifest itself, and we will feel the effects. For instance, if you are asked to make a presentation before a large group of peers and you are not a public speaker, this fear will attack you. "What if I blow it, or make a fool of myself," is a fear of failure. So, we all have experienced this fear at times in our lives. We either conquered the fear or it conquered us. It becomes a big problem when it is the dominating motivation in our life, because it carries a negative effect on every decision.

If you find yourself in a situation where this fear is controlling your thinking, use your seed list, and quickly conquer those fears. If you do not, that fear may show its ugly head when it is decision-making time in a sales situation. To be able to relate to an individual with a fatalistic motivation, you must take full responsibility for the decision, be the doctor of sales, and tell them why they are making a wise buying decision. You must reassure them that you are there to take care of their wants, needs and desires. This fear creates a need to be taken care of, and you, the doctor of sales, must fill that need. (In the next chapter we will take more time working through each of the motivations and their needs).

The Exasperator

The next motivation, which has a lesser intensity of fear, is the exasperator. The exasperators are exactly as it sounds — exasperating! It is a fear motivation that causes people to argue with you about anything and everything. If you say it is a beautiful day, the exasperator will say the opposite. It is interesting how while you are talking to them, someone else comes along and remarks about it being a lousy day and the exasperator will make a 360 degree turn and proclaim what a lovely day it is. Why do exasperators argue so much? Their fear is loss of position or strength. Probably their greatest fear is that someone will overshadow or overpower them, and so they are always prepared to stand their ground. Exasperators, because of their fear, tend to over-correct and are generally very physically-oriented. They are so physical that they must overpower everybody in their work. You see, with an exasperator, you are not their friend, you are Their Friend! They own you!

Enmity

Enmity is a feeling of upheaval and unrest that is created everywhere exasperators go. We cannot be around exasperators very long and maintain peace of mind. They will make sure of that. They will try to upset your best day. I am not saying that exasperators can get under your skin and upset you, but they can test your patience a lot! If you understand their motivations and that they are naturally argumentative, not just to create enmity, but to reassure themselves of their position, then you will not let their behavior bother you. Just accept them as exasperators and that is just the way they are.

I have a very good friend who is an exasperator. He argues with me about everything and anything. He is the kind of guy who, when you go out to lunch with him, everyone in the room knows you are there. When the waitress or waiter asks for your order, he says, "No need to ask him what he wants, he doesn't know!" Everyone looks at the idiot (me) who does not know what he wants to eat. Of course he speaks so loudly that everyone in the restaurant hears him. When the waitress or waiter comes with the tab, he is the one who always says, "No need giving him the check, he's too cheap to buy. I'll take it!" Everyone turns and looks at the cheapskate (me). I refuse to argue with anybody, so I just let him buy my lunch!!

One day I was mowing my lawn when my neighbor walked over with his two children, all of them in their swimming suits, heading toward our pool. Because exasperators are physically-oriented people, they tend to reward you with physical things. If you do something nice for them, they will give you something or do something for you. I had previously told him that he could swim in the pool anytime.

So, now he sees me mowing the lawn and says, "Mind if we swim in your pool?" I said I did not mind at all. And then he added, " If you let my kids swim in the pool, I'll mow the lawn for you." I responded, "You go swim with your kids and I will mow the lawn. (There was about an acre of grass, which is a lot to mow.) Once again he insisted that he mow the lawn, and once again I told him that I would do it. Finally, he said, "Get out of the way and let a man mow the lawn!" Being "Mr. Nice Guy," I let him mow the lawn and I went swimming with his children. There is no point in arguing, exasperators always win. In relating to exasperators, you have to realize that you can either let them win, or argue with them, and even then they will win the argument, in their mind.

Enslave

This same man telephoned me one day and the first thing he said was, "Who've you been talking to, anyway?" I replied that I was talking to a friend, and he said, "A friend? I thought I was your friend." So, I responded, "Well, you are my best friend; that was just an acquaintance."

Exasperators own you. These are the clients or customers who believe you should cancel other appointments in order to give them your time.

Energetic

Because people with this motivation are physically-oriented, they like to do physical things, and they tend to have great energy. They are normally athletic and they like to do physical work, such as construction. Can you see an exasperator barreling down the highway in his big "eighteen wheeler?" He comes upon a Volkswagen doing about 55 miles and hour and he is doing 70! He doesn't just go around the Volkswagen; he comes roaring up behind the car and honks his horn. Of course the little Volkswagen "bug" pulls over and the exasperator goes flying by. Can you see the power of making Volkswagens get out of your way?

Or how about this one: The "earth mover." The earth mover is a piece of equipment that is used in highway construction. You are cruising down the highway when suddenly you see a person holding a stop sign. This person is not too big, but will make you stop just where they want you to be. They are semi-exasperators. All of a sudden, you understand why you were stopped where you were. There is a big piece of equipment coming out of the hillside, and it is aimed right at you! Then just before it hits you, you duck and it goes roaring by. The guy driving the earth mover has arms like "Popeye." Can you see the power of making people duck? A man in Kansas City told me he drives one of those rigs...a big man, about six-foot-four. He said, "They really do aim at cars. In fact, they keep a tally of how many people they can make duck in one day. The guy who gets the most tallies in one days gets free beer from all the other crew members.

Another profession exasperators enjoy is being a "policeman" with the badge of authority and the pistol of power! A couple years back I was caught in a radar trap for traveling 15 miles above the speed limit. I pulled over and watched in my rear-view mirror as the policeman got out of his car. It seemed he just kept getting up. He was six-foot-five, wearing a helmet and chin strap, and his pants were tucked into his boots. He walked like John Wayne, and you could hear the kettle drums, boom, boom — boom, boom, as he walked towards me. He came up to my window and flipped open his ticket book, which is covered with metal so it does not get soggy in the rain. If I had a running board, I just know he would have put his foot on it! He looked down at me, and with a high, squeaky, falsetto voice, said, "Let me see your license." I sat in that car and nearly died for the next thirty minutes. I bit my cheek and my tongue — and anything else I could find — just so I would not crack a smile. I knew if I did, I would be in jail for at least thirty days.

How about the criminal lawyer who does not care whether his client is innocent or guilty, just as long as he wins the fight. Or the hard sell salesman who could sell "snowballs to the Eskimos." Incidentally, exasperators are known for their one-liners, and they do a lot of funny stuff, usually off the top of their head. You wonder if they stay up all night thinking of funny things to say.

Enforce

Exasperators never ask you to do something, they order you. That is why they make great "First Sergeants." For you who are, or have been in the military, you know the kind of person to whom I am referring. They never ask you to do anything; it is always an "order."

Enrage

Do not get exasperators mad at you, because I guarantee they will poke you in the nose for a little while. They will even resort to physical pressure if they are pushed. Their fear is loss of position and strength, and the only way you can relate to exasperators is to let them win or give them recognition for their position or strength. They will start the argument and you must let them win.

When I was 16, I got an infection in my foot, and I went to the local family doctor to get a penicillin shot. Unbeknownst to me, the local family doctor does not give those shots — the local family nurse does that job, and this particular nurse was an exasperator. She came into the room, and her bedside manner left much to be desired. As she walked into the room she said, "All right, drop your pants!" Now, that is not a nice thing to say to a guy, first thing. She could have said, "Hi, how are you today? Would you please drop your pants?" or something to that effect. When I was sixteen, I was a little bit of a "smart aleck," so when she told me to drop my pants, the only thing I could think to say to her was, "I will, if you will." I want you to know that was a bad thing to say to an exasperator nurse. She said, "You drop your pants or I'll shoot you right through," and I want you to know that when she hit me with her needle, I could feel it clear up into my shoulder. Do not get an exasperator nurse mad at you because they will get even — like missing the vein several times when taking blood, etc.

The exasperator's fear is so intense that if you do not allow them to establish their position or give them recognition for that position, they will argue with you all day, and they will not buy from you, just to prove that they are better than you. They need to know their position is established. Again, there are two ways you can do this: one is to let them win the argument, or you can give them recognition for their power or position. A statement like, "you mean you are in charge of this entire department?" carries a lot of recognition and will let exasperators know that you recognize their power or position. Exasperators buy, they spend money, they work hard, and they are very trustworthy people. They are the kind of people who give you lots of referrals. But you must establish a relationship, and you do that by recognizing and satisfying their needs so that their fears are gone.

After my friend has beaten me in an argument, we will get along great the remainder of the day. He is fun to be with, very skilled, and tremendous with his hands. But, most people do not like him because he is always arguing, or putting people down to make himself look big. He is conceited! I really know, however, that he is just fearful that people will not recognize his position.

If you can understand people's motivations, you can relate to their needs, and when you can do that, you have established a relationship. Then all the things I have covered in this book will fall into position.

The Appraiser

The appraiser's fear is "ambiguity" or a "non-structured environment." The appraiser needs to have a road map, things laid out and planned, or a good sense of predictability. If it is not exactly as it should be, it causes intense fear, and so the tendency is to look for facts, figures and details. We call appraisers perfectionists, because they are detail-oriented and demand perfection of everyone, including themselves. They are very easy to recognize because if you were to say, "Isn't it a lovely day? It must be 70 degrees." They would respond, "It's 71 degrees." They will always correct you a little bit and this drives some people crazy. You need to understand that appraisers are not correcting you to put you down (like the exasperator), but rather to help you, because they believe if you are going to say something, you might as well be right. In fact, number one on the list describing the appraiser is "absolute."

Absolute

Appraisers are most comfortable if they can deal in absolutes, which cause them to be very conservative people. People with this motivation will not enjoy work that requires "people" skills. They are not comfortable with the responsibility of solving people problems, or relating to customers or clients. They tend not to be people-oriented. In fact, they have a little difficulty separating people and things.

If people expect others to be perfect, they will be disappointed. In dealing with mathematics, $2 + 2 = 4$, but in dealing with people problems, $2 + 2$ sometimes $= 3 \, 1/2$, and sometimes $4 \, 1/2$. You need to be flexible when dealing with people, and appraisers sometimes have difficulty doing that.

The appraiser says, "Just give me an office back in the corner where no one will notice me and I will be happy." As a salesperson you need to understand how to relate to this motivation. If you talk in generalities, as salespeople tend to do, you will drive an appraiser right "up a tree." They do not want to hear approximately, in the neighborhood of, or right around. They want absolutes.

Accurate

The reason appraisers always correct you is because they are helping you to be accurate. Incidentally, never argue with appraisers because they are usually right. They will not argue unless they have all the facts and details, and so they are sure before they make an argument. They do the necessary study and research to make sure they are correct. So, when an appraiser says, "Well, actually it is..." just respond by saying, "Well, I did not know that. I appreciate your help."

Accountable

When you give appraisers a job, and ask them to keep a running diary of what they do, they will write a book, detail upon detail and page upon page, because they love reports. For you who are in government, and especially the Federal government, you will realize a high percentage of the career people have this motivation. It is a great place for appraisers to work because there is a lot of paperwork and forms to be filled out. I once saw an expense account of an appraiser, and one of the entries in the account was $.10, and beside the number were the words "pay toilet." If you are going to keep track of your expenses, you keep track of all of your expenses. You will not let a little thing like that go by.

Anti-Social

Appraisers tend to stay away from crowds and crowded places, especially social gatherings. In social situations, people talk about nonsense things or make "small talk." To appraisers this is a waste of time. They would rather spend the evening locked in a room by themselves, creating something on their computers. To them the computer will always find the correct answer to problems.

Actually

Actually is a good word, especially when you are talking to appraisers. If you want to get their full attention, this word will do it. Remember from an earlier chapter on body language that when people move forward in their seat, it means they are curious and their mind is open. Well, when you say to an appraiser, "Actually...," they will move forward. If there was ever a word in the dictionary that will open their mind, it is "actually," because now you are getting "past the fat and down to the bone."

Appraisers enjoy work that demands perfection, such as accounting, research science, mathematics, architecture and engineering. All of these fields have great appeal to people with this motivation. I am not saying everyone who does detailed work has appraiser as their highest motivation, but they enjoy detail type work. Do not generalize with appraisers. Be specific, and if you do not have all the details, you must tell them you will get back to them with the details they need to make a wise buying decision. And, be sure you do!

Relater

You will be able to relate to the relater because a high percentage of salespeople have this motivation as their high motivation. The relaters are the "people-oriented" salespeople. They love people in general. They buy things, say things, and wear things, based upon what people are going to think about those things.

Ridicule

Ridicule is the relater's greatest fear. Because they are so people- oriented, people become their god, and they have to please everyone. Therefore, they buy clothes, wear certain hairstyles, say things, and join clubs to get acceptance and recognition by the important people in their world. They want everyone to like them, even people they are not fond of, or might even dislike.

Respect

Relaters will do things to gain your respect based upon their performance rather than their personage. If you do not freely give them that respect or recognition, they will ask you, " How am I doing?" four or five times a day. What they really are saying is, "Will you please give me a little recognition for what I have done?" When you are dealing with a relater in a sales situation, you need to tell them how much you like their possessions, such as their automobile, their suit, their home, or the way they have decorated their residence. All these things are important to relaters. They work hard in order to give you many reasons for a compliment. They just stroll along and smile at everybody and see everything that is happening everywhere. The most important thing in the world to relaters is other people's opinions of them. You cannot walk past a relater without being seen, whereas an appraiser might not see you at all; and, of course, an exasperator will "run over you."

Receive

This motivation causes people to live by the law of fair exchange, "giving to receive." They not only give things, although they like to give things, but they also do nice things for people. They never forget a birthday or anniversary, and expect you to say, "Oh, you shouldn't have." If relaters give you a gift and your only response is, "Thank you," they will add, "Oh, you don't like it very much do you?" Did I buy the wrong size or color? What is wrong with it? Do you know why they are so upset? It is merely because you only said, "Thank you." In their mind you should have said, "Oh, you shouldn't have!" In fact, if you know they spent a lot of money on the gift, you should say, "You paid too much!" If they bought you something really special and you did not say all those things, they may take it back!!

Responsible

Relaters want to have some responsibility. They do not want to be the "top person" on the organizational chart, but they like to be second or third in command. A great position in a local civic or social association for the relater is "Program Chairman," (not President). As Program Chairman, everyone knows them, and they can introduce the program. As president, they would be responsible for the entire activity, which carries too much responsibility. If they were president and something went awry, they would look bad to their club members and peers.

In speaking to numerous service organizations across the country, I often find program chairmen who are relaters. I always recognize their fear because all through lunch they ask questions about my presentation. They want to know if I have spoken to a service club previously, and if so, was I well received. Sometimes I give them a little scare and tell them that the last group booed me a bit, but it wasn't too bad! That is definitely not what they wanted to hear, so they introduce me with great fear and trepidation.

As I speak, I throw in some humor and make my presentation as entertaining as I can. Normally, after the program, people tell the program chairmen how much they enjoyed the program and, as I am leaving, the chairmen are all smiles because I came through for them. Relater chairmen are afraid people will not like the program and that would be a reflection on them, which, in their minds, would be rejection because of poor performance.

Reactionary

This fear-motivation causes people to live in a reactionary state. Everything they do is based upon how other people will accept or reject their performance.

They do things because of our response to the things they do. If relaters think we will like something, they will say or do that which they think we would like. When we do not like it, it "blows them away."

The relater wants us to respond positively to everything they do. It is important to them because when we respond to them as they expect, it is always favorable, and that is pure acceptance of their performance.

Can you see how relaters might have a problem with the exasperator who is always looking for something to argue about or an appraiser who is always correcting the things they do and say? Relaters tend to avoid these types of people, especially the first thing in the morning. Relaters need to get a good start with some acceptance. Exasperators also need to establish their position the first thing in the morning, so when you put the two together, they both lose. Relaters like to do people-oriented work, such as teaching, nursing, ministry, counselors and sales. In fact, I would say probably 80% of salespeople have relater as their high motivation.

Love Motivation

The love-motivated person is one who has recognized and conquered the four fears — fear of rejection, fear of ambiguity, fear of loss of position, and fear of failure.

They must recognize these fears each time they arise and conquer them before they create problems in their life. They replace the four fears with five loves:

Love of Self.   *They know who they are and have a good inward relationship.*

Love of Authority.   *They have good upward relationships. When you have love-motivated employees, you smile a lot! Working with a love-motivated customer makes selling "fun work."*

Love of Family.   *Love-motivated people think of employees and prospects as family, as opposed to being just employees and prospects. They love their area of responsibility and have good downward relationships.*

Love of People.   *Love-motivated people love people in general. They have great outward relationships. When you meet them, you feel as if you have known them for a lifetime, because they are warm and friendly, easy to get to know, and cause you to relax in their presence.*

Love of Productivity. *A love-motivated person works when no one is watching. They do the little things everyone else fails to do, such as reading a little more, studying a little harder, or making a few more telephone calls. When we do all of these things, we are more productive.*

They are more friendly than the "relater," but never get upset when people dislike them. They believe, "If people don't like them, they must have a problem."

The love-motivated person is more of a perfectionist than an "appraiser," but knows the difference between things and people. They are flexible with people and perfectionists with things. They are more dynamic, enthusiastic and motivated than the "exasperator," but they lead rather than push. And, they are more relaxed than the "fatalist" but never run from responsibility; in fact they assume responsibility whenever necessary.

Everyone has all five of these motivations, but there usually will be one that dominates, and a second and third that greatly influence their thinking and decision making. If you are able to determine your prospect's number one motivation in the first five minutes of the sales interview, you will then be able to relate your presentation to their wants, needs, and desires. As you get to know your customers, their second and third motivations also will be revealed to you, which will give you knowledge of how to build high value in your product or service.

The following are five questions you can use in your first five minutes that will help you better understand your prospect's high motivation. These are not technical questions; and they are not related to just one product or service. They are general and can be used in any situation. The answers are a sampling of those I have received over the years in response to these questions, as relates to each of the five motivations.

"Isn't it a lovely day?"

Fatalist:	*"Well, I don't know. The weather is the weather; I guess it is OK." (Very non-committal)*
Exasperator:	*"It is a lousy day." (They will argue about anything.)*
Appraiser:	*"Yes, it is a lovely day, 72 degrees, 10% chance of rain." (Exact)*
Relater:	*"It is a fantastic day to play a little tennis." (Always relate the question to doing something with people)*
Love-Motivated:	*The love-motivated person listens to the question, and is the only one who really answers it. Fear-motivated people relate the question to the weather, whereas the love-motivated person says, "It is a fantastic day! What does the weather have to do with it?" The question was not, "Isn't the weather nice?" The question was regarding the "day" itself.*

"What is your occupation?"

Fatalist:	*Enjoys non-creative work, such as working on a production line, which carries little or no responsibility.*
Exasperator:	*Enjoys physical work, where they can flex their muscles.*
Appraiser:	*Enjoys working with facts and figures — detail work.*
Relater:	*Always enjoys people-related work. It does not matter what the job is, as long as it is working with people.*
Love-Motivated:	*They like any of the above; however, they tend to become a leader in whatever field they choose because "cream always rises to the top."*

"How do you like your work?"

Fatalist: *"Work is work! If you don't work, you don't eat."*

Exasperator: *"It's tough; perspiration runs off me like sweat."*

Appraiser: *"Well, it's a fine job. Two weeks vacation, retirement benefits, a great medical plan."(They tend to tell you all the details surrounding the work and not the work itself)*

Relater: *"Oh, they're fantastic people to work with!" or "The work is OK but the people are hard to work with." (They never work for anyone, or have anyone work for them. They always work "with.")*

Love-motivated: *"Work?" What do you mean, work? This is my life!" (They do the kind of work they want to do, regardless of pay, benefits, or what other people might think)*

"Tell me about your children"

When people talk about their children, they are really telling us everything we need to know about them. If I were to ask you about your children, and then ask your spouse and the children's school teachers the same question, all of you would give me a different response. You would not be telling me about your children at all, but rather, you would be telling me how you relate to your children.

Fatalist: *"Kids are kids; another mouth to feed."*

Exasperator: *One man replied, "My son plays 'first-string' football." Another response was: "My kid is the 100-yard dash, 220, and relay champion of the state!" I said, "Wow, he sounds terrific. Is he going on to college?" The man replied, "What you do you mean, he; it is a her!" I was talking to his wife just a little later and she said, "My daughter has the lead in the school play, sings in the a cappela choir, and is the class vice president. (The father had exasperator motivations which caused the "sports or athletic" abilities to shine. As a relater, the mother related to her social achievements.)*

Appraiser: *"We have fine children; 3.0 grade point average." (They tend to tell you how intelligent they are.)*

Relater: *"I have fantastic kids. My son is the president of the student body at the pre-school," or "My child is the most popular student in the school."*

Love-motivated: *"My children are the greatest." (They do not qualify the statement.)*

"How would you describe your father?"

I have found that asking about "mothers" does not work in this situation. We revere apple pie, the "flag," and mothers in our society. We just do not say bad things about "mom." However, we have license to say anything about "dad!"

Fatalist: *"That old drunk? He never did a day's work in his life."*

Exasperator: *"My dad was a man's man. He was tough; chewed nails and spit rust!"*

Appraiser: *"I had a fine father who provided well for us, put us through school and bought us the National Geographic Magazine."* I thought this answer was a classic. If, when asked to describe your father the first thing that jumps into your mind is that he bought you the National Geographic Magazine, you must be an appraiser.

Relater: *"Dad and I were like two peas in a pod; we were buddies."Or on the reverse side, "Dad was a great man, but he was never very close to us kids."*

202

Love-Motivated: *"Dad was a great man in his own way, although most people never really knew him." The man might have been an alcoholic who beat his kids three times a day, but love-motivated people focus on the good side of people.*

When you are relating to people, whether it be your boss, prospects, or other sales agents, if you can understand their motivations, you can understand their needs. In the next few chapters, we will look at prospect's needs as well as the needs of salespeople. That will help you put all of this into focus. When you meet people, you not only study and evaluate them, you accept them for who they are. **If you will listen to what they say, and more importantly, hear why they are saying it, they will tell you their motivations.** With that information you can direct your presentation to their needs.

When you make your presentations based upon needs, you are the "doctor of sales," and that is success. You will enjoy higher closing ratios, as well as repeat and referral business, because you are playing the role of the doctor.

CHAPTER 18

THE PROSPECT'S NEEDS

☞ *Needs of the Fatalist*
☞ *Needs of the Exasperator*
☞ *Needs of the Appraiser*
☞ *Needs of the Relater*

We have spent a great deal of time covering wants and needs. In this chapter, we will take another look at the five motivations as they relate to prospects or clients, based upon their needs. Remember, if you can understand your prospect's values, you can create value in your product or service as it relates to their value system. Values create wants, needs and desires, so as you satisfy your prospect's values you will also be satisfying their wants, needs, and desires.

There is a difference between wants and needs; wants are physical and needs are psychological. A want might be a four-bedroom home, and a need might be a four-bedroom home, next to a doctor's house. That would add a little prestige and satisfy the needs of a relater who places a high value on what people think. Or, a want might be a four-bedroom home and a need might be a four-bedroom home that is well-built and will last through World War III. Exasperators have a need for something that has strength because they place a high value on establishing their position.

205

A man was having his annual interview to determine whether his performance merited a raise in pay. He was, indeed, offered a sizable raise; however, his response was interesting. He asked if in lieu of his raise he could drive one of the company vans home each evening.

This, of course, was a great deal for the company. That particular van was on the back parking lot, subject to vandalism by the neighborhood children, including broken windows, air being let out of tires, etc. This would allow them to have more company name recognition in the community, as well as someone taking care of the van by keeping it safe, clean and serviced. And, they saved the money which would have gone to the raise in pay.

We would say this man wanted a van, but he needed a van with the company name inscribed on the side; then as he drives down the streets of his neighborhood everyone recognizes that he is a company man. When he parks the van in his driveway, people say, "He must be a VIP. He drives a company van!" He wanted the truck but he needed the recognition. His raise was more than enough to cover payments on his own new truck. He rationalized the fact that his raise could purchase his own new van by saying, "Well, I would have insurance and upkeep; I would have to sell it when it is old; and trade-ins are always lower than the value of the vehicle." He had lots of reasons, but the fact is he needed the recognition.

If you can understand needs, you can base your presentation on those needs, which are the "hot buttons" in sales. Needs are what turns customers on most about your product. Can you now understand why it is so important to get to know your prospects and customers in the first five minutes? When you can determine motivations, you can then know your prospect's needs.

Needs of the Fatalist

The fatalist is, as you already know, is a person who has a "fear of failure," and as a result, fatalists tend to run from responsibility. If I have a fear of failure, what would I be looking for in our sales relationship? I need someone who will take responsibility for me and take care of me so I can feel secure. Fatalists need security. If you say, "Don't worry, I'm going to take care of the entire thing," they will know they have come to the right place. Understand that fatalists do make money. There are fatalists who work hard every day of the week. They do not have a lot of responsibility, but they make good money and they buy from someone.

If you can understand and relate to their needs, they will buy from you. As I mentioned, if the product or service you are selling is too expensive, you might have a bit of a problem with them because normally they are not in the higher income bracket. When you are the doctor of sales, you simply assure them that you will take care of all the details.

Does this put responsibility on your shoulders? You had better believe it; you will work harder for a fatalist than for any of the other motivations, because you have to do everything. If you give them something to do, it will not get done. I had some people at an employment service tell me that when people with this fear motivation come in for employment and they are sent out for an interview, often they will fail to show up at the interview. Their fears are so great that they do not believe they will get the job anyway, so why waste time going on an interview.

If fatalists are working in a job without a lot of heavy responsibilities, they will be very secure in that position and stay on the job for years. I have met people who have worked at the same position on a production line their entire adult life, without a promotion. A promotion would mean more responsibility and they do not want that. They are secure; they know that if they will come to work eight hours a day, five days a week, they will get their paycheck, including cost-of-living raises each year.

One of the mistakes corporations make is that they promote some people too quickly, especially if those individuals have a fear of failure. One of the major causes of turnover in personnel is a result of individuals being put in a position of authority who have too many fears to handle the responsibilities of the job.

The following illustration gives a good picture of relating to a fatalist in a sales interview, after the salesperson had recognized that his prospect was fatalistic.

Ron, a real estate agent, has just met Paul Jacobs, a potential customer who was ushered into his office by the receptionist. Following the initial greeting, Ron said, "Pull up a chair and get comfortable, sir. What are you looking for in a home?"

Paul, looking toward the floor, responded, "Oh, I'm not sure. Something I can afford, I guess." Are you married? Ron asked? Paul responded that he was in one word. Ron continued with, "Do you have any children, Paul?" "Yes," he replied; "I've got five." "Could you tell me a little bit about them?," Ron asked. Again Paul gave a vague answer, "What do you mean?" Ron replied, "Well, ages, boys or girls, etc."

Without looking up Paul said, "Three boys — 5, 9, and 12, and two girls — 3 and 7." Ron continued, "Sounds like a nice family to me." "Yeah, they're all right" Paul answered.

Ron continued pulling information from Paul, "Where are you working, Paul?" He said, "I work for the Peters Construction Company now. I was building boats for Elmer's. I was there a year and then they let me go. Off season, you know. No one buys boats in the winter. This job I've got — it's OK, but I'm out in the cold a lot, and my shoulder bothers me." Ron asked Paul if he was buying his present residence? "No, I'm renting, but I have to move. The landlord says I have too many kids for a two-bedroom apartment. He never did like us. He had to think of a way to get rid of us."

Are you picking up any fatalistic traits thus far?

"Are you looking for something to buy?" Ron asked. "If I can afford it, I am. I have no downpayment, but I understand that the government has some types of loans I might get." "Well, there are some loans available," Ron added, "Let me ask you a few questions and see if you qualify for some government assistance."

During this entire interview Paul never looked Ron in the eye. Fatalists very seldom make eye-contact, because they might see rejection in the other person's eyes. They already feel bad enough and do not need anything to make them feel worse. Paul also is non-committal; he avoids solid answers. Fatalists do not want to commit themselves because with commitment comes responsibility. In the first five minutes Ron was able to recognize Paul as a fatalist and started looking into the possibility of some type of secure government-backed loan. It was probably the only type of financing for which Paul would qualify; however, if he should qualify, Ron has a sale and has been productive. Ron recognized Paul's needs, and was able to do a good job for him.

There are ways to help the Paul's of the world, and there is great satisfaction when you are able to make it happen. If you are a love- motivated salesperson, you give without expecting anything in return. You give service and you do the best you can for the prospects who walk through the door because they happen to be alive and breathing air. You do not prejudge them or feel you are wasting your time on a loser. And you make sure they are a qualified prospect, which, in this case, Paul was. If on the other hand they are not, you  simply tell them you do not think you can help them. That also is doing a good job for the prospect. But if you can help them, you take all the responsibility for the fatalists, and as you do that, they feel comfortable with you.

If we had pursued this a little further, Paul would have eventually made eye-contact with Ron. After he felt secure with Ron and knew he was being taken care of, he would start looking directly at Ron. You will find that people can go from fear to love-motivation, if you give of yourself to them, because your love dispels their fears.

In fact, over a period of time you can literally lift customers to the point where they become love-motivated—when they are in your presence. That does not mean they are love-motivated people all the time, but when they are with you, they ride on your love-motivation, which, incidentally, is why you are really successful as a salesperson.

Needs of the Exasperator

Some salespeople will say, "Who cares?" Very few salespeople enjoy working with exasperators. Exasperators are usually hard-working individuals. They are the kind of people who do what they say they will do, even if they have to knock the world over in the process. They are great to have on your team, and are very good customers and clients. If you establish a relationship with them and they are loyal to you, they will give you repeat and referral business.

I would estimate that nearly one-third of our population fits into this motivation, so we need to know how to successfully relate to exasperators. Have you ever heard someone say, "That is not my kind of customer?" What those salespeople were really saying was that they do not know how to relate to a type of person's needs. When needs are satisfied, and fears are conquered, they then become love-motivated people. If you do not want to hang around exasperators, satisfy their needs, and they will no longer be exasperators.

The exasperator's need is for position; they must know that you recognize their position. They will make sure you do, either by winning an argument or receiving the recognition they need. This is not that difficult to do because exasperators do a lot of things with their hands. They build fireplaces, patios, garages, and occasionally, their homes. They are also proud of what they have done. It does not matter what you are selling. If you walk into the home of an exasperator who has built his own fireplace and give him recognition for his work, he will listen more closely to what you are selling.

Some years back I was District Manager for a Life Insurance Company. We know, in the insurance business, the most difficult people to sell to are the exasperators. First of all, exasperators know they will never die; and secondly, if they should die, they do not want to leave all their money to their wife's next husband! That would be the same as losing the last argument.

I had an appointment with a couple one night, and it did not take me long to discover that this man was an exasperator. He was a truck driver who drove the "big rigs." He was tough! He had his sleeves rolled up showing a tattoo on his arm, he talked tough, and everything in his life pointed to his physical strength. In my first five minutes I said to him, "You mean you drive one of those big trucks? I don't think I would last two hours behind the wheel of one of those huge things!" That was recognition of his position. He said, "Sure you can. There's nothing to it." When he said there was nothing to it, and I had just indicated I could not handle the job for two hours, he knew I was a weakling and he was strong. If he had said, "I'm sure you could do it," that would have made me his equal. He did not believe that. By letting me stay as the weak person, he had established his position and I could begin my presentation.

As I was about to close the sale I said, "Now, this insured savings program is going to help you in several ways." At this point his wife spoke up and said, "Well, we just don't believe in life insurance." The husband interrupted her and said, "Aw, be quiet, and let the guy do the talking." The exasperator was "on my team," and when he told his wife to let me do the talking, I shut up and began writing, because it knew it was time to close the sale.

This man did not buy an insurance policy from me because I gave him recognition for his strength. He bought the program because for the first time, ever, he heard a presentation of life insurance with a retirement benefit that would pay all of his money back, plus an income for life, and he planned on living a long time! He was able to hear what I was saying because his mind was open, and when his mind was open, I was able to conquer his fear. I am not saying you can "sell snowballs to the Eskimos." You still must build value, answer questions, and close the sale. However, knowing people's motivations will give you the opportunity to open their mind, and to make your presentation fit their needs. I talked to another life insurance agent who sold an insured savings program to an exasperator who framed and hung it over the fireplace, so that all of his friends would know how much he loved his family.

If you are in the real estate business you should ask exasperators questions that allow them to gain a position. "Are you a handyman?" or "Are you a person who can replace a few boards and hinges, spread a little paint and increase the value of hour home with your own efforts?" If you get positive answers you can then make statements such as, "With a little work, you can increase the value of this house by ten thousand dollars." Another good statement would be, "Well, it sounds like you know how to get a job done. I want to show you the basement of this house because with your skills, it would be very simple to turn it into a recreation room."

Male or female, exasperators love to get their hands involved in a project and they are creative enough to see possibilities as you point them out. Once their position is established, they will recognize your position and let you be the doctor of sales. Now you can do the driving, open the door of the house for them, etc., because you are in control of the exasperator. If you can understand the exasperator's needs, then you can relate your total presentation, from approach to the close, to the customer's values, and the only logical thing to do is "buy."

A woman I have known for many years once told her customer, an exasperator, to step into a shower. Then she asked him to bend over and pretend to pick up a bar

211

of soap. She asked if he bumped anything when he was bending over, and he replied, "No." "You see," she replied, "that shower was made for you." She told me that this couple signed the earnest money deposit sitting on the toilet! This motivation causes people to be physically-oriented, so you must be able to relate your presentation to satisfy their need for things within the home that covers this area of interest.

Another real estate agent told me of a client, also an exasperator, who was in competition "pistol shooting." The gentleman had remembered seeing a home on one of their tours that had a cellar, rather than a basement. The cellar had an unfinished, dirt floor. It was a musty, damp, eye-sore that made this house almost impossible to sell. The agent and the customer revisited the home, and while in the cellar he told the customer, "This house was built with you in mind. You can have a practice "pistol range" in your own basement. And again, the customer made an offer, and wrote a check for his earnest money deposit in that dirty old cellar. The same house had a garage, separate from the house, that leaned to one side, with 2 x 4's holding it up. Other agents had said prospects invariably would say that there was a serious problem with the garage whenever they showed this particular house. This agent took his customer into the garage and asked, "What would you do to straighten this garage if you were to buy this home?" When you understand an exasperator's motivational needs, you will choose the product or service that best fits, and make your presentation by focusing on the high value the exasperator places on proving physical skills and abilities. Exasperators enjoy fixing things, and if the value is increased in the process, that is even better.

It is important that you forget your "relater" motivations when you are working with an exasperator, such as thickness of the carpets, or the people living in the neighborhood. Basically, exasperators like a little elbow room and they want a house so strong that it will stand through World War III. Whatever your product or service, you must be able to relate to the exasperator's need for position and strength, if you are to build a high value in your product, and meet wants and needs.

Another real estate agent relayed his favorite "exasperator" story to me regarding a house he had showed in which farm animals, including chickens, had full run of the home. On the drive to the house, the agent told his prospects that the house was a mess! He said, "Even you, with all of your skills, would never be able to handle this house. However, I am showing it to you, just in case you might be able to see some potential." The agent degraded the house so much that the wife began to wonder why they were even going to look at the house, but her husband wanted to see it. When they arrived at the house, the owners had cleaned the house and put the animals outside, and it was not nearly as bad as they had been led to believe. The wife could even see some real possibilities. The agent said, "with a little work, you two could increase the value of this home by thousands of dollars." They agreed and bought the home. The agent told me that they went to work on the house — cleaning and painting — and it became quite a showplace.

No matter what your field of sales, always relate it to the physical world when you are working with an exasperator. They need a position, and that position must always be based on "physical" things. You need to prove to them that their position will be stronger as a result of the service or product that you are offering. In a multi-level marketing opportunity, assure them, "You are the boss." In insurance, you can say, "You might live forever (and I hope you do), and this money will never run out — you will not live to spend the last check."

Needs of the Appraiser

Appraisers fear ambiguity, which creates a need for details, facts and figures before they can purchase anything. This motivation will manifest itself more quickly than the other four.

A typical first-five-minute interview with an appraiser prospect follows a common pattern. It appears the person is saying, "My high motivation is appraiser." Some are such classic answers we might think they have already read this book or have attended one of my seminars.

Illustration:

Q.   *"Hasn't this been a lovely day?"*
A.   *"It sure has. It's 78 degrees out there with 42% humidity. That's extremely low for this time of the year, you know. I believe it is the lowest humidity for this date since 1978."*

Q.   *"Is this the first time you have been in to see us, or have you done business with our company previously?"*

A.   *"Back in 1987, one of your agents showed us three houses. We didn't buy, but we did look."*

Q.   *"You've lived in this area for quite a while?"*

A.   *"Next month it will be 23 years and 6 months. We have "actually" lived in two houses during that time."*

Q.   *"What is your line of work?"*

A.   *"I work for Webber, Shultz and Smithson. I'm a CPA there, serving fourteen clients."*

Q.   *"How long have you been with them?"*

A.   *"23-1/2 years. They bought me to this area originally."*

Q.   *"Do you have any children."*

A.   *"Oh, yes. We have three. There's Jerry Jr.; he's 18. Beverly Dawn is going to be 15 on August 12th, and Bobby is 11-1/2."*

Q.   *"Does your wife work?"*

A.   *"Well, she works at home, but occasionally she works part-time if we need her at the office."*

By now, the real estate agent knew all she needed to know to begin her sales process. She said, "It is really nice to get to know you, but now let's talk about real estate. I am sure we can find a home that fits your exact needs and at the price that fits your housing budget."

The appraiser needs details and that is why he gives details. Remember, we project outwardly what we need inwardly. If I need my position established as an exasperator, I will attempt to establish that position. If I need details as an appraiser, I am going to give details. In the first five minutes, it is quite easy to get a good response by simply asking general questions and knowing exactly what motivation is dominant in your prospect. Once you know the motivation, you are able to select the product or service that best fits the prospect's needs and values, and you are able to make your presentation so that it will relate to that particular prospect. You are then communicating to the prospect's needs and values, and when that is true, you have created a client, and you will enjoy repeat and referral business.

When the "doctor of sales" has told me what I want to hear, I will not go to anyone else. Probably no one else has even been able to understand and relate to me this way. I know I am being taken care of by the "doctor of sales."

Since the appraiser needs details, they like to measure things, read all the data and statistics, see diagrams, and hear words such as, actually, facts, bottom line, and calculate. If "calculate" does not fit into your presentation, find a way to slip it in some place, because appraisers love calculations. I have been told by real estate agents that appraisers will measure the most unusual things: thickness of carpets, size of window sills, etc. If you are in real estate and your prospect is an appraiser, bring your tape measure along for the prospect's use.

For those of you who sell intangibles, your company spends a lot of money on brochures, charts, diagrams and projections. The appraiser is the customer for whom those details were printed. Pull them out of your attaché case; the more you have the better it is. Relater salespeople do not like details, so they usually place the brochures, with all the charts and graphs in the bottom of their attaché case. Appraisers need that information. The appraiser will read everything in the packet, including "printed in the USA," because they love details. As the doctor of sales, if you have satisfied their need for details, they have no reason to "think about it," or "sleep on it." Appraisers are notorious for thinking about and sleeping on, things. The reason for this is that most salespeople talk in generalities. The appraiser gets back to the office, does a little work on the calculator, and determines exactly what the product will cost. The problem is, the salesperson is not there to close the sale. As the person in authority in the sale, you must recognize an appraiser, and present as much detail as possible. You may think they are bored, but they are not. In the process of giving them the details, appraisers feel comfortable and secure. They are completely at ease and are confident that a sales agent who knows what he or she is doing, is taking care of them, and telling them what is best for them.

Needs of the Relater

The relater motivation causes individuals to be people-oriented due to a need for recognition. Everything they do is usually motivated by needing a compliment. Whatever your product or service, if your prospect is a relater they need to believe that your product is the most popular of its kind on the market, and that everyone is buying it.

A life insurance agent told me that he had one specific policy that he said was "The most popular policy that I offer." In fact, that was his closing line, and most times it was very effective. He did not realize until he sat through my seminar that the people who responded positively to that closing statement were relaters. He had found that every time he used that line, a high percentage of prospects would buy from him. They wanted to do what everyone else was doing. It must be the "best" policy if "everyone" else was buying it, right?

The following will give you some answers received from relaters during the first five minutes (the first close). These answers will be warm, soft and "feely," with a lot of "fluff and stuff." Having fun is important to the relater, and being nice to be around or sharing all the good times, is a measurement of how much acceptance a person will receive from a relater.

> *Q.*   *"Isn't this a beautiful day?"*
> *A.*   *"Oh, I tell you, it is gorgeous. In my opinion, this is sun-bathing weather."*
>
> *Q.*   *"Well, it is just beginning. It's nice to know that we have a whole summer ahead of us, isn't it?"*
> *A.*   *"I love it; it has to be my "favorite" season."*
>
> *Q.*   *"Let me get to know you and your family a little bit so I can better understand your needs. Begin with your husband. What can you tell me about him?"*
> *A.*   *"Well, he is just a great guy. Everybody loves him. In fact, he's been promoted twice in the last year and a half. He's really moving up quickly."*

Q.   *"He sounds like quite a guy. Do you have children?"*

A.   *"Yeah, we have a little guy, Jeff, and he's four — the future president, I'm sure! Then, of course, there's the "belle of the ball," Patty; she's two."*

Q.   *"Well, I can certainly see you have a fine family. You need a home for your growing family. You also need something you can really be proud of; the type of house where you could have a housewarming party and show it off to your friends."*

A.   *"That sounds perfect. Can we see it today?"*

A housewarming party? Oh, yes. That idea really appeals to relaters. They buy houses for their friends' approval, you will remember. They must have the best doctor in town, shop at the best stores and join the most popular groups. That is the only way relaters can let everyone know how well they are doing, and they need acceptance from their friends and peers.

Did you notice how she talked about her children? — future president, and belle of the ball? After reading this book you will never again look at people the same as before. You will begin listening to what people are saying, and hearing, with a broader understanding, why they are saying it. People tell you everything you need to know about their values in their general conversation. Then you need only to satisfy their wants and needs.

When this real estate agent is showing this woman a home, she will probably say, "This is the room where you will entertain all your friends. Look at these carpets. Aren't they plush? You just feel like you're wading in them. This home was decorated by Stone's Interiors on Fifth Avenue. Mrs. Stone is one of the finest in the area. There is a lot more to see in this home. You will be excited about the huge family room and the lovely master bedroom. Every room is equally as nice as this and your friends will be as impressed as you are."

Relaters are people conscious and are quite concerned about membership in their social circle, club, or church. They especially care about the neighbor next door. If there is a physician, or the principal of the local high school living in the neighborhood, the relater will tell you. I am not sure why those two are so impressive, but relaters place them in high esteem. Also, if you can show them how they will be the envy of their friends, they will buy your product, regardless of the need or the cost.

Multi-level marketing is a great vehicle for relaters. Statements such as, "We're in the people business," or "we have social events, rallies and meetings," really excite relaters. They are joiners. Most relaters go to church to be a part of an organization, rather than to worship God. You have heard of the "boys night out," or the "girls shopping spree." These are groups of relater men or women, spending an evening acting like boys and girls.

Relaters love group activities because they come alive in a "group" situation. No matter what product or service you are offering, make sure that in your presentation their need for relationships can be fulfilled by purchasing your product or service. If you cannot satisfy this need, you will have great difficulty selling to relaters. They have so many friends, that you will see a great deal of referral business from a client with this motivation. On the other hand, they will also spread the negative word if they are not satisfied with your product or service.

It may appear as though I am putting people down, or focusing on their negatives. Not so! We are looking at fear motivations and the effect those fears can have on our customer's decisions. Everyone has the ability to be a love-motivated person, if only they will conquer their fears. Any person can become and achieve whatever they choose, if they also choose to make a "weed and seed" list. No one is locked into any one motivation; it is just a matter of which motivation we allow to control our thinking. If you can understand what motivation is controlling your prospect, you can recognize a person's needs and values, which will help you do a better job for each customer you meet.

Needs of the Love-Motivated Person

The love motivated person is motivated by a love of relationships and productivity. When we look at the "five loves" of the love-motivated person, we find that all of them are types of productivity. To recap, the first love is a love of self; you are more productive when you have accepted yourself.

The more we can recognize "who we are" within ourselves, the more productive we will be in our lives. And, the more recognition and love we can give to those who have authority over us, the more productive that relationship will be. The more love we give, the more effective we will be in relating to those over whom we have authority, and the more productive that relationship will be. The more love we express to people in general, the more productive we will be in our social life. Therefore, all of the loves are dimensions of productivity. The love-motivated person is productive in all areas of life.

If you were to choose the ideal customer — the one who walks through the doorway and immediately believes in you and has an open mind — you would have chosen a love-motivated person. The greatest problem, of course, is that we believe only five percent of our population allows this motivation to control their thinking. Therefore, it becomes necessary that you become a love-motivated person, recognize the four fear motivations, and satisfy the needs of each which ultimately will dispel your customer's fears and lift them to a love-motivation.

Responses to questions in your "first close" from the love-motivated person will be open and honest, and will give you all the information you need to do the best job possible for this customer. In this format, I have chosen to use real estate illustrations, because you can easily relate to them.

I have worked with sales organizations that sold "diamonds," and with sales organizations that sell "bull semen." However, no matter what the product or service being sold, the relationship between you and your customer is much the same. The following is a look at the first five minutes of a real estate presentation to a love-motivated person:

Q.	*"Isn't this a beautiful day?"*
A.	*"I'm having a great day, and I've been looking forward to meeting you. You were so kind and helpful on the telephone."*
Q.	*"Thank you. I want to get to know a little more about you before we talk property. Is that OK?"*
A.	*"That's fine."*

> *Q.*   *"I've found that I can do a better job for my customers if I have a little understanding of their background. How long have you lived in the area?"*
>
> *A.*   *"My husband and I moved here in 1992, and he started a business which became very successful. He passed away two years ago. Thank heavens he left me very well-off financially."*
>
> *Q.*   *"Why are you thinking about moving now?"*
>
> *A.*   *"Well, I've been living here all alone for two years, just kind of rattling around in this big house. My children and grandchildren visit me often, but they live in the area, and seldom stay overnight. So, you see, I really don't need this much house."*
>
> *Q.*   *"How much would you like to downsize? Have you considered the number of bedrooms you want, or do you have a price range established in your mind?"*
>
> *A.*   *"Price is no object, but I don't want a house that's so ostentatious that it's an open invitation to burglars. But I would like for it to be a home that is really nice, and comfortable."*

I am often asked whether people are ever that open with a salesperson, and the answer is "yes." When prospects have no fear motivations causing them to be closed and hesitant, they will tell you everything you need to know in order to be the "doctor of sales." The agent in this case had no challenge getting to know the client; she was totally open. She did not mind admitting she was well-to-do, and she did not cry when she spoke of her husband's passing.

A relater would have cried, however. They believe they are supposed to cry a lot in those situations. The exasperator might say, "The old man kicked the bucket," and the appraiser would possibly say, "For the past two years, three months and six hours, I have been alone in this world."

This customer talked about her husband dying and leaving her very comfortable, which was very positive, rather than her looking for sympathy. In fact, the agent could not offer sympathy because she had ended by saying that her husband had left her "well-off."

Let us continue a little more of the conversation between this agent and her customer, while viewing the property, which, incidentally, the woman purchased.

> **Agent:** *"The good thing about a townhouse is that you have the benefit of owning your own home, and yet you have the security of your neighbors close by."*
>
> **Customer:** *"I like that. And I think the upkeep would be much simpler for me."*
>
> **Agent:** *"I agree with you. Here's the master bedroom. You will notice the rooms are a nice size, but they're not so big that you'll rattle around in them."*
>
> **Customer:** *"Let me tell you something. I'm at a point in my life where I would like to have the freedom to travel, and not have to worry about my home, and I think you've found the answer for me."*
>
> **Agent:** *"Great. In this home, you will have room to entertain your family, and have a spare bedroom for your guests. You'll also have the comfort and luxury to which you are accustomed, but with the advantage of low maintenance and high security. I believe it is the best home I can show you, based upon your needs."*
>
> **Customer:** *"I'm convinced; let's do it!"*

This agent recognized the needs of the customer and then was able to point out everything that was of value to her customer. To an exasperator or an appraiser, none of those things would have been of value. But for a love-motivated person, in this particular situation, it was the most productive move the agent could suggest, and immediately the customer agreed and purchased the home.

Most likely you have seen yourself in all five of the motivations. That is normal; we all have a little of each. Your spouse however, will be able to tell you where you really are. At about age 35, one of the five motivations will become dominant, and the majority of our actions and reactions will be affected by that major motivation. Our second and third motivations will have a lesser impact on our values and the decisions we make daily. This does not mean that we are locked into one motivation and cannot change. The challenge is that we get comfortable with our self-image, and accept our fears as, "It's just the way I am." We call this maturity, or more appropriately, "a rut." We get into a rut that feels comfortable and it intensifies with age.

When we reach our fifties or sixties, the top three motivations are firmly in place and our behavior is highly predictable. If you find you have a fear-motivation that needs conquering, just add it to your seed list and in time that fear will dissolve.
This looks simple on paper, but there are thousands of variables, and it would be impossible to list all of them. This is the basic foundational material you need to understand people's motivations. You will need to apply your own creativity to your particular sales situation, which varies from prospect to prospect.

Also, you will most always be dealing with mixtures, such as an exasperator husband and a relater wife. Because all five motivations come in different shapes and sizes, you need to get to know your customers early in the interview so you will know which motivation is controlling their thinking. This is vitally important because motivations can change within the same person from day to day.

Each time you get together with your customers, take the time to determine which motivation is in control. When you can understand their motivation and recognize their needs, then you can create value in your product or service, based upon their value system, not yours.

Get out of your shoes and into theirs, have empathy, and talk about satisfying their needs. The doctor of sales does that, and it is the difference between failure and success. I know you can be the doctor of sales if you will choose to approach every sales relationship with this teaching in mind. Read this chapter again and again, until it is second nature that you sell needs, and not wants.

CHAPTER 19

Behavioral Deficiencies

☞ *The Fatalist Salesperson*
☞ *The Exasperator Salesperson*
☞ *The Appraiser Salesperson*
☞ *The Relater Salesperson*

In the last few chapters, we have been looking at your customers and other people, but this chapter is dedicated to looking at "you." I will hit close to home and talk about salespeople, based upon the motivations of life. My purpose here will be to step on your toes a few times, so that you can recognize yourself in some of the areas that can destroy your effectiveness. My goal is for you to see your areas of need, conquer fear motivations, and move on to love-motivation.

I have never met a person who said, "I really like being an exasperator. I think I will stay right here." It is only that most exasperators do not realize where they are. When they choose to, they can be love motivated people; more productive, more energetic, and more effective in every area of their life, simply by conquering exasperator fears.

We will look at how salespeople fit into each of these motivations. If you recognize yourself in one of the four fear motivations, use your seed list to make the corrections you need to become love motivated.

The Fatalist Salesperson

The fatalist has the most intense fear — the fear of failure. It is literally impossible for a person with a high motivation of fatalist to be happy or content in a sales job where they must be dependent on commissions, because commissions are dependent on being productive. That then puts the responsibility squarely on the shoulders of the fatalist who will not stay on the job.

When we assist corporations in interviewing people for sales positions, we will not even consider a person with a high fatalistic motivation as a qualified applicant. They simply have great difficulty accepting the responsibility that accompanies sales. Fatalists can be successful as a retail clerk in a situation in which the customer comes to the store, makes a decision as to what they want to purchase and carries it to the clerk, so that the clerk can take their money.

The CEO of a very large department store chain told me he did not want salespeople; he wanted clerks. There were two reasons for this: first, the store sold merchandise at very low prices so they could not afford to pay the "salary" required for a "salesperson." Secondly, they based their entire sales force on turnover in personnel. They ran their business under the premise that if they kept an employee only a month or two, they never had to give the employees a raise in pay, benefits, retirement or hospitalization. So, everyone was paid minimum wage. The interesting part of that story is, that department store went bankrupt, nationally.

Among the opposites of this sad scenario are the Nordstrom Brothers, who believe the public is looking for the doctor of sales, someone to take care of their needs and someone who knows what he or she is doing. Nordstrom invests much time and money into training their sales staff, making sure each salesperson gives the service for which they are well known.

The fatalist does not want that role, so they feel comfortable in the clerking position. You have bought something, probably something quite sizable, and when you were paying for the item you felt as if you were doing the clerk a favor. You also find that true occasionally with waiters and waitresses. Then they wonder why their tips are so small!

I was with a friend in a restaurant in Los Angeles and the waitress was having a bad day. She was rude and sarcastic, and it was easy to see she did not like her work. My friend said to her, "Why don't you get into some line of work that you really enjoy. We can clearly tell you don't like waiting tables." She replied, "Oh, shut up!" and left. That was the last we saw of her that evening. We had to ask the cashier for the check, so that we could pay our bill.

You will find that fatalists are so passive in a sales situation, they have difficulty initiating action, which means they never establish a sales position. If there is no sales position established, there is no authority, and, therefore, there is no responsibility. We could carry that one step further and say that with assumed responsibility comes opportunity. When people say, "I never had opportunities like other people," or "I never have been lucky," they need to understand, opportunity comes only when people are willing to take on the responsibility that comes with opportunity.

The fatalist motivation can show itself at any time, and will usually hit a person when it is time to close the sale. The fear of asking for the order and the possibility that the customer might say "no" is enough to cause a salesperson to develop a weakness in closing. Sometimes the customer has to make the decision to buy, and then ask the salesperson to assist in the close!

Remember we all have this fear within us, and we will either conquer it, or it will control us. When you know it is time to close the sale, tell yourself that it is better to try and fail, than to never try and fail. You might be surprised at how easy it is to close sales if you just tell the prospect what you want them to do and what that can mean to them.

A friend, who has a great deal of fatalist fear, recently went into a "new" line of work. He told me he had become a sales representative for a large company in our area. I stopped by to see him one day when I was nearby and discovered he was a clerk out on the display floor, and his job was to tell people where to go to pick up the things they wanted. When not busy with a customer, he was stocking shelves. They titled him a sales representative, and he did assist customers in finding what they wanted. It was very comfortable for him because his only responsibility was to make sure everything got on the right shelves and that he pointed people in the right direction.

The Exasperator Salesperson

The exasperators like a selling job with a challenge, because they enjoy the hard sell. I heard about a guy in door-to-door sales who knocked on someone's door and when it was opened, said, "I'm with the ...(company name)....." The woman of the house slammed the door in his face. So, he went around the house to the back door and knocked again. When the woman answered, he said, "Hello. I hope you're not as crabby as the lady who opened the front door!" She laughed, let him in, and purchased his product! The exasperator just barges in, and takes over. That is power! When two of them meet on a corner, they really have some "war stories" to share.

Exasperators like pressure-selling and they have all the sales techniques down pat. They know how to coerce you into a position where you just cannot say "no." Can you see the power in that? Their needs are actually satisfied by overpowering people. This type of salesperson is the type who has given sales a bad name over the years. That is why people lock the door, and turn out the lights when they see a salesperson approaching. Exasperators will plunge into any situation, because they like a challenge. They are the salespeople who do the war hoop before they come in, and when they have done that, you had better watch out, because they will come through the door!

This type of salesperson is unaware of the prospect's wants, needs, or desires, and does not really care. They only are interested in giving their sales pitch and making a sale. They think they will never see this customer again anyway, so who cares! This approach to sales works on an average of two sales out of every ten appointments. This is not a bad closing ratio, but you have to see a lot of people to make a living. You also can develop ulcers or die of a heart attack at age forty-five from the stress of pushing. The exasperator continually pushes, dominates and oversells; so they are forever breaking new territory and they never get a referral because they are so pushy. In fact, the customer will warn the neighbor not to let the salesperson into their home.

When you find yourself with a number of exasperator tendencies, it is normally a fear of losing a sale, so you over-compensate. Realize, if you can create value based upon needs, you do not have to push. People automatically want to buy things that satisfy their needs. Do not be guilty of trying to shove your products down your customers' throats.

Most salespeople have some of this motivation as a part of their make-up. If it is the third motivation, it can give the tenacity a person needs to be successful in sales. Make sure it is covered with love-motivation and it will assist, not destroy, your sales relationships.

The Appraiser Salesperson

Appraiser salespeople love details and tend to be very technical in their sales presentation. Their thinking is, "If I were having someone give me a sales presentation, I would want them to give me all the details and the technical data. That is the information I need to make a decision to buy. The problem here is that if they are making a presentation to a relater, they will be turned off completely. Relaters are not at all interested in the technical side; they merely want to know what the product will do for them, not how it is manufactured. Because an appraiser likes details, they become super-detailed in their presentation. In fact, they are so detailed that they talk about things that are not worth mentioning. I have witnessed appraisers getting so caught up in the most minute details that the customers become bored. I know you are not boring, but some of your prospects have possibly been a little bored when you have talked about all the things that interest you and were not at all of interest to them. You need to be aware of that tendency. Appraisers do not remain in sales very long unless they are selling "high tech" equipment or a product or service that requires an in-depth presentation. They do not like commissioned sales, because there are no guarantees of income, which makes it difficult to budget. Because they tend to be perfectionists, if they miss one sale, they tell themselves that they must be no good as a salesperson. It is at this time that they decide to get into a field that better fits their abilities. In most cases, this person will revert back to a job that they did not enjoy previously, but they are comfortable with the responsibilities of the job description, and it offered a salary-plus-benefits package. They may be more than qualified for the job, and the management team will probably appreciate their work, but they will not enjoy going to work on Monday mornings.

I had the opportunity to work with a sales organization that sells encyclopedias. These salespeople work by appointment only and call on prospects in their homes. The following illustration is a dialogue of a sales presentation by an appraiser to a young couple with two very young children. The salesperson has tremendous knowledge of her product as well as the need for the product in families just like this one, but she sells from her frame of reference rather than relating to her prospect's wants, needs, and values.

Illustration:

Mr. Cook: **"Our children are quite young, so I don't think this is the time to buy encyclopedias."**

Salesperson: **"I can see you are a very intelligent man, and are very well educated, so I am sure you believe in the value of a good education. Our books are designed to help your children toward the start of their personal pursuit of intellectual development. I am sure you agree with this premise, Mrs. Cook!"**

Mrs. Cook: **"Oh, yes."**

What she has said is true, and it does have value for the Cook family. The problem is, however, she did not relate to Mr. Cook's concern, by creating curiosity and opening his mind. So now she has a man with a closed mind, who is probably offended that she is trying to get his wife to agree with her, which means she is disagreeing with him. With the positive response from Mrs. Cook, she plowed ahead into her presentation, filled with "twelve cylinder" words, that she knows will impress the Cooks.

> *Salesperson:* *"An illustration of the superiority of our context and illustrations is shown here in the "A" volume in our offering on "Animals." You can see how your children will be enthralled with this entire expose. Let me read you an excerpt from this volume on The Intelligence of Animals. Most animal behavior is based on instinct and they are born with this knowledge. It has nothing to do with reasoning. That is, animals do certain things without learning, or without knowing exactly what will happen. When a moth breaks out of its cocoon, it is ready to begin its life's work....."*

It is about here that the Cooks begin thinking of ways to get this salesperson out of their home. They are not listening to what she is saying; in fact, they are making eye contact with each other and speaking volumes! And, the salesperson continues, "...It can fly about and find its food in the sweet juices of plants, without having to learn how. Instinct directs the animal to carry out certain actions in order to keep alive. If instincts guide the animal in an unusual..." At this point Mr.Cook interrupted the spiel; he had heard enough.

> *Mr. Cook: "I think we get the idea."*

> *Salesperson:* *"What is your reaction to what I have shown you, Mrs. Cook?"*

She was attempting to get more response from her ally who had supported her earlier.

> *Mrs. Cook:* *"Well, uh, it is all very interesting. I do feel, however, that we will need to discuss the purchase of this type of material prior to making a decision."*

> *Salesperson:* *"Well, I understand and I am in total agreement with*

> *you, because you must remember, a child's mind is a*
> *very precious commodity."*

Mr. Cook: *"We agree and we will give this some real thought and*
            get back to you."

Salesperson: *"OK. I will look for your call."*

This salesperson left that appointment thinking she had a sale, and that they were going to think it over, and call tomorrow, or the next day, for sure. They will not call and probably will not accept a call from her. You can see that the salesperson was interested in telling her story about her great product. She believed if she could get all of this great information presented to the Cooks, they would have to purchase her books. The fact is, the encyclopedias she was offering would be tremendous for the Cooks and their children, if only she had made a presentation geared toward the children's age group.

The beautiful pictures of animals would help the children learn the names of the animals and how they look. And they could mature with these books helping them at each level of their understanding and need. Instead, she was so concerned about impressing the Cooks with her vocabulary and great knowledge, that she forgot who was going to use the encyclopedias.

Appraisers like to show off their vocabulary. A man introduced himself to me some time ago by saying: "I'm Dr. Jones: BA, MA, Ph.D." I was impressed!! I replied, "I'm Orv Owens, SS, DVBS." Dr. Jones replied, "I do not believe I understand what that means. What are those degrees?" I answered, "Well, the "SS" is Sunday School, which I have attended all my life and "DVBS" is Daily Vacation Bible School, which my parents made me attend every summer." He was not impressed!

Appraisers like to impress you with their knowledge, and to appraiser salespeople, product knowledge is important. The problem here was that when she was talking about an encyclopedia for a four-year-old child, she needed to get down to that level of speech, even when talking to the parents. If she could have created value where the need was, the Cooks would have bought her books. She did not lose the sale of the encyclopedias because there was no need, or because the product was not of high quality and great value. She lost it simply because she was so much of an appraiser that she could not get out of her shoes and into the shoes of her prospect and make a presentation based upon their area of need.

Do not allow your appraiser motivations to get in the way of communicating with your prospects. If you have seen yourself in what you have just read, add to your seed list some positive thoughts about your ability to relate to people based upon their area of interest.

Empathy is vital in any sales relationship, and it emanates from our having an intense interest in our prospects. We must learn to be flexible with people and a perfectionist with things; and then we will become more love-motivated. Always remember, you do not sell a product or service, you sell a relationship, based upon meeting the wants and needs of the customer.

The Relater Salesperson

Relaters, because they are people-oriented, tend to be very warm and friendly. The warmth they give is, "I want to be your best friend." Therefore, their smile, friendliness, and desire to get to know you, is based upon their need for acceptance. If they do not feel they are receiving what they deserve from you, they get very "cold." If you disagree with them, or are not impressed by them, they will have hurt feelings, and will withdraw or pull away from you. Therefore, if you are the customer of a relater and you do not buy, they may be offended.

I had an experience with a car salesman a few years ago that illustrates how relaters think. I was looking for a blue Lincoln with a white vinyl top and velour upholstery, and Carol, my Director of Public Relations, found two dealers in our area who could get this car for me.

One dealer had the exact car I wanted, with the white vinyl top. The other dealer had a blue on blue. I preferred the blue with a white top so that was the dealership from which I decided to make my purchase. The salesperson who had talked to us earlier was not in when I arrived, so the sales manager said he would take care of me. He invited me into his office, and sitting on top of the desk was a trash can — next to me — which the sales manager ignored. This appeared a bit tacky to me, especially in a Lincoln dealership.

The telephone rang as we were discussing the details of the purchase, and he commenced to talk with a friend about his most recent golf game for about ten minutes. During this time I was left twiddling my thumbs! Finally, he finished his conversation, and had just begun to get back into the details of the sale when the telephone rang again. This call was from another friend. I left his office and went out into the showroom and looked at a few cars.

When he finished his call he came out to the showroom and said, "Let's get back to business! With all of this equipment this car will cost you..." (he named a price) I said, "That's very interesting, but I have lost interest in purchasing a car from your dealership." "But this is the car you want," he said. I agreed, "That is true, and it's at a good price as well. However, when I visit a dealership to purchase a luxury automobile I expect to be treated quite differently than I have been treated in your place of business." All the way out the door he was asking me what he had done wrong.

I was willing to accept my second choice, which, in fact, cost a little more than the blue with a white vinyl top, but I refused to purchase my automobile from anyone less than a doctor of sales.

Relaters care what you think. The relater sales person was more concerned about what his friend would think than he was in taking care of his customer — me! They were close friends, and possibly his friend would not be his friend the next day, if he had preferred me over the friend. He could not take that chance, and he lost the sale.

The relater motivation will cause people to be very friendly and to talk to anybody anywhere. They are easy to get to know, because they love people, and the more friends they have, the more successful they feel. You are their best friend until you step on their toes a bit, or you do not do exactly what they expect you to do. Suddenly, they give you the "cold shoulder," and the friendliness is dead. They will then go to someone else who will satisfy their needs.

Relaters are people-oriented salespeople and that is good. The problem with the relater is that they look to people to get what they want, rather than to give what the people need. Being people-oriented means you have people skills and the ability to talk to people and enjoy working with them. This capability can be valuable in the sales field, but does not guarantee sales effectiveness. To be effective in relationship selling, you must have empathy for the customer, and that is where the relater has difficulty. Relaters sell based upon their own interests, rather than those of the customer.

When relaters are impressed with a product or service, they think everyone is interested and will see the same value. They have great difficulty selling a product or service that would not be of interest to you. You will find these customers have a totally different value system from yours, but are buyers and need you to relate to their values. This is difficult if your relater motivation is high because you want everyone to see the real value — yours — rather than buying a product and regretting later.

The exasperator's values are totally different than those of the relater, so they will not be impressed with a relater salesperson pointing out their favorite features.

A relater real estate agent took a couple into a model home that he just knew they would love. The problem was the husband was an exasperator, and was not going to fall in love with any house. This is how the sales presentation proceeded:

Agent:	*"You're going to love this room! I just love its decor, don't you? It's warm and comfortable."*
Dave:	*"It looks like a lot of extra cost to me. I'm looking for something that's a little more simple."*
Sue:	*"Dave, I love it. It's everything I've ever wanted.*
Dave:	*"I don't think so! I'm looking for something that's well-built and easy to keep up."*
Agent:	*"Dave, you're going to be impressed with this neighborhood. Some of the nicest people in the world live here. They have activities going on all the time."*

Sue: *"That sounds like fun!"*

Dave: *"It sounds like 'no privacy' to me! All I need is some dumb neighbor sticking his head over the fence twice a day."*

Agent: *"The neighbor next door is the principal of the local high school and they're a great family."*

Dave: *"No way! My last principal threatened to kick me out of school. I don't need a neighbor like that. I'll see you out in the car, Sue."*

Sue: *"Don't worry about it. He talks rough like that all the time."*

Agent: *"I don't think I showed him a thing he liked."*

He was right. He did not show Dave a thing he liked, because he did not direct his presentation to an exasperator. You will notice that Sue was with the real estate agent throughout the presentation, because they were both relaters.

In this sales situation you saw another variable, and that was that you will often be required to relate to more than one motivation in a sales presentation. This is not only true in relating to two people, but sometimes a person will have two motivations very close in intensity, and you must recognize each motivation, and satisfy the wants and needs of both. As a love-motivated salesperson, you must be able to wear all hats.

If you have a high relater motivation such as was true in this case, and expect acceptance and appreciation from Dave, you will never get it. Dave is already in the car, waiting to see the next house. If the real estate agent had been a love-motivated salesperson, he would have recognized Dave's needs and pointed those things out to him. There were sufficient things in that home to turn Dave on: the strength of the house itself, the fence around the back yard, and the room for a shop in the garage.

At the same time, he could have satisfied the relater needs of Sue with things such as the decor and the neighbor next door. Be careful not to see yourself in your presentation, rather than relating to the customer's wants and needs. If you do, you will only be effective with people who are of the same motivation.

The relater salesperson likes to trade: "I'll buy from you if you will buy from me," or "I'll give you a discount on my product, if you will give me a discount on yours." The problem here is that no one makes any money. Relaters are the first to discount their product rather than build value. They will do anything to make a sale, because making a sale is acceptance, recognition, and appreciation. So then, a relater will give up profits and position, or even lose face, in order to save face when he returns to the office.

I met one person who led his company's sales force in sales for a month and yet had to quit because he did not make enough to pay his overhead. The reason for this was that he sold his products at wholesale. He did not make a dime that month, but he had great acceptance. That tells us that the relater's need for acceptance is greater than their want for money; or, need for recognition is greater than want of productivity. The company liked that salesman but he could not afford to continue working for them. Relaters love people, but more than that, they love people to love them.

I believe sales managers are hired to pump up relater salespeople and that sales meetings are conducted for relaters. At 9:00 a.m. on Monday, the sales manager says: "It's going to be a great week! We are going to write goals on the board, and you are going to sell more than you have ever sold in your life!" When relaters leave the meeting they are ready to set the world on fire. At about 10:30 a.m. they come crawling back underneath the door, crying, "Nobody wants to buy from me! I guess I'm just not a salesperson." The manager says, "What do you mean you are not a salesperson? You are one of our best. See all those houses out there? Those are people who are waiting to hear you knock on their door." Now, the relater salesperson is all pumped up and hits the pavement again. Sales managers are cheerleaders.

Relaters make great salespeople when they get their own fears out of the way! If the fear of rejection and ridicule are causing you to play the role of the relater salesperson, add to your seed list statements that build your self-image and self-esteem. Start thinking of yourself as the "doctor of sales," establish a sales relationship with your customers, and tell them how your product or service will meet their wants and needs based upon their value system. Use your tremendous people skills, rather than allowing them to get in your way.

The Love Motivated Salesperson

Are you now ready to hear about yourself? Hopefully, by now you have decided to be a love-motivated salesperson. You will know your effectiveness in the sales field by your creativity, productivity and consistency.

Creativity:

Number one on the list of love-motivated traits is creativity. The love-motivated sales salesperson is a creative individual. In the interviewing process, we often ask people about their hobbies. If they respond that they are musicians, singers, dancers, writers, or possibly a poet, then we know they are creative people.

If you are creative in one area, you tend to be creative in many areas of your life. I like hiring creative people, because they will channel that creativity into sales relationships. If you do not feel creative, add it to your seed list. I happen to know that you are creative, but that you have "created reasons" not to develop your natural "ability to create."

You were "created to be creative," and you find your greatest happiness when you are creating something. That is the fun of sales: meeting a prospect, and then creating a client; or finding a solution to your customer's problems. Salespeople are happier people than most, because the sales field is so creative. The more you exercise your creative ability, the more it becomes a capability. Never say you cannot be creative because, in fact, you are creative.

Productivity:

The second word on our list of love motivated traits is productivity. Love-motivated salespeople do the things that are the most productive for their customers. This is not always making the sale. Sometimes, it is saying, "I do not think this is the best time for you to buy." When a salesperson says that to you, would you think of buying from any other salesperson when the time does come to buy?

One real estate agent oversold a house to a family. She had done such a good job, however, that when she told them that they could not qualify for this particular house, they insisted that she keep their deposit until she could find a house for them. That couple felt this real estate agent was productive, and that they could trust her to do the right thing, and find a home within their buying power.

Consistency:

A love-motivated salesperson is consistent. The relater is a people-oriented salesperson; the love-motivated salesperson is relationship-oriented.

Being relationship-oriented means that you are aware of the values, wants, and needs of a customer, and your total function is to help your customers make a wise buying decision. Because this is your "job description," or the kind of person you are, you are the same every day — morning or night, at busy times, or when you find spare time.

With this consistency, the customers believe they know you and can trust you. They never see you have a bad hair day, or down time. Of course, this means you must work like crazy to maintain this consistency. You must control your own decisions, expose yourself to positive input every day, and do a thorough reading of your seed list — on a daily basis.

We want to be relationship-oriented salespeople because it not only satisfies the customer, but it also brings tremendous self-satisfaction, just knowing we are being highly productive.

The love-motivated person is so concerned about people and their needs, that they are able to establish so strong a relationship that the customer thanks them for coming to their home or office. When you are a love-motivated salesperson, you are always welcome. In fact, you are not only welcome, you are a cherished part of their lives. You function in a role that helps them be happier and more productive.

People in our world today are looking for love-motivated salespeople who are willing to take charge, conquer fear, take responsibility and understand their concerns. In fact, they want their salesperson to understand the things they do not understand.

They feel good when the salesperson not only sees their needs, but also can tell them about needs of which they were not aware.

You have the ability to be a love-motivated salesperson. Possibly you have not developed those abilities into capabilities, but you do have them. If you have not developed these abilities, it is merely because you have not worked at developing them. You do this by creating the seed list. This has been a major theme throughout this entire book, and I hope the message has gotten through to you. The only way you will ever develop your abilities into capabilities, and become the person you want to be, is to become that person, subconsciously.

When your fears are conquered, you will become a love-motivated person, and your sales techniques will turn into relationship techniques — selling by relationship rather than by coercion.

And then, you will truly be the "doctor of sales" and will have mastered Relationship Selling.

EPILOGUE

Over the years I have met many people in management and sales who have said their life was changed by a book, a seminar, or a person who offered them some good advice. They say, "I would not have enjoyed the success that I have, had it not been for ...," and then they mention that person, or book, or whatever it was that had such impact upon their life. My response to that kind of statement — especially if the comments are directed toward something I have taught — is that any change, development, increase in productivity or achievement you have made is a result of applying principles of success in your life. Success does not just come your way, you must pay the price. You really deserve all the credit.

Some of you, while reading this book, have underlined or highlighted lines that you will review over and over again. Some of you will use sections from this book in training your staff members. Others — and I hope this is not you — will read half of this book, place a bookmark inside, and plan to get back to it soon; but not finish the book. Whatever impact this book has on you will be simply because you have applied the concepts of relationship selling into your everyday life. It must be a lifestyle rather than a sales approach to have total impact on your life.

In studying people over the last thirty years, I have learned that the most successful people in any profession relate to their family, friends and strangers the same way they relate to clients, patients and customers. Those who try to put on a persona of being a relationship-oriented person come off as a phony or a person putting on an act. This normally results in creating fear in the prospect and loss of a sales relationship. Please do not try to do this, choose to do this. Doing is "performance" only, and being is "personage," — the kind of person you are. When you have adopted this philosophy as your own and have chosen to be a relationship-oriented person, you will begin seeing how much potential you really have to reach any goal you may set for yourself.

Many companies that I have consulted with over the years have adopted this philosophy into their mission statement. These companies hire people who can understand what they are all about, and dismiss staff members who have difficulty buying into and becoming a relationship-oriented person. Increase in productivity has been a testimony of the value that our society places on a business or professionals who care about their clients.

Word of mouth advertising — which is continuously both positive and negative — is the most powerful advertising because the hearer believes it to be true. A reputation in a community has great impact on how much business you will enjoy. Today your prospects, clients, customers or patients will determine whether you are in business to meet their needs or just to make a buck. The result will be repeat and referral business, or loss of business.

If you have read through this book, read it again. You will get far more out of the first chapter, after having read the final chapter. My challenge in making this book a meaningful experience for you has been to create an understanding of the concepts so that you can apply them in your day-to-day life. There is little value in reading something and then saying, "That's interesting," and forgetting it. It is my desire to help you understand the success principles that have been making people successful from the beginning of time so that you can use rather than abuse them. You are doing everything covered in this book. You are either doing it right and enjoying great success, or you are doing it wrong and wondering why you cannot reach your personal goals. Use these principles rather than abuse them and you will be on a path to tremendous success. I call it "The Psychology of RELATIONSHIP SELLING - Developing Repeat and Referral Business."